The Colour Encyclopedia of
AIRCRAFT

OCTOPUS

The Colour Encyclopedia of
AIRCRAFT
by Nigel and Nicola Macknight
foreword by Miss Sheila Scott OBE

Text/Captions: Nigel Macknight
Picture Research: Nigel & Nicola Macknight
Design: Terry Godfrey/Trevor Hall/Dave Allen
Special Artwork: Russell Brown
Oil Paintings: Courtesy of Airfix Products Limited
Editorial Consultant: Bill Gunston

First published 1980 by Octopus Books Limited
59 Grosvenor Street London W1

Copyright © 1980 Octopus Books Limited

ISBN 0 7064 1303 2
D.L TO.553-1980

Created by Starless Productions
20 Edward Avenue Bobbers Mill Nottingham NG8 5BD

Produced by Mandarin Publishers Limited
22a Westlands Road Quarry Bay Hong Kong

Printed in Spain

CONTENTS

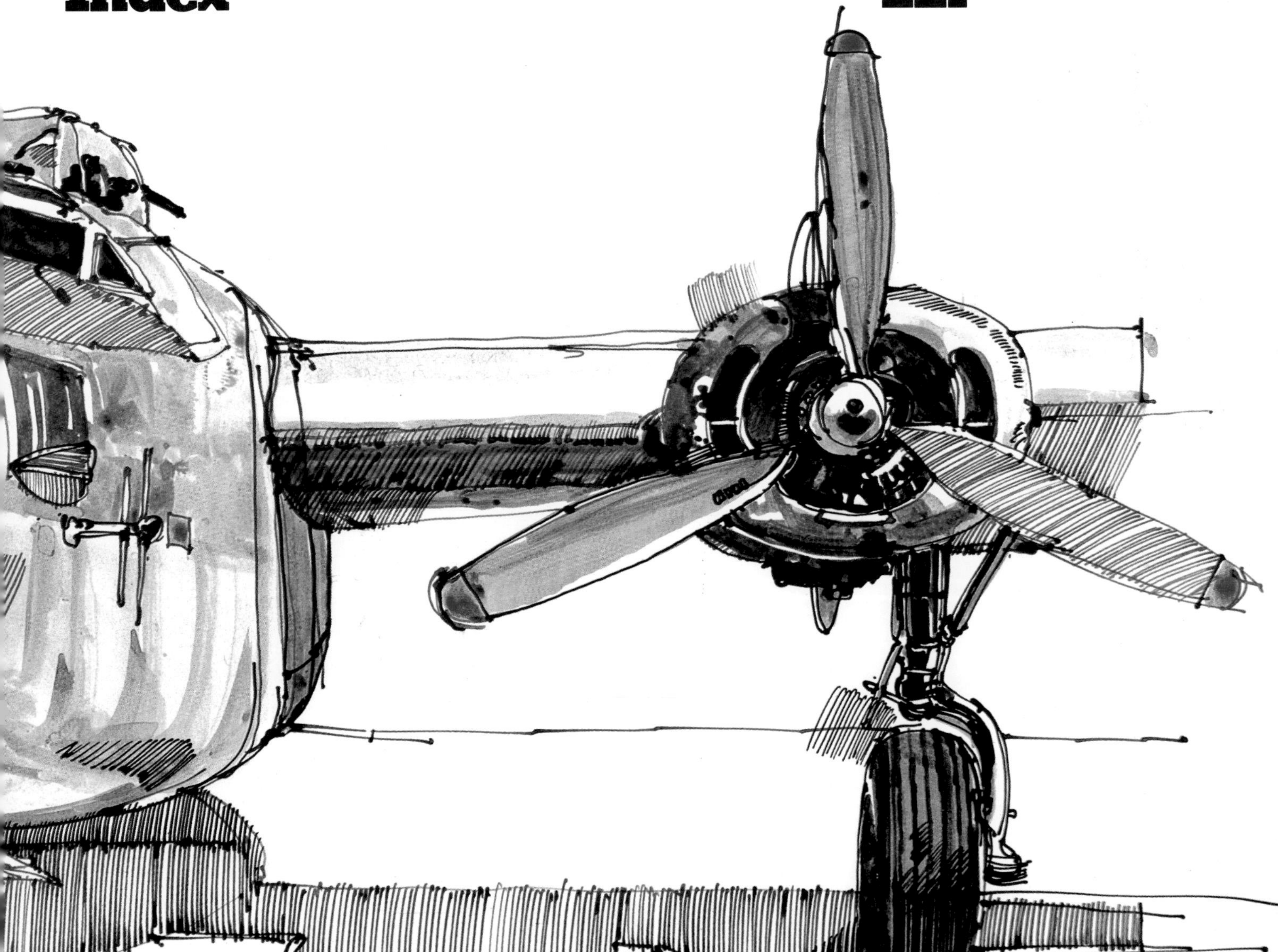

Foreword by
Miss Sheila Scott OBE
breaker of over 100 long distance flying records

Man does not grow wings easily! Yet the sky that surrounds us contains the very air we breathe and is vital to every living thing.

Lovers of the sky often find it difficult to express to others what they really experience. Is it merely being in charge of a very efficient machine, or conquering the problems posed by the elements, overcoming instinctive fears, or just another way of earning a living? Undoubtedly for most there is another ingredient . . .

This comprehensive and interestingly presented book by Nigel and Nicola Macknight goes a long way towards illustrating that indefinable extra dimension. Writing in an informative and yet relaxed style, the authors have skilfully combined the more colourful work of specialist photographers with contrasting interpretations of flight by various artists. The result is a book that optically 'takes off' – a refreshing view of the machines of the air and the element in which they fly.

Having sampled all kinds of flying machines, from balloons and helicopters to jet fighters, I am particularly delighted to recommend this beautiful book and contribute the foreword to it. May all who read it be tempted to experience the joys flying offers.

Otto Lilenthal makes a test flight suspended beneath a frail glider.

The Pioneers

Man's desire to fly from place to place like the birds has resulted in one of the most fascinating adventure stories of all time. In his earliest attempts at flight, Man's first instinct was literally to flap his arms (suitably modified with the addition of crude 'wings' made from wood and feathers) and hope for the best. It took him centuries to realize that birds had been adapted by evolution to take to the air in this way and that a man would have to develop his own methods if he wished to soar through the air.

The differences between birds and humans as far as flight is concerned are painfully real. Birds have hollow bones that are amazingly light, yet very strong. A bird's whole anatomy, particularly its muscles, is purpose-built to provide an output of energy far greater in relation to its weight than any human could generate, even over a short time. The average bird's heartbeat rate of 800 times a minute, compared with a human's average rate of 60 beats per minute, is ample evidence of this difference in energy output. In short, the millions of years of evolution that have perfected the ability of birds to fly left humans with a lot of catching up to do!

Despite the obvious drawbacks, many gifted minds were turned to the task of

Below: Orville Wright makes the first successful powered flight on 17 December 1903 at Kitty Hawk.

achieving flight by means of flapping wings. Perhaps the most famous of the early thinkers was the Italian genius Leonardo da Vinci. He was born in the fifteenth century and was the towering figure of the Renaissance. He was a painter, anatomist and philosopher and also studied the flight abilities of birds to find out what enabled them to take to the air. It was then that da Vinci made a vast number of calculations relating to manned flight and left behind a wealth of drawings and diagrams. But despite the amount of research he did, none of da Vinci's creations ever left the ground.

Far greater progress took place when inventors began thinking in terms of building craft in which to travel, rather than merely imitating the birds by wing-flapping. These craft first took the form

Above: **Blèriot hits the headlines.** *Below*: **The Vickers 'Gun Bus' of 1914.**

of balloons and later gave way to un-powered gliders. It was in a balloon that Man first successfully became airborne after centuries of futile attempts to 'grow wings'. The Montgolfier brothers, Joseph and Etiènne of Lyons, France, discovered the lifting properties of hot air and began to build balloons to take advantage of this. At first they experimented by sending dogs and ducks and other animals aloft. In 1784, they persuaded a colleague to make the first human ascent. Almost at the same time

the even greater lifting properties of a newly-discovered gas called hydrogen were being realized, and hot-air balloons began to fade into the background.

Early hot-air balloons were rather clumsy and their flights were of comparatively short duration as no suitable fuel existed which could be carried in sufficient quantities to keep the brazier alight that supplied hot air to the balloon envelope. All this changed when the hydrogen balloon came in on the scene. At this period in history the balloon was regarded as something of a novelty act belonging to a fairground and this attitude prevailed for at least one hundred years. It was not until the beginning of the twentieth century that ballooning

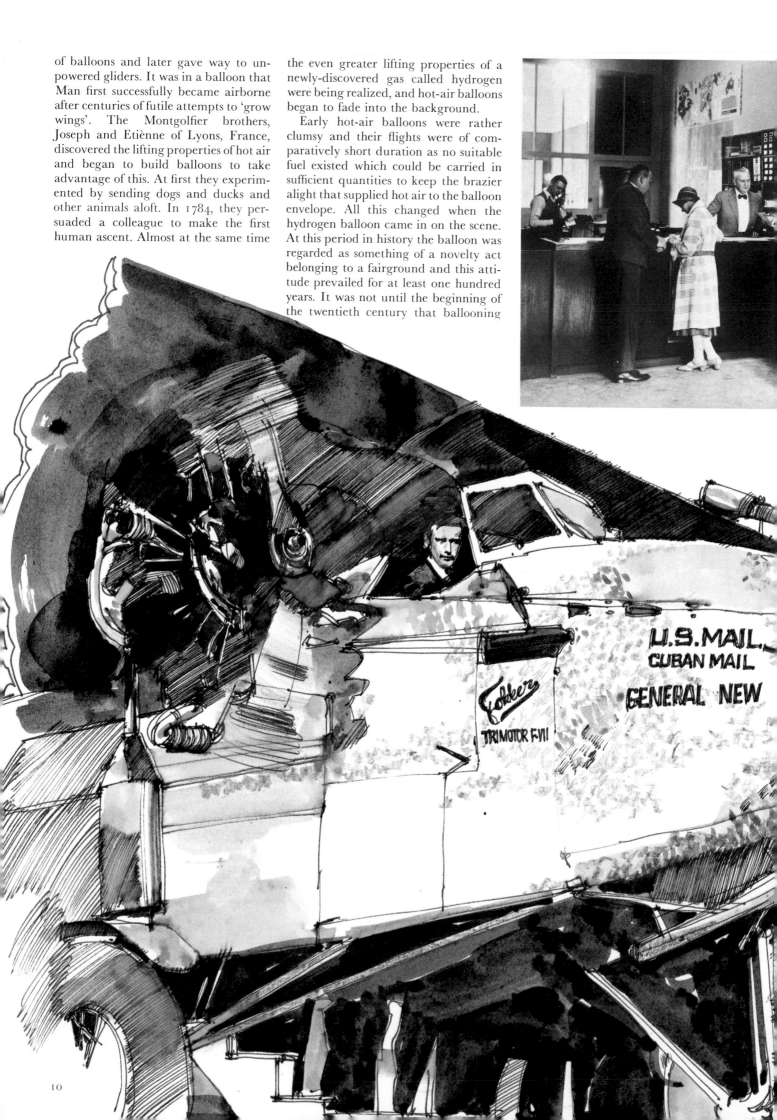

Above and right: Striking comparisons between the reception areas of major airports past and present. Computer-controlled booking networks and increased mechanization have kept pace with growth.

Pioneers of a very different kind – but pioneers nonetheless – were the operators of the first air mail services. High-speed postal deliveries are something we take for granted today, but the early services were plagued with difficulties.

took on an air of respectability, when it became a fashionable pastime of high society.

Ballooning's social popularity however was short, for by 1908 most rich and influential people interested in taking to the air had discovered a new and even more exciting fashion in the form of the aeroplane. As the motor car had already made mechanical contrivances respectable, the balloon was more or less laid aside. Fortunately, just after the First World War there was a slight revival of interest in ballooning, and as a result the sport never completely died out. There were national and local clubs in France, Germany, Belgium, Holland and Switzerland and a few balloonists soldiered on in the United States.

Meanwhile, the airship – a steerable, cigar-shaped type of balloon – had been having a somewhat more chequered career. The first successful airship appeared around 1900, the most imposing being the big rigid-framed products of Count Ferdinand von Zeppelin in Germany. Zeppelin operated successful air services before the First World War, and his airships were subsequently used for bombing raids on England from the outbreak of the conflict. The development of better fixed-wing fighters provided an effective defence against these German giants, however, and heavy losses led to the withdrawal of airships from bombing operations. After the First World War, airships returned to make long-distance flights in the hands of civil operators, but a series of heavily-publicized disasters shook the public's confidence in them. In any case, fixed-wing aircraft were now beginning to overcome the airship's principal advantage of long range and by the late 1930s, airships had almost disappeared from the skies.

In the 1950s a worldwide rekindling of interest in ballooning began. This fresh wave of enthusiasm is still sweeping the world, and just as in days long gone by the shape of a distant balloon against a blue summer sky is by no means uncommon today. Like gliding, ballooning is a 'pure' sport. Balloons cannot travel where the balloonists want, except to a limited degree, as prevailing winds and air currents will determine the course of the balloon. Together with the silence and gentleness of the flight, this is undoubtedly one of its greatest attractions in these days of supersonic travel and

The legendary Supermarine Spitfire helped the RAF to win the Battle of Britain and set new standards for others.

increasing air pollution. Today it is the hot-air balloon that dominates the scene, as modern propane gas cylinders are relatively light and are readily available. When connected to a burner unit which looks like a bigger version of a camp stove, the propane gas cylinder provides a clean, powerful, yet safe source of heat to keep the balloon aloft. Much of the popularity of hot-air balloons in modern times can also be attributed to the widespread availability of polythene and other impervious man-made fabrics for producing light yet tough balloon envelopes. These materials have the additional ad-

vantage of being relatively easy to work.

Work is continually underway to develop more efficient burners and envelopes, and this steady progress has never been better demonstrated than in the summer of 1977, when the first flight across the Atlantic Ocean by balloon was achieved.

As with all aspects of aviation, commerce has crept in to play its part. Many balloons now double-up as aerial advertising hoardings, the publicity potential of this idyllic sport being plain for all to see. At first, conventional balloons made their flights in much the same way

as before, bearing the trademark of some well-known company or product on the envelope exterior. But now things have developed one step further. The latest trend is towards balloons that are 'total' advertisements. These take the form of gigantic inflated light bulbs or sparking plugs. There is even one extraordinary balloon shaped like an enormous pair of jeans!

Whatever shapes they appear in, balloons will continue to provide endless enjoyment for the people lucky enough to own and fly in them, and they remain a fascinating spectacle for the rest of us at ground level.

Balloons may have provided Man with his first means of getting airborne, but it was gliders that turned him in the direction that eventually led to a complete conquest of the air. Brave pioneers like Otto Lilienthal of Germany proved that gliders were closer than balloons to the goal of true flight. Lilienthal had enough courage in his convictions to leap from the tops of high cliffs, suspended beneath the graceful wood-and-fabric gliders he had so carefully designed and fashioned with his own hands. In many ways, Lilienthal can be regarded as the father of the very popular modern sport of hang-gliding, though his experiments were to have far greater implications than mere sport on the wider field of aviation as a whole in the years that lay ahead. Unfortunately, Lilienthal himself was killed in a flying accident when testing one of his latest designs.

It was of course the Wright brothers of the USA who took all aviation experiments to their logical conclusion, when

Below: **The world's first pressure suit, designed for the pilot of the Bristol 138A in 1936. Today's pilots (right) are more comfortable.**

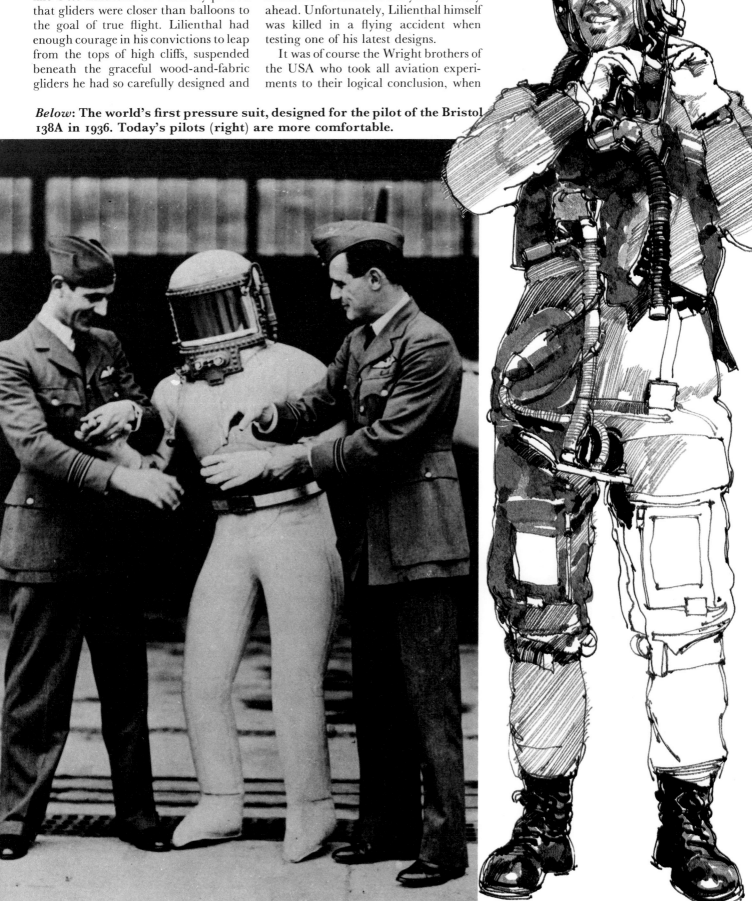

Orville Wright, under the watchful eye of brother Wilbur, lifted off from the beach at Kill Devil Hills, Kitty Hawk, North Carolina, at the controls of their frail little *Flyer* to make the first powered aeroplane flight in history. Over the years leading up to this epic achievement many hundreds of dedicated inventors, engineers and physicists had contributed to the fund of knowledge that the Wright brothers drew upon when building their successful machine. But to the Wright brothers went the final distinction of bringing all the calculations and experiments to fruition. The Wrights themselves did a tremendous amount of experimentation with unpowered gliders before taking the bold decision to fit an engine, and even went so far as to conduct a series of tests with scale models in a crude wind-tunnel.

It is probably fair to say that the aerodynamic knowledge required to build a successful powered aeroplane already existed before Orville Wright actually made that epoch-making first flight on 17 December 1903, but it was the right type of engine to power the aircraft that had previously been lacking.

After the sensational performance of the Wright brothers in America, the next aeronautical event to hit the headlines occurred in Europe, when Louis Blériot became the first person to cross the English Channel in a fixed-wing aircraft. A car accessory maker by trade, Blériot took the *Daily Mail* newspaper's cash prize of £1,000 for his gallant endeavour, and took special pride in the fact that the flight was made in a machine of his own design. His cross-Channel journey began at Calais, took 38 minutes to complete, and ended in a ploughed field near Dover Castle.

Now that Man was beginning to gain some degree of mastery over this whole new realm which lay above him, there began a series of daring pioneer flights that blazed the trail for today's commercial airliner routes. The first of these took place on 14–15 June 1919, when two test pilots from the Vickers company of Great Britain, John Alcock and Arthur Whitten-Brown, made the first landplane crossing of the Atlantic Ocean.

Flying a specially-converted Vickers Vimy twin-engined biplane bomber, left unpainted for lightness and loaded to the brim with fuel, Alcock and Whitten-Brown headed out over the Atlantic from St John's, Newfoundland and immediately encountered heavy storms. By dint of sheer courage and determination they landed sixteen hours later in a peat bog near the Irish coast that they had mistaken for a firm green field. This error of judgement was understandable after a flight of that duration, particularly as no injuries resulted, and they returned home as national heroes. As well as winning a *Daily Mail* cash prize of £10,000, both these intrepid airmen were honoured with a knighthood.

Above: **Built to probe the limits of high-speed flight the Douglas X-3 Stiletto had tiny razor-sharp wings and a long, pointed fuselage**

Below: **The Fairey Delta 2 research plane established a new World Air Speed Record of 1,132 mph in March 1956 with Peter Twiff at the controls**

Epoch-making flights of the type flown by Alcock and Brown grabbed the headlines with unerring regularity in those swashbuckling days of the pioneer aviators. Perhaps the most impressive example of sheer airmanship was that exhibited by the crew of the triple-engined Fokker F-VII *Southern Cross*, when they made the first flight across the vast Pacific Ocean. The flight-deck crew of the *Southern Cross* comprised of Australians Captain Charles Kingsford-Smith and Captain C.T.P. Ulm, while two talented Americans, Harry Lyon (navigator) and James Warner (radio operator) occupied the rear cabin.

In order to span such a vast expanse of water, the *Southern Cross* needed to be very heavily modified from its original airliner configuration. Every available space in the Fokker's airframe was crammed with extra fuel tanks, as it would have been impossible to fly such a long journey with the normal fuel capacity. This had the inevitable drawback of increasing the overall weight of the aircraft, so the undercarriage legs and fuselage structure were heavily reinforced. In addition, flexible fuel pipes were fitted to withstand the prolonged periods of

Characterized by its crescent-shaped wing, the Handley-Page Victor was the last of the RAF's nuclear 'V-bombers'.

A Boeing 747 – the first of the 'jumbos' is a symbol of progress

vibration from the engines. In the extremely likely event of an emergency landing being necessary, a large valve was fitted beneath the main fuel tank which would enable its entire contents to be dumped in mid-air in just 50 seconds.

When planning their assault on the Pacific, Kingsford-Smith and his team came up with another novel idea to ensure their safety if ditching became necessary. They planned to saw off the outer engines and the fuselage and use the big monoplane wing as a huge raft! With this ingenious scheme in mind, a small distilling plant for producing fresh water and a supply of rations were installed in the wing before the flight took place.

On the morning of 31 May 1928, with months of careful organization behind them, the crew of *Southern Cross* took off from a misty Oakland Airport, San Francisco, and set course for Honolulu, 3,893 km (2,408 miles) away. The first leg of the journey was completed without incident, but the longest stage – to Suva in the Fiji Islands some 4,800 km (3,000 miles) further – was yet to come. To span such a great distance and yet pinpoint a tiny island in the middle of the ocean was a daunting challenge, but Kingsford-Smith and his crew braved blinding rain squalls, a troublesome starboard engine and a temporary loss of radio contact with the outside world to land on Suva

with only a few drops of fuel remaining in the *Southern Cross*' fuel tanks.

Armed with a whale's tooth – a Fijian good luck charm presented to them by the oldest inhabitant of Suva – the intrepid foursome then set off for Australia. Although this was the shortest leg of the journey, it turned out to be by far the most gruelling. Relentless storms tossed the *Southern Cross* around the sky as if it were a paper kite, while torrential rain cut visibility from the cockpit drastically. To make matters worse, Lyon's compass broke down, but Australia proved too big a target to miss and Kingsford-Smith and his crew touched down at Brisbane at 10.13 local time. Behind them lay 11,755 km (7,347 miles) of ocean.

The men who flew their aircraft on first flights across oceans and vast expanses of land easily qualify as pioneers, but women too played their part. Jean Batten, Amy Johnson and, in more recent years, Sheila Scott captured the imagination of the public with their record-breaking long-distance flights just as readily as men like Blériot and Kingsford-Smith. The headlines have also been stolen by various attempts at speed and altitude records, first flights across famous mountains, and the first mail-carrying flights.

The pages that follow show the fruit of the pioneers' courageous efforts.

AIRLINERS
Flying for Everyone

Along with such inventions as the telephone, television, radio and the motor car, passenger aircraft have played a leading part in the communications revolution of the twentieth century. This form of travel has made it possible for ordinary people to reach almost any place on earth in only a matter of hours, in standards of safety and comfort that the pioneer aviators could never have dreamt of.

The story of passenger air transport really begins with dirigibles. These huge hydrogen-filled aircraft were built around a metal framework and driven along by propellers. In Germany in 1900, Count Ferdinand von Zeppelin flew his first airship, the LZ1, over Lake Constance, on the border between Switzerland and Germany. That design was not a complete success but by 1910 he had his massive LZ7 *Deutschland* running very smoothly indeed. During the years leading up to the outbreak of the First World War, Zeppelin's Delag company operated seven such 22-seat airships on a network of routes all around Germany. Delag made almost 1,600 flights, carried around 34,000 paying passengers and covered well over 100,000 miles between 1910 and 1914.

By 1914, commercial aviation in the USA was well underway, with the world's first scheduled air service for paying passengers being operated to and from St. Petersburg and Tampa, Florida, between January and March 1913. This 25-minute flight across Tampa Bay was flown by a tiny two-seater 75 hp Benoist biplane flyingboat. In its short but distinguished history the 'St. Petersburg-Tampa Airboat Line' carried over 1,000 passengers without incident.

Military pioneers

In those very early days of powered flight, the majority of 'passenger' services were run by military authorities to transport urgent mail and VIPs. This was particularly true of the RAF's Communication Wing, which began making regular flights between London and Paris to ferry officials to the First World War peace conference, held in the French capital in January 1919. This service was operated by modified single-engined Airco DH.4s and lumbering twin-engined Handley Page o/400s, both types having originally served as wartime bombers. By September of that year, when the final flight was made, a total of 934 people and 1,008 bags of mail had made the journey, and the Communication Wing had claimed the honour of having undertaken the first passenger flight across the English Channel by night. Both during and just after the First World War, similar military air

Airship LZ127 *Count Zeppelin* first crossed the South Atlantic non-stop in May 1930, and was typical of these early lighter-than-air giants.

Dressed in her most immaculate outfit, a wealthy passenger is helped aboard a Luft Hansa Fokker F.II. The 'Airboy' helping her was also responsible for carrying luggage.

services were also operated spasmodically by France, Germany, Italy, Switzerland, Russia and the crumbling Austro-Hungarian empire, using a wide variety of both modified and standard bomber aircraft.

In the immediate postwar years, of course, there was a surplus of ex-military aircraft around – and plenty of experienced pilots to fly them. Joy rides became a popular pastime with the mar-

velling masses at fairs and fêtes, and it was at this time more than any other that flying really captured the public's imagination. One enterprising Englishman, Claude Graham-White, even built a rather frail 100 hp biplane called the *Charabanc* to cash in on this new-found enthusiasm for 'barnstorming'. It had the, then, remarkable feature of an enclosed cockpit and could carry up to ten fare-paying passengers at a time, but by

now even more ambitious individuals were ready to operate scheduled passenger aircraft services as soon as the wartime restrictions on civil aviation activities were lifted.

First off the mark was, somewhat surprisingly, a German company called Luft Reederei. They inaugurated a daily service linking Berlin, Leipzig and Weimar in February of 1919, using a variety of modified bombers. These aircraft were basically unsuitable for the job, as they provided little in the way of creature comforts for the passengers they carried. Bomber aircraft hastily modified and pressed into service to carry passengers, like the LVG CV.I, accommodated their occupants in open seats fully exposed to the elements.

Corrugated metal

A more suitable form of passenger transport was clearly overdue, and it came in the shape of the Junkers F.13. This was a single-engined aircraft of German design and construction with comfortable enclosed accommodation for four passengers. As the world's first purpose-built airliner, the F.13 entered service on 25 June 1919 and was amazingly advanced for its time. For while 'stick-and-string' biplanes ruled the skies, the sleek new Junkers model was a low-wing monoplane with superb handling characteristics and an outstanding performance. A notable feature of the F.13 was its unusual *corrugated metal* fuselage and wings, designed to provide great structural strength without imposing extra weight. A total of 322 F.13s had been built by the time Junkers ceased producing them in 1932, these having performed a wide variety of civilian passenger and military cargo carrying duties throughout the world. Some idea of the outstanding reliability and air-

worthiness of this early design can be gathered from the fact that the very first F.13 built was still flying regular pleasure trips around Berlin at the outbreak of the Second World War in 1939.

In Britain, meanwhile, several airlines had come into existence, including such famous names as Aircraft Transport and Travel, Handley Page Transport and the Instone Air Line. Of these the AT & T introduced the world's first daily international airline service, operating between London and Paris. Flying a DH.16 with four passengers in the enclosed cabin, pilot Cyril Patterson took 2 hours 25 minutes to make the journey, and collected a grand total of £84 in fares! From that point on, passenger flights across the English Channel became more and more popular and among the best known aircraft to fly this route were Handley Page's 110 km/hr (70 mph) 0/400s and Instone's lone ten-seater Vimy Commercial *City of London*, an adaptation of the famous Vickers wartime bomber.

Forced landings

As time went by air routes were extended to other European cities, so that by 1922 Daimler Airways (the successor to AT & T) was flying regularly from Manchester to destinations as far afield as Berlin, using a variety of de Havilland aircraft. During that same year the company successfully introduced the DH.34 biplane to take over from its eight-seater DH.18 airliners. This model had accommodation for nine passengers and made its maiden flight just one week before it entered commercial service – a far cry from the seven year proving period endured by Concorde much, much later!

In those early days long-distance flights were somewhat unpredictable, mainly due to the unreliability of the

The Junkers F13 was extremely advanced for its time. The unique corrugated metal construction made for unequalled strength and durability. Here, the passengers are greeted aboard by the aircraft's captain.

aeroengines then in use. For example, one famous flight from London to Paris in the early twenties involved over a dozen forced landings through engine failure and took almost 24 hours to complete! Pilots embarking on such flights were normally given a hefty wad of notes by their employers to pay for their passengers' on-going bus or rail tickets in the event of their journey by air being abandoned short of the advertised destination. As if mechanical faults were not enough in the way of discouragement to early air travellers, there were also the problems posed by adverse weather conditions and difficulties in navigation. To help overcome the setbacks encountered when travelling long distances in conditions of poor visibility, some Handley Page airliners pioneered the use of onboard Marconi radios to enable their crews to keep in touch with airports along the way.

Railway accident!

However, the vast majority of early airliners enjoyed no such luxury and navigation for them was often a case of studying a map and keeping a careful lookout for roads, rivers and railway lines as they slid past the cabin window between patches of cloud. In very bad weather this procedure became rather difficult to say the least, and there was more than one instance of two low flying airliners colliding in mid-air because their pilots were both following the same railway line in different directions! Even in good weather though, conditions in the open cockpits of these early types were often cold, wet and windswept for passengers and crew alike. Most companies provided heavy coats, goggles and even helmets for their passengers, who often had to endure violent shocks when

Above: **An unusual passenger. Even crocodiles were weighed before a flight.**

their aircraft came in to land on the muddy grass fields which often passed for runways in those riproaring early days.

Despite the numerous hardships encountered, the sheer speed of air travel continued to attract more and more paying customers throughout the 1920s. As a result, airline companies in Europe were constantly improving their aircraft and looking further afield when planning their routes. Together with transcontinental flights in America, many of the world's major air routes – now taken so much for granted by the modern jetsetter – were opened up between the two world wars, in pioneering flights that now rank as milestones in aviation history. Often with woefully inadequate machines one airline after another faced and overcame the difficulties of covering long distances over mountains, deserts, oceans and forests, setting up facilities along the way to make their path a little easier each time.

Flyingboats

Meanwhile, in France, ex-wartime bombers such as eleven-seater Farman Goliaths formed the mainstay of that country's first commercial airlines, and in those days France led the world in building up its route network. Most of the early French airline services were internal, linking cities such as Lyons, Lille, Marseilles and Paris.

However, by 1920 there were also flyingboat flights to Corsica and mail

Below: **The spirit of early passenger flight is captured in this painting.**

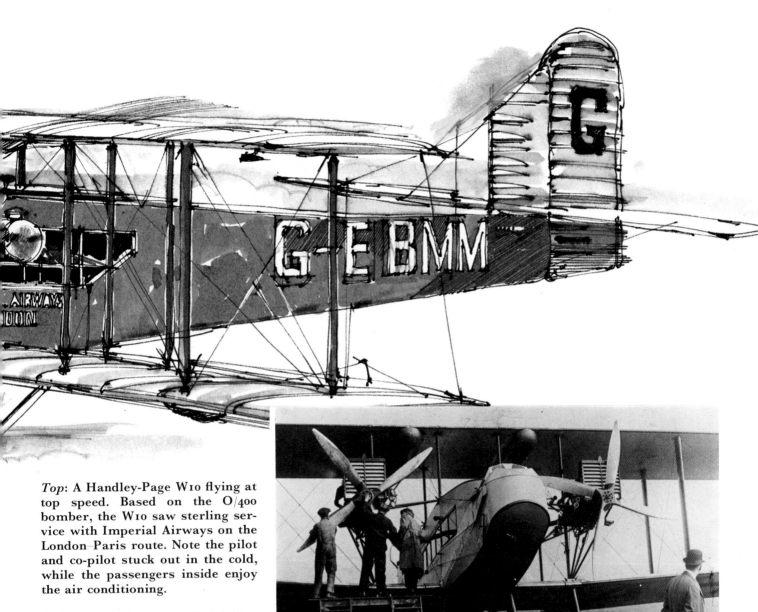

Top: A Handley-Page W10 flying at top speed. Based on the O/400 bomber, the W10 saw sterling service with Imperial Airways on the London–Paris route. Note the pilot and co-pilot stuck out in the cold, while the passengers inside enjoy the air conditioning.

Above: **Early airline maintenance facilities were crude to say the least.**

flights on from there across the Mediterranean to Casablanca in North Africa. From the French point of view however, Casablanca was just a stepping stone on the way to their money-spinning West African colonies, so the route was next extended to Agadir on Morroco's Atlantic coastline. Then, well-known flying-boat constructor Pierre Latécoère overcame enormous climatic difficulties and the threat of medieval-minded nomads to build a chain of landing fields and supply dumps south across the burning wastes of the Sahara desert. This epic pioneering had been completed by mid-1925, so it became possible to travel or send mail direct from Paris to Dakkar in West Africa, using Latécoère's sizeable fleet of Breguet 14s and war-surplus Salmson reconnaissance aircraft.

By that time there were also many scheduled services between Paris and London, for there was a growing market on that route. Unfortunately, too many airlines were offering the same service, making it unprofitable for all of them. As a result, Britain's leading airlines got into financial trouble in 1923, forcing the government of the day to inject £1 million into a new company called Imperial Airways which would unite all

the larger private firms under a single patriotic banner. In Holland, a state airline called KLM had been similarly established as early as 1919, and Denmark followed suit in the following year. Belgium's national airline, Sabena, was founded in 1923 and in 1926 Germany's leading airlines joined together to form Luft Hansa. One by one, the famous names of today were staking their claim to the rich bounty their owners believed lay ahead in the field of commercial air transport.

By this time, Great Britain was determined to establish air services to Australia via India, and to open up a route to southern Africa, thus spanning her vast Empire with a reliable and swift means of transportation. One of the treacherous desert sections of the eastern route had been opened for mail deliveries by the pilots of the RAF's Desert Air Force in 1922. Flying round-nosed, lumbering Vickers Vernon biplane transport air-

craft, the intrepid flyers often had long furrows ploughed into the featureless earth to help them find their way. However on 7 January 1927, the first commercial through flight from Basra on the Persian Gulf set off for Cairo, which was reached in two days.

Three Engines

The aircraft used on this lengthy journey was a de Havilland DH.66 Hercules biplane, one of five specially commissioned for Imperial Airways' long haul to the East. The Hercules was a fine aircraft, but its 'stick-and-string' construction was regarded as quite antiquated even then. Moreover, as aero-engines in the mid-twenties were not powerful enough to keep a twin-engined machine in the air if one failed, the Hercules had three aircooled radials of 420 hp each, just to be on the safe side. With eight passengers and the two crew members seated up at the front in their

Hannibal **over the Pyramids in Egypt.**

open cockpit, these grand old machines could cruise at around 170 km/hr (110 mph) in 650 km (400 mile) stages between refuelling stops.

For the next two years, political disputes in the Middle East prevented Imperial Airways from completing their England-India route, but on 30 March 1929 an Armstrong Whitworth Argosy biplane called *City of Glasgow* left Croydon Airport in London (then London's main airport) on the outward leg of the first-ever through flight. As France and Italy were in dispute at that time, the passengers had to travel between Switzerland and Genoa by train. From there, a Short Calcutta flyingboat took them to Alexandria, where a Hercules conveyed them the rest of the way to India with eight stops in between. The whole journey cost each passenger £130 and took seven days one way – slow by modern standards, but a remarkable achievement nonetheless, considering the equip-

ment at their disposal.

The Argosies were certainly a great improvement on earlier airliners and soon earned an enviable reputation for their economical and reliable service. Their two crew members were still stuck out at the front in the open, but inside the well-appointed cabin there were wicker seats for up to twenty passengers and an excellent view for one and all. Seven Argosies were specially designed for Imperial Airways' long-haul routes, and they served in the Middle East, India and Africa until the mid-1930s. They probably had their greatest moment when they inaugurated the celebrated 'Silver Wing' service between London and Paris in 1927. On these flights seating was reduced to eighteen to make room for a steward, who provided a superb buffet meal.

British routes finally reached Australia via India and Singapore and new aircraft were introduced to supercede the

Argosy and Hercules, reducing the journey time to twelve and a half days. These included a few four-engined Short Scylla biplanes and Armstrong Whitworth Atalanta highwing monoplanes, as well as the last of the big biplanes – the legendary Handley Page HP.42.

'Aerial Galleons'

Right from the very outset, Handley Page HP.42s were in a class of their own. They were massive fabric-covered biplanes at a time when sleek all-metal monoplanes were all the rage. Yet in nine year's service on busy European routes and lengthy, leisurely journeys throughout the British Empire these slow but steady 'aerial galleons' won jealously-guarded reputations for safety and dependability which have seldom been matched in the history of commercial air transport.

Despite its apparent outdatedness, with a mass of heavy bracing struts between the wings, 'two up, two down' uncowled engines and triple-finned biplane tail unit, the HP.42 was one of the world's first four-engined airliners. The prototype, named *Hannibal*, made its maiden flight from the factory airfield at Radlett, Hertfordshire, on 17 November 1930, piloted by Squadron Leader 'Lofty' England and Major John Cordes. What the HP.42 lacked in external streamlining was more than compensated for in terms of elegant comforts within. Its low ground clearance enabled passengers to step directly into the cabin, without the need for cumbersome portable stair units. Once aboard, the privileged passengers found inlaid wood panelling, comfortable armchairs, big picture windows, two lavatories and passenger operated controls for heating and ventilation.

This flagship of the Handley Page company was truly a Pullman carriage of

An interesting comparison in passenger cabins. Travel by air in the early days was for the privileged few who could afford it. Airliner interiors were accordingly sumptuous.

the air. It was designed exclusively for Imperial Airways of London, the foremost British airline of the interwar period. Two different versions were produced, the HP.42E (Eastern) for India and South Africa Empire routes, and the HP.42W (Western) for the cross-Channel 'shuttle' and European services. Four examples of each model were ordered by Imperial at a cost of £42,000 each and on 11 June 1931 *Hannibal*, although it was an 'Eastern' version, took over the London-Paris 'Silver Wing' service from Croydon to Le Bourget before leaving for its regular base at Cairo in August. By early 1932, all eight HP.42s had been delivered.

Slow Touchdown

These giant silver biplanes were particularly known for their slow touchdown speeds, permitting operation from very short landing areas. The HP.42's *forte* however could also be its Achilles' heel, for cruising at a sedate 150 km/hr (95 mph) it could be severely embarrassed by strong headwinds. One captain remembers taking more than an hour to cross the English Channel at its narrowest point in the teeth of a gale! Nonetheless, for a return fare of eight pounds and fifteen shillings, the 'Silver Wing' service proved extremely popular with businessmen. Passengers departed from the airways terminal at London's Victoria Station in the morning and were deposited 'refreshed and relaxed' on the rue Lafayette in the heart of Paris a mere three hours 34 minutes later, after a comfortable flight lasting two hours 15 minutes. 'Speed without hurry' was Imperial Airways' proud slogan.

Personal Titles

In keeping with the general air of luxury and elegance that surrounded the HP.42s wherever they flew, each aeroplane had its own personal title emblazoned across the curved silver nose area in bold black lettering. The HP.42Es were named *Hannibal*, *Hanno*, *Horsa* and *Hadrian* and carried twelve passengers in the forward cabin and twelve in the rear. The centre section of the fuselage where the engine noise was greatest was cleverly used as a cargo hold for mail and baggage to keep the passengers free from undue distraction. The HP.42W models, *Heracles*, *Horatius*, *Hengist* and *Helena*, seated twenty and eighteen passengers in fore and aft cabin areas respectively, with slightly reduced baggage space. An operational crew of three was carried, comprising captain, first officer and radio operator, with one or two cabin attendants.

HP.42E 'Eastern' models flew out of Cairo to Karachi and Delhi, making overnight stops *en route*. As the London to

Frankfurt Airport is symbolic of today's highly-automated approach to air travel. It contrasts with the picture of Berlin Airport taken in 1928.

Delhi journey took six and a half days to complete, it is not perhaps surprising that the crews and passengers tended to strike up a friendship along the way. It was not unusual of the captain to entertain his charges to dinner at the end of a long day's flying, and on the occasions when a landing at one of the Imperial's unattended desert fuel stores became necessary, he was not above asking one of his passengers to help fill up the aeroplane's tanks for the onward journey!

In all, the Imperial Airways fleet of HP.42s jointly logged more than 100,000 flying hours and flew a total of ten million miles without any passenger injury.

Today, only the highly polished propeller of *Horatius*, hanging in splendour on a flying club wall in the south of England remains to echo the magical spirit of this majestic bygone era.

Elsewhere in Europe, such countries as France, Germany, Italy and the Soviet Union had by this time established flourishing airline industries. After a seven year series of proving flights, the Dutch airline KLM finally began carrying passengers between Amsterdam and Jakarta in 1931. Much of the credit for the existence of this air route, which was the world's longest when inaugurated, must go to the aircraft of Anthony Fokker. During the First World War this

industrious Dutchman had made his name building warplanes for the Germans. In the interwar period he established a great reputation with a whole series of single- and multi-engined airliners, characterized by their sturdy construction and thick, high-mounted wooden wings.

Perhaps Fokker's most famous airliner was the triple-engined F-VII, used to pioneer a number of important air routes and frequently hitting the headlines when making epic journeys in the hands of early aeronautical adventurers. These included the first flight over the North Pole in 1926 (Richard Byrd and Floyd Bennett in the *Josephine Ford*) and the first flight across the Pacific Ocean in 1928 (Charles Kingsford-Smith and his crew in *Southern Cross*).

Despite all the progress being made by Anthony Fokker and his fellow Europeans, it was in the USA that the greatest leaps forward in airliner design had been made between the wars. Commercial flying there had begun immediately after the First World War with a fleet of American-built DH.4s and Standard JR-1 mailplanes, whose operators performed their duties in something of the spirit of the 'Pony Express'. By 1925 a comprehensive pattern of internal routes served the continent, with aircraft often following lines of fiery beacons by night to cross from coast to coast in less than two days.

When the US Post Office entrusted the handling of the mail to private enterprise in the following year, the floodgates were thrown open for commercial air operations on an unprecedented scale. Competition for Post Office contracts was very stiff, and this situation produced an attitude of intense salesmanship that could hardly fail to attract large numbers of paying passengers when transporting people became the main priority. Many

ISLAND AIRLINES

of the smaller airlines went bankrupt or merged with larger ones when this spirit of competition cut air fares to the bone, and so it was that the 'big four' airlines – TWA, American, Eastern and United – finally emerged at the top of the tree.

Flying Coast-to-coast

Small airliners like the exquisite bullet-shaped Lockheed Vega had up to now played a prominent part in the development of fast passenger services and vital mail deliveries, but to cater for the heavy demand much larger machines were soon taking to the air in great quantities. Typical of its time was the triple-engined Ford Trimotor, affectionately known to millions as the 'Tin Goose'. A highwing monoplane with a stately appearance and more than a passing resemblance to the Fokker F-VII/3 that had been its designer's inspiration, the Trimotor became the first great American contribution to the world of civil aviation. It had the same corrugated metal skin that characterized the earlier Junkers F.13 and made its maiden flight in 1926. Over 200 'Tin Geese' were eventually built, some flying even to this day on services to remote Latin American townships that would prove uneconomical for any other airliner to operate.

By 1933, transcontinental routes in particular had become great money-spinners in the USA, whose airlines cried out for more, bigger and better aircraft. These duly appeared in the shapes of the revolutionary Boeing 247 and Douglas

The beautifully-streamlined Lockheed Vega was built entirely of wood.

DC-2. Unlike the Fokkers and Fords that had gone before, these new monoplanes had their wings mounted low down on the fuselage and were beautifully streamlined. Both had retractable undercarriages and comfortable seating for ten and fourteen passengers respectively. Their powerful radial engines combined with their streamlining to give them a much higher top speed than had previously been possible. But more importantly for the continued growth of commercial aviation, these planes were the first which could fly safely, and even gain altitude, if one engine happened to fail.

The DC-2 possessed a slightly better performance than the Boeing 247, but both were worldbeaters. It was the Douglas type that began the first eighteen-hour transcontinental services in 1934, with foreign airlines like Lufthansa and KLM adding their names to the swelling DC-2 order books soon after. When the Douglas company announced a slightly larger successor (the DC-3) soon after, it was not perhaps surprising that this went on to become the most famous and successful airliner of all time.

The original DC-3s were developed for American Airlines and first saw service on their non-stop New York-Chicago run in June 1936. Such was their success that they were put on general sale, being sold as either fourteen-seat 'sleeper' models or 21-seat 'dayliners'. Powered by two 1,000 hp Wright

Affectionately known as the 'Tin Goose', the legendary Ford Trimotor was America's first great contribution to civil air transport. In its 4AT version the 'Tin Goose' was powered by three Wright Whirlwind radials.

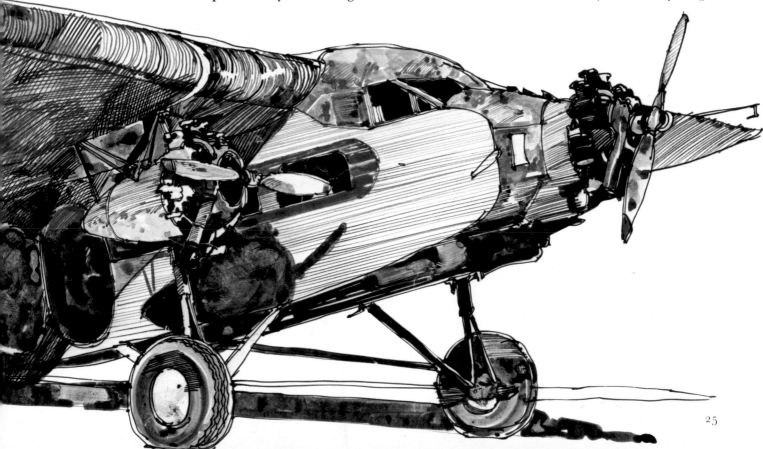

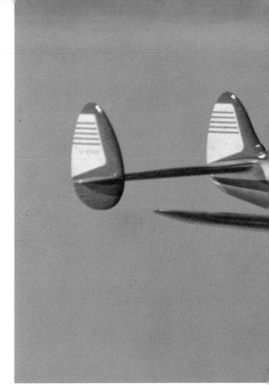

Cyclone radial engines, these marvellous aircraft immediately reduced the journey time across America by another two hours. By the time DC-3 production ceased, virtually every airline in the world had at one time or another operated the type. It was built under licence in several countries, including the Soviet Union, and saw outstanding wartime service as the immortal Dakota. A much later version demonstrated even greater versatility, for it saw combat as a 'gunship' during the war in Vietnam! Many hundreds are still flying today in every corner of the world.

Enter Electra

In an attempt to keep pace with Boeing and Douglas in the lucrative twin-engined airliner market, Lockheed introduced an elegant ten-twelve seater called the Electra in 1935. Easily recognizable with its twin tailfins, the Electra had a neat retractable undercarriage and a useful maximum speed of 320 km/hr (200 mph). It was something of a challenge to Lockheed to build such an aircraft, as it was constructed entirely of metal, whereas their previous products had been wooden machines like the bullet-shaped Vega. That neat retractable undercarriage mechanism almost became the prototype's downfall when it failed to lock down properly after an early test flight. The pilot just managed to maintain control as the Electra touched down on the runway and the fault was rectified before mass production began.

Electras could carry the same number of passengers as Boeing 247s, but in doing so could fly faster, higher and further. At $36,000 they were also the cheapest planes in that sector of the market, and so proved highly competitive. Electras went on to serve with such famous airlines as Braniff and Pan American and were also ordered by operators in Britain, Australia and New Zealand. A

sad footnote to the story of the Electra is that Amelia Earhart, the most famous aviatrix of the 1930s, was flying an Electra on a round-the-world record attempt when she disappeared without trace in the Pacific Ocean in 1937.

Spurred on by the success of their DC-3, the Douglas company realized that it was now well within their capabilities to produce an even larger airliner, possibly even doubling the number of engines. The end result of this thinking was the DC-4, with ample accommodation for 54 passengers in its pressurized cabin. This design found much favour with the airlines, and a military variant known as the C-54 Skymaster was widely used in the transport role, many later being released onto the civilian market. At around the same time Boeing produced the Stratoliner, using the wings and engines of their famous B-17 Flying Fortress bomber.

Although Australia, New Zealand, Canada, Japan, South Africa and various South American countries had all developed commercial airlines before the

A United Airline stewardess in military uniform.

The shape of the Lockheed Electra was a familiar sight for many years.

Second World War, most of their operations were suspended when the fighting commenced and their aircraft taken over for military use. Of all the world's national airline services, only the USA's internal flights continued on any great scale during the course of the war. As a result, when peace returned, the American airlines and planemakers were already geared up to spread around the globe.

Meanwhile, on the technical side the war had encouraged a great increase in the size of aircraft, considerable improvements in their design, and the development of quite sophisticated communication and radar systems. In the immediate aftermath of the war, though, many airlines found themselves very short of both suitable aircraft and facilities. Great Britain's premier airline BOAC, for example, began a London-Buenos Aires service in 1946 using modified wartime surplus aircraft like Avro Lancastrians (derived from the Lancaster bomber), Junkers Ju 52/ms, and of course DC-3s.

An elegant newcomer

Across the Atlantic DC-3s also took care of most postwar internal services in the USA, while ex-wartime DC-4s commenced scheduled services between New York and London in 1945, making two refuelling stops on the way and taking 24 hours to complete the journey. By February 1946 however, the transatlantic services of both Pan Am and TWA had been taken over by an elegant newcomer called the Lockheed Constellation. Shaped rather like a very long cigar, these beautiful, four-engined aircraft could carry 43-60 passengers at a cruising speed of 490 km/hr (300 mph) and came as a vast improvement on earlier types.

A study of the Lockheed Super Constellation in flight.

A DC-6B of the Swiss Airline Balair basks in the sun outside its hanger.

In an attempt to compete with the 'Connie', Douglas stretched their DC-4 to accommodate up to 86 passengers, gave it four big 2,400 hp Double Wasp engines, and so produced a worthy rival – the DC-6. This sturdy machine, of which 170 were built, began to fly 'across the pond' in 1947 in a journey time of only ten hours. It was followed by the DC-6B, with room for up to 102 passengers, whose most outstanding feature was its range of over 4,800 km (3,000 miles). The DC-6B proved to be one of the most outstanding and economical piston-engined airliners ever built, with many of the 288 examples that entered service still flying to this day.

As is usual in the fiercely competitive world of commercial aviation, Lockheed retaliated with an improved version of the Constellation in 1947, boasting an increased fuel capacity that enabled it to make nonstop flights from New York to Paris. This model also became the first aircraft to operate a regular round-the-world air service in June of that same year. Aiming to meet postwar requirements at the luxury end of the market, Boeing brought out the mighty Stratocruiser in 1949. This impressive four-engined doubledecker with rows of seats on the upper deck and lounges and bars below was descended from the massive B-29 Superfortress bomber of Second World War vintage.

On its upper deck the Stratocruiser could seat 50-100 passengers, or could alternatively provide 28 bunks and five seats. Although some of the 55 Stratocruisers built had problems with their engines, they were fast, had a useful 6,700 km (4,200 mile) range and were popular with passengers and crew alike. Several were sold abroad for first class long-haul services, and with airlines such as BOAC they continued in this role until they were superceded by jets in the late fifties.

The Turboprop

By the time Constellations, DC-6Bs and Stratocruisers entered service, a better type of aeroengine known as the Wright Turbo Compound was becoming widely available. Lockheed took the brave decision to convert the Constellation to such powerplants and 'stretch' the length of the fuselage in 1950, this resulting in the serpentine form of the Super Constellation. Douglas followed suit by producing the DC-7, similar in most ways to their DC-6B but having Wright Turbo Compound turboprop engines and increased seating capacity. To the DC-7 went the distinction of flying the first nonstop transcontinental service in the USA, taking just eight hours to cross from coast to coast. With the addition of wingtip fuel tanks, the 'Super Connie' achieved the same feat soon after, and still further refined versions of both types went on to make the first nonstop scheduled flights across the Atlantic. These wonderful machines made possible such 'dream flights' as Europe-Japan over the North Pole and represented the pinnacle of piston engined aircraft development.

Although American airlines and planemakers dominated the postwar civil aviation scene in no uncertain terms, the British made a valiant and fairly successful attempt to reassert their expertise when Vickers introduced their turboprop-powered Viscount in 1950. Designed for economical operation over short and medium distances, the Viscount was a real winner as far as passengers were concerned with its big cabin windows and smooth, quiet ride high above the clouds. Its introduction on certain routes doubled the demand for tickets almost overnight and eventually led to sales of 444 Viscounts to airlines all over the world – including the USA. Another notable British turboprop airliner was the big Bristol Britannia, designed for use on much longer routes. Unfortunately the Britannia took to the air a little too late to realize its full potential, for just one year later Boeing's worldbeating 707 appeared and Britannia sales stuck at a mere 85.

The Comet

Turboprop airliners occupy an important place in the history of aviation, but nowadays the international scene is well and truly geared to jet propulsion. The first jet airliners entered service in 1952, when BOAC began selling tickets for flights between London and Johannesburg in the revolutionary new de Havilland Comet 1. Powered by four Rolls-Royce turbojets buried in the wing-roots, the Comet 1 seated 36 passengers in great comfort and more than halved flying times over long distances with its ability to fly at very high altitudes where the air is thin and offers less resistance. For example, it cut the London-Tokyo time from 86 hours to a mere 23 at a

stroke.

In their first year of operations over a dozen Comet 1s flew with BOAC and Air France, and de Havilland's order book was bulging. Then, between 1953-4, three aircraft disintegrated in mid-air with the loss of everyone aboard. All Comets were immediately grounded pending a full investigation and the world's newspapers buzzed with horror stories about the dangers of mass transportation by jet aircraft. The makers

eventually traced the cause of the tragedies to metal fatigue in the aircraft's skin, leading to the pressurized fuselage bursting open with indescribable violence.

It was four more years before de Havilland and BOAC felt able to launch a heavily revised Comet 4 back into service. Reasonable sales were achieved, and a great deal had been learned about the problem of flying large numbers of passengers at very high speeds, but by this time the worldbeating potential of

Cathay Pacific is one of the multitude of airlines to operate the Boeing 707.

A Comet 4-B of Dan-Air displays its sleek lines as it soars off the runway.

the original Comet 1 had been lost and bigger and better American jet airliners were already entering service – notably the famous Boeing 707.

Big Jets

Back in 1952, the Boeing company had invested around $20 million to develop a big jet airliner. Just two years later, drawing from the vast amount of experience they had accumulated building large jet bomber aircraft postwar, they rolled out their prototype. Pan American placed an order almost immediately and with this endorsement further orders began to flow in from all around the world. By October 1958 the first transatlantic 707 services got underway and ushered in the era of relatively cheap mass air travel. Nowadays, the imposing lines of this graceful sweptwing aircraft with its engines slung underwing in big pods is a familiar sight the world over in a number of variants, varying from the short-range Boeing 720 to the impressive 707-420 Intercontinental. By the late-seventies around 1,000 examples of the 707/720 family had been built, these having flown a combined total of over 40 million hours, carrying approximately 600 million passengers in the process. Not slow to enter into competition for big orders in this area of the market were the Douglas company, who built a very similar aircraft called the DC-8.

Meanwhile, Britain tried to break into the big jet market with the VC10, which began its airline career in BOAC colours in 1964. This distinctive aircraft, with its high T-shaped tail and four Rolls-Royce Conway engines clustered in pairs on either side of the rear fuselage was especially designed for the 'hot and high' conditions encountered on many of BOAC's intercontinental routes. Carrying around 150 passengers at a cruising speed of 930 km/hr (580 mph) the VC10 was a fine ambassador for Britain's aviation industry wherever it flew, but the Vickers company found it virtually impossible to compete in a market so totally

dominated by the giant American plane-makers. The Soviet Union, with their 'captive market' state airline Aeroflot, had no such problems selling the very similar Ilyushin Il-62, which commenced its flying career on the Moscow-Montreal route in 1967.

Slightly smaller in size, though no less important, are the short- and medium-range jetliners that are now so familiar to plane spotters the world over. The first of these to fly, the Sud Aviation Caravelle from France, took to the air on its maiden flight in 1955. They are still to be seen in various countries today, but have passed their heyday and are much rarer now than they were. The Caravelle has beautiful lines, but the thing most important airport spectators marvelled at when the type first entered service was the steepness and speed of its initial climb after takeoff.

The 'Jumbo Jets'

Similar in basic configuration to the Caravelle even to the point of having both engines mounted on the rear fuselage, are Britain's BAC One-Eleven, Holland's Fokker F.28 Fellowship and USA's McDonnell Douglas DC-9 and Boeing 727. All serve in large numbers worldwide, though the American types outnumber the others by quite a considerable margin. The trijet 727 was built as a result of design studies by Boeing that indicated the need for a

Boeing's superb 727 is the world's best-selling jet airliner by a substantial margin with the 2,000 sales mark now in sight.

The Trijet 737 is the smallest model made in Boeing's range. It has been specially designed to permit operation from short runways.

A DC-9 of the Dutch airline KLM.

short- to medium-range jet airliner to replace the many piston and turbojet engined aircraft then being phased out of service. Three engines were chosen for reasons of economy and to accomplish the desired 960 km/hr (600 mph) performance, while special highlift flaps were incorporated to permit operations from relatively short runways.

By late 1964, several airlines reported their need for an aircraft capable of carrying slightly more passengers so Boeing introduced the 727-200 version, featuring a substantial increase in cabin length. Success for the new model was immediate, as more and more world airlines chose to make largescale purchases. On 29 November 1973 the 1,000th 727 was rolled off the production line at Renton, Washington; the first time in history that any commercial airliner had reached this figure. With production still proceeding at a cracking pace and the 2,000 sales mark within sight, the Boeing 727 is easily the world's best-selling jet airliner.

The smallest member of the Boeing family of jet airliners is the short-range 737, powered by two underwing Pratt & Whitney JT8D engines – the same type that powers the trijet 727. Despite its smaller external dimensions, the stocky 737 has the same cabin width as any other contemporary jetliner, except of course for the wide-bodied 'jumbo jets', like the European Airbus, McDonnell Douglas DC-10, Lockheed TriStar and, of course, the first of the 'jumbos' – the gigantic Boeing 747.

It is a sobering thought that the 747 is

Striking colour schemes are very popular as shown by this TAA DC-9.

twice as long as the total distance covered in man's first powered flight – by Orville Wright in 1903. Had Wright taken off beside the Boeing's tail, he would not even have reached the wings before coming back down to earth. The first prototype took to the air for its maiden flight on 19 February 1969, amidst a welter of public acclaim. A true heavyweight, it was soon dubbed 'Jumbo Jet' by the press and has since loaned this popular title to a whole new generation of wide-bodied jetliners.

Pan American inaugurated the first commercial services with the type in February 1970, this long-established airline having assured the early success of the 747 by placing a firm order for 25 aircraft virtually straight off the drawing board. The initial introduction into

regular scheduled service went remarkably smoothly, particularly bearing in mind the fact that airline and airport operators had no previous experience of handling such a huge aircraft. Predictably, orders began to flow in from all over the world as airlines clammered to cash in on the 'jumbo' revolution.

Although the 747 boasts truly enormous proportions, and is capable of carrying up to 500 passengers, it is of conventional construction. With its four engines slung well beneath the wings on streamlined pylons, it has been designed with the ease of maintenance as a top priority. Perhaps it is as a result of this that airlines operating the type report very favourably on its reliability. Passengers have certainly never been so well catered for. There are a variety of seating arrange-

ments to be found in the 747s of different airlines, but common to almost all of them are the two aisles that run the entire length of the aircraft. The ten-abreast seating configuration affords a level of comfort and spaciousness unmatched in previous airliner interiors and provides room for such luxuries as a lounge, a theatre, a spiral staircase to the upper decks, and various private seating areas. Passengers board the 747 through ten double-width doors, five on either side of the fuselage.

The flight deck, with arrangements for a crew of three or four, is on a level high above that of the main passenger cabin. In fact, because the crew are already so high off the ground even when the 747 is

Above: **Passengers on a 747 enjoy an in-flight movie.** *Below*: **The spiral staircase is a unique feature.** *Bottom*: **A British Airways' 747.**

A 747's engine dwarfs a technician.

sitting on its undercarriage, Boeing's designers seriously considered locating the flight deck beneath the aircraft's belly, in order to improve the pilot's forward vision during takeoff and landing. A downward-looking periscope was also considered during the early design stage, but both solutions were rejected when windtunnel tests showed that the line of the 747's nosecone would need to curve steeply down from the windscreen anyway, thus bestowing excellent visibility from the cockpit.

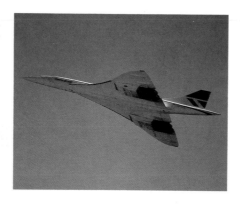

Concorde.

4.5 Million Parts

Boeing 747s are assembled near Seattle, Washington, in the largest building ever made. It's so large that clouds have been known to form in the ceiling! Here, the 4.5 million parts which go together to make each aircraft come in from all corners of the United States. The engines are made in either Connecticut, Ohio, or Derby, England (depending on the type of engine fitted), the fuselage in California, the nose section in Kansas and the tailplane in Texas. In all, some 15,000 companies manufacture the multitude of parts transported to Seattle for final assembly. Many of these components re electrical, for the 747 is fitted with some of the most sophisticated avionics (aviation electronics) ever flown. Its automatic navigation system, for example, is only slightly larger than a standard television set and weighs about the same. Yet it can provide completely automatic guidance – through any weather – to any point on the globe, with no outside radio contact. Amazingly, the 747's airframe is laced with many hundreds of kilometres of electrical wiring, while the 1,100 hp auxiliary power unit installed in the extreme tail section could cater for the entire electrical needs of a small town. Another interesting feature of the 747 is its ability to carry its own spare engine on a *fifth* pylon beneath the port wing. Thus equipped, the five-engined 'jumbos' are able to save their operators substantial air freighting costs by transporting their own spare engines for routine maintenance at faraway engineering facilities.

Flying Supersonic

As far as the future of airliners is concerned, there is little doubt that people will expect to travel even faster to their destinations in the years to come. The beautiful Anglo-French Concorde provides a fascinating pointer to the shape of things to come, though most experts agree that future supersonic passenger aircraft will need to carry far more people to really pay their way. Despite its economic shortcomings, Concorde is by far the most glamorous shape in the skies, enabling businessmen who can afford the fare to reach faraway meeting places.

Transatlantic journeys at over twice the speed of sound seem a far cry from Count Ferdinand von Zeppelin's massive hydrogen-filled dirigibles, yet the same pioneering spirit that forged the first air routes can still be seen today through the glossy coat of technology.

A McDonnell-Douglas DC-10 of the West German state airline Lufthansa 'rotates' at take-off.

AIR RACING
Contests in the Sky

There have been air races for as long as there have been aeroplanes that would stay in the air long enough to complete even the shortest course. In the early days, many victorious pilots would have had to admit that their success was due to the fact that no other aircraft had been able to stay up long enough to pass the winning post! Before the First World War, in the years from 1909–14, aero-engines were unreliable, aircraft were tricky to keep airborne and often they were only marginally safe to fly over any distance, while their pilots and designers were still almost totally ignorant of the laws of nature that let man take to the air at all.

The first international air race meeting in the world was organized by the French in 1909 at Reims. 38 aircraft turned up, of which 23 actually flew. There were daily speed prizes for ten-kilometre (six-mile) circuits of the airfield and on the last day a two-lap contest was held for the Gordon Bennett Trophy – the first air racing prize in history. It was won by Glenn Curtiss of America, flying a tiny biplane of his own design called the *Golden Flyer*, at 75.7 km/hr (47 mph). He flew at around 14 m (50 ft), the altitude record at this meeting being only 155 m (508 ft). The Gordon Bennett was the most famous of the prewar air racing events and was won the following year by an Englishman named Claude Grahame-White. 'Whitey' as he was known, was a famous and much respected pioneer pilot who founded Hendon aerodrome in North London, where many local races were held. It was also famous as the site of the great Royal Air

The first air racing meeting took place in Reims in France in 1909 and, as can be seen here, the aircraft entered were extremely frail and basic.

Force Pageants held during the years between the two World Wars and although it is now closed as an operational airfield, it remains as famous as ever as the home of the magnificent RAF Museum.

Charles Weymann of the USA won the next Gordon Bennett contest in a Nieuport racer at 125.5 km/hr (78 mph), and the next two events were taken by France, with their glorious Deperdussin racers. These 'Deps' were the first purpose-built racers in the world, marvellously-streamlined wooden monoplanes, with huge rotary engines that enabled the French pilot Marcel Prévost to win in

1913 with a fastest lap of almost 204 km/hr (127 mph). Not only was he the first man ever to fly at over 200 km/hr, but he broke the World Air Speed Record three times in the course of the race! In 1920, when the event was revived after the First World War, France won it again, this time with a Nieuport-Delage 29 which achieved 271 km/hr (168 mph). That was the end of the famous Gordon Bennett races, for under the rules, France, having won it three times in succession, became the permanent holder of this coveted trophy.

'Spin-off'

The year 1920 was also notable for the appearance of a very advanced American racer called the Dayton-Wright. This monoplane featured an enclosed cockpit and a retractable undercarriage which gave extra streamlining. It retired during the course of the race but serves as a good example of the stimulus given to aircraft designers by the challenge of international race meetings. In fact, a very interesting picture emerges from these events: advanced 'one-off' types specially-designed for racing purposes began to form the basis for subsequent production fighter aircraft. Indeed, one of the justifications for spending what later became hundreds of thousands of pounds or dollars on racers was the use to which the knowledge gained in races could be put into new fighter designs.

The same situation exists to this day in such fields as motor car racing, in a process we now term 'technology spin-off'. For example, from his compact little pre-1914 racers, Edouard Niéport evolved the famous Nieuport Scouts that served with such distinction in the First

Henri Biard standing in the cockpit of his Supermarine Sea Lion II in 1923.

World War, while Louis Bechereau, who designed the Deperdussin, used the knowledge gained in racing to create the superb range of Spad biplane fighters.

The 'spin-off' process was occasionally reversed when, for example, the 1920 winner of the Gordon Bennett was a carefully-prepared and very special version of a standard French fighter! The 'Dep' had enjoyed a great moment of glory some time earlier when a few months before the 1913 Gordon Bennett, Prevost won the very first Schneider Trophy air race – easily the most famous aerial contest in history. One of the beautiful Deperdussin racers has survived to this day and can still be seen in the *Musée de l'Air*, the well-known air museum in Paris.

Schneider Trophy

The background to the Schneider Trophy, which led to the most famous series of air races ever held, is not generally known. Jacques Schneider, the son of a wealthy French steel and armament manufacturer, announced that he was offering a trophy for seaplane competition in 1913. As a keen racing motorist and balloonist, he was determined to advance the cause of flying – particularly in his native country. It seemed to him that the future of long-distance flying lay with flyingboats and floatplanes, as most of the surface of the world is, of course, water. Moreover, he had wisely decided that a speed contest would offer most stimulus to advancement in design and it was argued that restrictions in landing speeds necessary to permit the use of existing aerodromes on land would cramp achievement of really high top speeds. Water 'aerodromes', on the other hand, could be as long as required.

His idea was enthusiastically received and the first contest took place at the curiously named Monaco Hydro-Aeroplane Meeting in 1913. The word 'seaplane' was not at this time in general use and had, in fact, been first proposed by none other than Winston Churchill. Seven entries were received for the first race, but three of them were knocked out in the elaborate trials and seaworthiness tests beforehand. Three French and one American pilot took part in the actual race and only two of the French pilots completed the 28 gruelling ten-kilometre (six-mile) laps. As already seen, the winner was Marcel Prévost, with Roland Garros (later to become the first French fighter ace) in second place. The other French pilot, Espanet, and the sole American, ex-Gordon Bennett Trophy winner Charles Weymann, both flying Nieuports, retired during the course of the race.

This first contest for the Schneider Trophy was a very small affair, tacked on to the tail end of the Monaco meeting, and it served chiefly to emphasise the unreliability of aeroengines at this period of time, a fact already well known. The second meeting, also held in Monaco harbour the following year, attracted entries from five nations, including Britain. Not counting reserves, there were four French entries, two from Britain, two from the USA, and one each from Switzerland and Germany.

On paper, that year's event sounds like a rather dismal affair as races go. All four French entries fell out one by one with mechanical troubles, while one of the British aircraft and the solitary German crashed during pre-race trials. The race was finally won by the other British entry, Howard Pixton, flying a specially prepared Sopwith 'Schneider', with Burri of Switzerland second. Both American entries withdrew when Pixton's times were published, knowing they could do no better. The race caused a lot of excitement at the time, one reason being that the winning speed was very high.

Up to this point in history, nobody really considered Britain to be of any great importance in the aviation world.

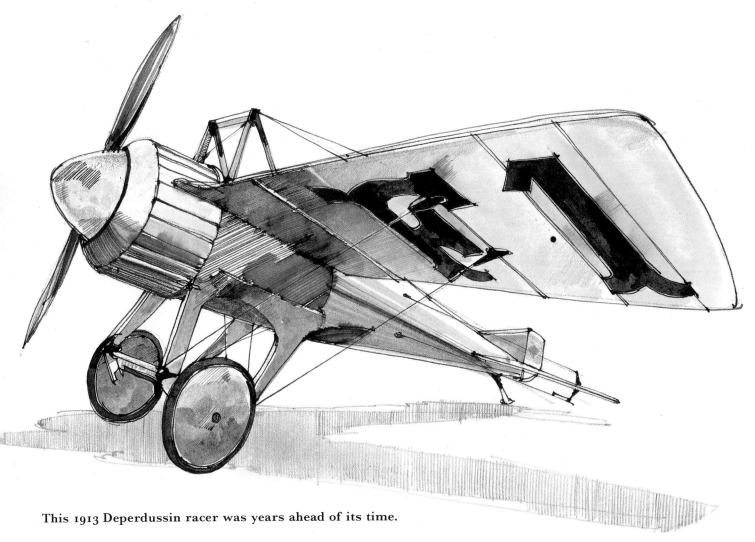

This 1913 Deperdussin racer was years ahead of its time.

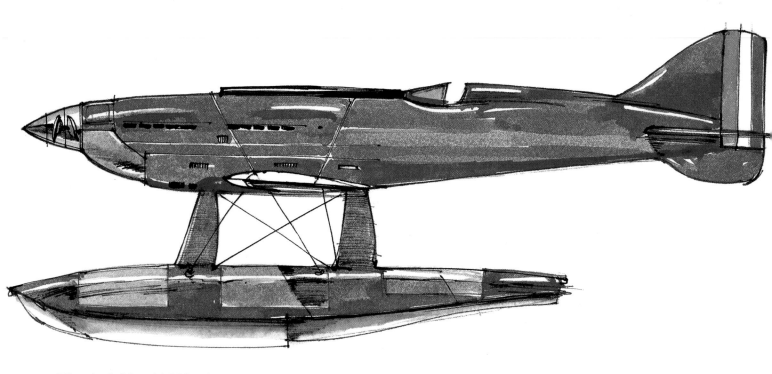

The sleek Macchi MC72 broke the World Air Speed Record in 1934 with a speed of 705 km/h (441 mph).

Now Tommy Sopwith and his chief engineer Fred Sigrist had not only put Britain among the leaders in aviation at one jump with the excellent little 'Schneider' but laid the foundations for a long line of world-beating fighter, aircraft, from the Sopwith Pup, Camel and Snipe of the First War to the Hurricane, Typhoon and Tempest of the Second, right through to the Hunter and vertical take-off Harrier of modern times. Tommy Sopwith's high standards of fighter design established a strong tradition that was carried on by the famous designer Sydney Camm when Sopwith's company became part of Hawker Aircraft in the 1920s.

It was Britain's privilege as winner to

was not therefore awarded, but as recognition of Janello's brave effort it was decided to ask Italy to stage the next contest.

In 1920, however, only the Italian team took the trouble to enter, so they had to content themselves with the mandatory once-over crossing of the finishing line by a single aircraft to claim the Trophy as their own – a hollow victory

indeed. In the following year's competition the field was slightly larger (it could hardly have been smaller), but the sole French entry was damaged during preliminary trials and two of the three Italian aircraft retired with mechanical troubles. As no-one else had entered it

organize the next contest. This was held at Bournemouth in 1919, after the First World War had ended. Unfortunately, the meeting was a complete and utter failure for two main reasons. The organization was very poor, and the whole area was blanketed by thick fog. All three British entries retired after just one lap and only Janello, a plucky Italian contender, held on for all eleven laps (the race was only for ten, but lap-counting was always a headache for pilots, particularly in poor weather conditions). It was only then discovered that he had mistaken a boat for one of the turn-markers, so none of his laps had taken a correct course. The Schneider Trophy was left to a solitary Italian to take the 'honours'.

If Italy gained a third consecutive win in the 1921 contest (1919 did not count) she would keep the Trophy for good, so it is not surprising that both France and Britain were roused at last to serious competition. The race took place at Naples and was won by Henri Biard, representing Britain in a Supermarine Sea Lion at 234.5 km/hr (145.7 mph). The Italians came in second, third and fourth. The French machines withdrew just before the event got underway but this was a most exciting contest nonetheless. Just before it started the Italians suddenly brought the trials date forward, but failed to prevent the British entry being ready in time.

During the race, the three Italians bunched-up in an attempt to prevent Biard from overtaking. After a terrific struggle he got through, but the quickest of the Italians was only a fraction of a second behind him and it was a very close battle right to the chequered flag. It was obvious that the Italian team consisted of some very good pilots and that they had plenty of competition experience behind them. Britain would have to work extremely hard to stay in the running in 1923, but then an entirely new factor entered into the situation — the first appearance of an American team to challenge the Europeans.

Aviation development in the USA had been progressing by leaps and bounds and it was this breakneck progress which caused the Americans to introduce a new and somewhat disturbing approach to the Schneider Trophy competition. Instead of entering the usual team of private individuals, America was this time represented by a team of US Navy pilot officers and their fleet of immaculate Curtiss CR-3 racers.

The interest of America's armed forces in air racing becomes obvious later, but the implications of using powerful service aircraft, backed by military personnel and resources, were not lost on the privately-sponsored teams of Britain and France. Italy declined to field a team at all, as the known performance of the American aircraft convinced her that there was no chance of victory. France, the birthplace of the Schneider Trophy, was determined to take it home, but their attempt was dogged with ill-luck and not a single French aircraft completed the course in 1923. France never took part in the event again.

The US Navy's Curtiss racers, endowed with all that service support plus a staggeringly advanced engine and propeller combination, came first and

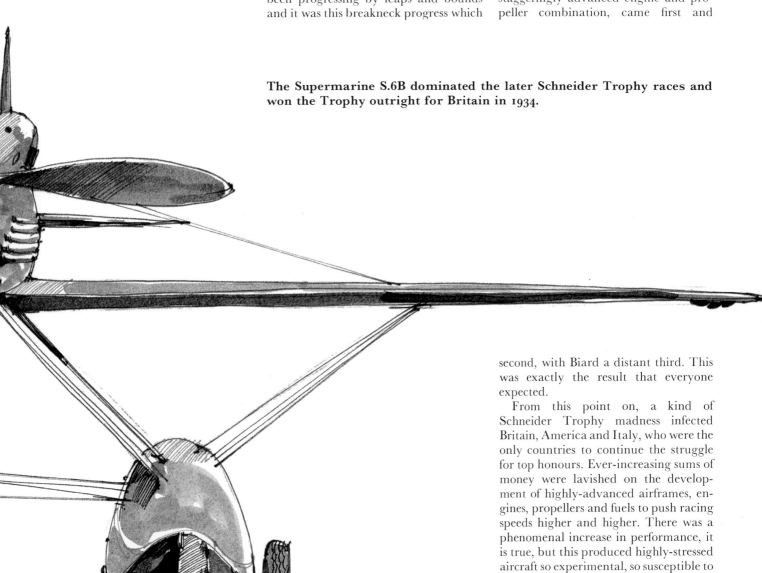

The Supermarine S.6B dominated the later Schneider Trophy races and won the Trophy outright for Britain in 1934.

second, with Biard a distant third. This was exactly the result that everyone expected.

From this point on, a kind of Schneider Trophy madness infected Britain, America and Italy, who were the only countries to continue the struggle for top honours. Ever-increasing sums of money were lavished on the development of highly-advanced airframes, engines, propellers and fuels to push racing speeds higher and higher. There was a phenomenal increase in performance, it is true, but this produced highly-stressed aircraft so experimental, so susceptible to unforeseen mechanical problems, that the Schneider Trophy story becomes a long catalogue of constant struggles against engine failures, of frantic last-minute redesign jobs and airframe rebuilding operations that seemed like an unending race against the downward sweep of the starter's flag. Gradually, even the British and Italian governments were drawn into the contest as winning became a matter of national prestige.

In 1924, no challengers were ready in time, and the US Navy very sportingly refused to make the mandatory once-over crossing of the finishing line to claim the event as their own, so the race was postponed until the following year. This generosity cost the Navy permanent retention of the Schneider Trophy, as they won it in 1925. The US Army's pilot was Lieutenant Jimmy Doolittle, who was destined to rise to fame as the first man to bomb Tokyo during the Second World War. He later became commander of the 8th Air Force, based in England, and as such was responsible for the daylight bombardment of Nazi Germany.

Great Britain and Italy learned a big lesson from the Americans' steamroller victories with superior equipment and both these countries entered highly-streamlined, very powerful racers for the 1926 competition. Despite their renewed effort, neither country's aircraft proved a

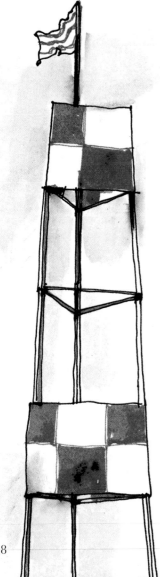

Jimmy Doolittle was the only pilot to master the extraordinary Gee-Bee which was characterized by the distinctive barrel-shaped fuselage. The other pilots were all killed.

match for the Americans. Britain came in second, the Italians third.

Time was too scarce for the private British designers to get a team of aircraft ready for the 1926 event, but the Italian planemaking company Macchi came up with a superb seaplane powered by a race-tuned Fiat engine of 880 hp and regained the Schneider Trophy at an average speed of 396.7 km/hr (246 mph). America was suitably impressed.

Britain successfully returned to the fray for the 1927 event, this time armed with two great advantages – the financial backing of its government through the Royal Air Force, and the first of a superb series of racing seaplanes designed by the brilliant Reginald Mitchell of the Supermarine company.

After 1927 it was decided to hold contests for the Schneider Trophy once every two years, to give designers and manufacturers more time to prepare their aircraft. The RAF team and their wonderful Supermarine racers, challenged only by Italy, won the event three times in a row in a blaze of publicity. The superb trophy was theirs for keeps.

The road to success had not always been smooth, however, for in 1931 the British government, keen to save money in those difficult times, announced that it would not be supporting the RAF in their plans to defend the Schneider Trophy. A personal cheque for £100,000 from Lady Houston to the Royal Aero Club saved the day, however, and the government consented to revive the RAF High Speed Flight. Rolls-Royce, aided by a specially-developed concoction of fuel, managed to squeeze no less than 2,350 hp from their race-tuned engine, enabling Flt Lt John Boothman to fly his graceful Supermarine S.6B to victory at an average of 547.3 km/hr (240.8 mph).

Both the USA and Italy had requested a postponement of the 1931 race to enable them to enter, but they did so only nine days before the contest and with no hope of raising finance for a further year the Royal Aero Club refused. Flt Lt Boothman later rose to the rank of Air Chief Marshal and gained a knighthood, while the S.6B went on to establish a new World Air Speed Record of 655.7 km/hr (407.5 mph) and provided the impetus that eventually led to the development of the legendary Spitfire fighter. The actual aircraft that attained this phenomenal speed is today in the Science Museum in

London. Between her great floats she guards the Schneider Trophy itself, placed there by the Royal Aero Club in the 1970s after it had been missing.

In the meantime, in Britain and America air racing had been developing along quite different lines. Claude Grahame-White had revived the racing at Hendon with the pre-war Aerial Derby, but in 1922 King George V offered a royal trophy – the King's Cup

– for handicap racing. This provided the stimulus for improving the breed of civil aircraft. From 1922 until the present day the race has continued. It is the oldest existing aerial race in the world and it has seen a lot of changes in the course of its long history.

In 1922, there were few new aeroplanes available and the first race was won by a commercial airliner entered by Instone Air Lines, and even that was a

The fabulous twin-engined DH.88 Comet *Grosvenor House* won the 1934 MacRobertson England–Australia race outright.

Formula One air racers are today's successors to such aircraft as the GeeBee of the 1930s.

converted DH.4 bomber. Frank Courtney won the second event in a civil-registered Siskin biplane fighter and Alan Cobham the third race in 1924, flying a big DH.50 biplane. For each of these events a separate trophy was awarded, a massive and imposing cup that seemed almost as big as the people who received it.

After this it became a challenge event, the cup being held by the winner for one year only. (One is tempted to wonder if the cost of a new cup every year prompted this sudden change in arrangements.) The first cup is still in possession of the Instone family and Frank Courtney still has 'number two' at his home in California. The late Sir Alan Cobham, winner of the third race, became famous for a series of pioneering flights and founded the firm of Flight Refuelling Ltd to develop, to the point of commercial viability, the art of transferring fuel from one aircraft to another in mid-air.

The first light aeroplane to win the King's Cup Air Race was one of the early Moths in 1926, flown by Hubert Broad, a de Havilland test pilot and Schneider competitor. In 1927 and 1928, Captain Wally Hope won twice in succession and later, in 1932, won it again to become the

only man to win the race three times. Atcherley, who had a long and distinguished career ahead of him in the RAF and who flew in the 1929 Schneider Trophy race, won the King's Cup in that same year. 'Batchy', as he was a known to his friends, was very lively personality and a great practical joker.

Captain Geoffrey de Havilland, a member of the famous family, flying one of his Leopard Moths, won in 1933 at 224.5 km/hr (139.5 mph) – a highly respectable speed for a four-seater light aircraft in those early days. All these races were held over courses running from several hundred to over a thousand kilometres long, with landing points at widely-spread airfields. Events often occupied two or three days with preliminary or eliminating rounds. Aircraft were handicapped according to the their estimated or calculated top speeds to ensure (in theory) that they all arrived simultaneously at the finish, thus placing the emphasis on the skill of the pilots. In practice finishes are usually more drawn out, but some excitingly close results have been recorded.

The last King's Cup Air Race before the Second World War was held in 1938, and was won by Alex Henshaw at the then fastest speed ever for the event, 380.1 km/hr (236.25 mph). The aircraft

he flew, a Percival Mew Gull registered G-AEXF, has recently been restored to airworthy condition and still flies from its original base at Redhill, Surrey. Its designer, Edgar Percival, watched it compete forty years later in the 1978 King's Cup event.

Air racing became properly underway again in 1949, when a new King's Cup was presented by King George VI. Flying had become so familiar during the war, that the public would no longer stand at a distant turning point to see the aircraft pass once overhead and vanish, so the Royal Aero Club (responsible for organising air racing in Britain) introduced short multi-lap courses for future events.

The main event is supported by a series of class races to make up a complete weekend of air racing and flying displays. This keeps competitors in the public's sight most of the time, while the constant jockeying for position and gradual closing up of the field adds to the excitement for pilots and spectators alike. If the handicapping is good the pilot of the slowest aircraft, after flying most of the race up front in splendid isolation, suddenly finds himself embedded in a mass of aircraft as he rounds the last pylon. One such pilot, flying a biplane normally used for aerobatic displays, once turned on a special smoke generator at the last pylon, much to the consternation of the rest of the pack! A short, closed circuit has the additional advantage of cancelling out the effect of the wind, making one less factor for the handicappers to worry about.

The first and so far only win by a jet aircraft was in 1957 when Fred Dunkerley, a Lancashire mill-owner, obtained 367 km/hr (228 mph) out of the Miles Sparrowjet, a prewar light aircraft converted to take two tiny jet engines. It rests today in honourable retirement at the Cranfield Institute of Technology. In 1960 Squadron Leader (now Air Vice-Marshal) John Severne gave the race its only royal win to date, when he flew a single-engined 'Tiger Club' Turbulent to victory, having persuaded his pupil, Prince Philip, to enter the aircraft for the race.

The event has only once been won by a woman, in 1930, when Winifred Brown of the Lancashire Aero Club was the first home in an Avro Avian biplane. Test pilot Charles Masefield set another record in 1967, flying his wartime North American Mustang monoplane fighter at 446.5 km/hr (277.5 mph) — the fastest winner yet. A series of supporting handicap events make up the modern calendar. Many of them carry points in the Air Racing Championship table, and one or more normally count as eliminating or qualifying rounds for the King's Cup race.

This form of handicap event, where speeds are adjusted to try and get a simultaneous finish, is almost unique to Britain. In other countries an event is usually decided by the maximum improvement over a given handicap, no attention being paid to arranging a close finish for the benefit of the crowd.

Things had not been moving at such a cracking pace on the other side of the Atlantic. For a country that had invented proper powered flying, America was in a curious position. The Wright brothers, once they had perfected their original Flyer – the first successful aeroplane in the world – did virtually nothing with it. Other American aviators, such as Glenn Curtiss, were a rare breed indeed– in sharp contrast with the hundreds of European designers. Also the American aviation industry had no time to design or build any modern warplanes (and thus try out all the latest ideas) before the First World War was over. Britain and France, on the other hand, each had huge stocks of powerful and very advanced aircraft available for very small sums at the end of the war, while America had to start virtually from scratch. Consequently, she did not show up well in the early Gordon Bennett and Schneider Trophy contests, until the service teams were entered.

Conscious of these disadvantages, and realizing that the country that developed the finest and fastest aircraft would reap huge rewards in this new and growing market, the Americans made great efforts to close the gap and in 1920, two months after the last of the Gordon Bennett races, the first Pulitzer race was flown. This was a speed contest round a course of 187 km (116 miles), sponsored by the newspaper family of that name, and attracted a total of 37 starters. Only 25 finished (the engines of the time did not take kindly to prolonged running at full throttle) but the race was watched by some 45,000 spectators and had a tremendous effect on the American attitude to air racing.

This public enthusiasm, and the intense inter-service rivalry between the US Army and Navy that it generated, were to help sustain the great American air races right through the next ten years. The Pulitzers had consulted the American armed forces before proposing the race, for it was obvious that from them would come the requirement for the fastest aircraft available. Fortunately this assured the future of racing in the United States for, in an era of limited military spending, an intense rivalry sprang up between the Army and Navy

Tom Summer's Formula One air racer at Mojave Desert in 1978.

to capture public attention and funds – especially for aviation research.

1920 was a significant year, because it was then that control of service aviation was handed back to the Army and Navy after two brief years of independence and the races became as important in terms of prestige as the annual Army-Navy football game. Success in either would often help to advance an officer's career. The first Pulitzer race was won by the first racing aircraft ever to be designed specifically for the US Army. This was the Verville R-1, which had lasted for only one lap in the Gordon Bennett event. It had been criticized as being too heavy, but its victory in the Pulitzer silenced the critics and set a pattern for all US racers and fighters for the next ten years with its very strong biplane airframe, which was carefully streamlined for extra speed and carried a powerful water-cooled engine right up front.

Not all the aircraft that took part in the race were so new, though some rather odd-looking experimental Curtiss triplanes took part. Thirteen of the entrants were wartime DH.4 bombers, which had a special class prize all to themselves. The Pulitzer race ran every year until 1929, but from 1924 onwards it lost its position as the premier National Air Race meeting. Other events took on more prominence and from 1925, when the allocation of service funds for purely racing aircraft ceased, it was contested at first with older types of racing aircraft and later with standard production pursuit aircraft, keeping alive the old interservice rivalries.

Sponsorship

Two new races now took over from the Pulitzer – those for the Thompson and Bendix Trophies, starting respectively in 1930 and 1931. But the 1929 Nationals, apart from seeing out the Pulitzer, were also significant for other reasons; for one thing, only five races on the card were now military, for the huge growth of civil flying in the United States was beginning to make itself felt. In the big event, in a free-for-all over 50 short, but extremely fast laps, both civil and military pilots competed directly for the first time in seven years. The race was won by Doug Davis in a civil aircraft with a fastest lap of 335.8 km/hr (208.7 mph). This was the first-ever civilian victory over the two services. His plane was the Travel Air *Mystery*, powered by a 'hotted-up' Wright engine of 300 hp, delivering 400 hp after special tuning for the race.

Credited with a sprint speed of 378 km/hr (235 mph) the *Mystery* was a real breakthrough in design, setting the trend for low-wing monoplanes in racing and, much later, in fighters. Doug Davis was killed in the 1934 Thompson,

Cliff Branch is one of the top pilots on the US air racing circuit.

whilst flying a Wedell-Williams of much the same layout. Other famous pilots who raced the *Mystery* were Jimmy Doolittle (promoting Shell Oil), Frank Hawks, a well-known breaker of long-distance speed records (sponsored by Texaco), and a most remarkable lady called Florence Barnes, described as 'women's answer to Wallace Beery' (a tough, gravel-voiced, extremely ugly Hollywood star of the thirties). Her Travel Air was financed from the riproaring motel she ran in the Mojave Desert outside Los Angeles.

The 1929 Nationals featured the first all-women events in air racing, the Women's Derby long-distance event, which was won by Louise Thaddan, who featured prominently in American private flying, while Amelia Earhart came third. She later made several famous flights before being lost over the Pacific on a round-the-world flight in one of the most written-about disappearances in aviation.

Sponsorship and participation by the big fuel companies was common in the USA. When Al Williams, one of the most celebrated competition and aerobatic pilots of the era, left the US Navy (where he had been a noted racing pilot and Schneider Trophy competitor) to concentrate on racing aircraft development he worked for Gulf Oil. His aerobatic displays in a big civil-registered Grumman Gulfhawk fighter were among the most talked-of events of the 1930s' aviation scene.

Seen in the perspective of history, perhaps the most significant event at the Nationals that year was the appearance of the first 'midget' racer, designed and built by Ed Heath. He marketed designs for home-built ultralight aircraft and built and flew a number of small racers, including the *Baby Bullet*. When it weighed-in at the 1929 Nationals it

tipped the scales at only 106.5 kg (235 lb) and had a wingspan of a mere 5.6 m (18 ft). It was however capable of 233 km/hr (145 mph) on a tiny 32 hp Bristol Cherub two-cylinder engine! The huge, overpowered 'special' racers of the 1920s and 1930s have gone for ever, but the 'midget' racer is still a major part of international contests and its construction and use in competition a fast-growing sport. These days, 'midgets' are known as Formula One air racers.

The Thompson Trophy was flown over a number of laps of a short course, a total of up to 480 km (300 miles) over a 16-km (ten-mile) circuit. The Bendix, on the other hand, was a long-distance race from the Californian coast to the home of all the Nationals, Cleveland, Ohio. This was a distance of about 3,200km (2,000 miles). The one exception to the usual pattern was that followed by the 1936 race, from New York to Los Angeles, when two ladies (Louise Thaden and Laura Ingalls) created a huge stir by coming first and second.

Official service participation was not generally a feature of these events, although individual officers sometimes took part. Many of the competing aircraft were the powerful 'specials' that followed the Travel Air *Mystery*. Most famous of these was the Wedell-Williams, designed by Jimmy Wedell. It was said that no plans or drawings existed, the whole concept being chalked out on a hangar floor!

With Pratt & Whitney Wasp engines of 450-900 hp it had an exciting career in the hands of several well-known pilots. Wedell came second in the 1931 and 1932 Thompsons, and won the event in 1933. These achievements were made all the more remarkable by the fact that Wedell had lost an eye in a motor cycling accident some years earlier.

Roscoe Turner, a flamboyant racing

and commercial pilot (who designed his own uniforms and kept a lion cub as a pet!) came second in another Wedell-Williams in 1932 and won the 1934 event on the same machine. In the 1932 long-distance Bendix race Wedell and Turner came second and third (another Wedell-Williams won) and were first and second in 1933, with other examples of the type coming first and second in 1934 and second in 1935. Joe Mackey wrote the final chapters to this success story when placed fifth and sixth in 1938 and 1939 respectively.

'Mr Smoothie'

The most spectacular of the big American racers was the Gee Bee series built by the Granville brothers. Built round a massive 800 hp Wasp radial engine, it featured the smallest possible airframe and took on the appearance of a flying barrel as a result. It was mean and vicious to fly and demanded incredible skill to race it at up to its maximum speed of nearly 480 km/hr (300 mph). So distinctive was its appearance that it became the symbol of American air racing in the 1930s. The only man who really tamed it was Jimmy Doolittle, who flew a Gee Bee to victory in the 1932 Thompson. The previous year's winner, Lowell Bayles, was eventually killed whilst attempting to race it, as were all other Gee Bee owners.

An increasing number of tiny hand-built 'midgets' with wingspans of less than 3.2 m (20 ft) and engines of 300–600 hp began to appear. These were capable of speeds around 320–350 km/hr (200–220 mph). One or two, like the unfortunate but beautiful *Mr Smoothie*

T-6s are so numerous that they have their own racing class. The races are always extremely closely-fought.

(which never raced) had even more power – in this case provided by an 825 hp Curtiss Conqueror.

One other racer worth mentioning was the curiously-named Wittman Bonzo, which featured a wingspan so short that many wondered how it even flew at all. It was designed, built and raced by Steve Wittman and was one of the trickiest and fastest 'midgets' in the game. He continued a successful and colourful racing career right into the 1970s. His first racer, *Chief Oshkosh*, flew in the 1931 Nationals and set a trend for innovation with a wing design many years ahead of its time. Wittman's greatest successes came in the postwar Goodyear event and in Formula One events. His home airport at Oshkosh,

where he became manager in 1931, is the site of the world's largest annual fly-in, the Experimental Aircraft Association Convention.

Both the Thompson and the Bendix were suspended during the Second World War but were restarted in 1946 and continued into the early 1950s. Both had by then become primarily jet aircraft events, but it became impossible to run the Bendix event under modern conditions and the Thompson Trophy gave way to the present 'Unlimited' races, which are among the most stunning spectacles ever to be seen anywhere in the world of sport.

Air racing of this type is open to any type of machine but the test of time has determined that the competitors most

Formula One air racing is also popular in Europe. Here mechanics are preparing for a British meeting.

likely to succeed are those equipped (some would say armed) with big ex-wartime fighters specially modified to push out their maximum performance in short bursts. These immensely-powerful machines storm around tight courses, usually situated far out in the desert areas of the United States where they can do least harm.

The courses are marked out by large, coloured marker-poles situated close to the public enclosures, in the same fashion as the courses used by 'midget' racers. Flying at extremely low levels – their wingtips have on occasion been seen to clip the sand – these monsters of speed hammer round and round the desert, constantly jockeying for position with the other snarling machines in the pack. Their cockpit canopies and other external protruberances are often redesigned by their mechanics to reduce them to the minimum possible size, thus reducing wind resistance and increasing the speed potential still further.

One enterprising individual tackled the problem of winning the closely-fought 'Unlimited' races by entering a four-engined Douglas DC-7 airliner (perhaps feeling that its massive wingspan would block the path of the faster and more nimble competitors who tried to overtake him!). This bold attempt met with little success, but it served to underline the fact that this exciting brand of air racing was indeed truly 'Unlimited'.

Formula One air racing was developed as a sport in the USA in the late 1940s. This was an attempt to bring some sanity to the reckless prewar art of pylon racing, as this form of short-course competition had attracted a variety of extremely dubious designs into the field with consequent loss of life and limb. A

'Unlimited' air racers in the pit area at Reno in 1968. Prominent amongst them are Ed Weiner's colourful Mustang and Darryl Greenamyer's Grumman Bearcat.

set of rules was devised decreeing that competing aircraft must have a minimum wing area, a propeller of fixed pitch and a fixed undercarriage before being allowed to compete. Minimum field-of-vision requirements were also drawn up in order to prevent the pilots sinking into the fuselage completely. Today's F1 racers are essentially similar to the earliest examples of their breed, though speeds have inevitably crept up as more has been learned about the complex art of squeezing out the maximum performance by means of fine tuning.

Pilots race anti-clockwise round a hexagonal course, with the turns marked out by aluminium pylons some 8 m (24 ft) high. The start follows the same grid pattern of present-day motor racing. Under the rules, a maximum of eight aircraft in a 3-2-3 pattern on the runway are allowed per heat. The *slowest* man in practice takes pole position, (in motor racing it is the *fastest* man) with the remainder reading back to the fastest men at the rear. As the flag drops, the pilots roar off, but they are not allowed to cut across each other's paths until the first pylon is reached. Thereafter it's every man (or woman) for himself and a further ten laps are flown after this first scatter lap.

The first man over the line is the winner and the whole race, including take-off and landing, lasts about twenty minutes. Formula One air racing has in recent years attracted an increasing number of European countries and Ger-

many, France and Denmark are all now actively involved in this spectacular sport.

There have, of course, been hundreds of other races run all over the world. Of these, the most gruelling are undoubtedly the long-distance international events geared to a single occasion, usually an anniversary of some kind. Two early occasions of this sort are seldom thought of as races, although they could be interpreted as such; they were the first crossing of the Atlantic non-stop in 1919 and the first flight to Australia.

It was unfortunate that the first true long-distance race, the so-called 'Pineapple Derby' in 1927, was something of a disaster. Fired with enthusiasm by Lindbergh's solo Atlantic crossing earlier that year, James Dole of Honolulu had offered $25,000 as the first prize in a race from California to Honolulu. Eight aircraft lined up at the start of the 3,924 km (2,439 mile) ocean crossing, but three crashed on take-off, three disappeared in the Pacific and only two made it to Honolulu. Not an auspicious beginning.

In 1934, the city of Melbourne in Australia was preparing to celebrate its centenary. One of the proposed attractions was an air race from England. The

Left: **As the name implies, any type of aircraft is allowed to compete in 'Unlimited' events but most are ex-Second World War fighter planes.**

idea caught on in a big way and financial backing for trophies and cash prizes came from Sir Macpherson Robertson, a wealthy confectioner. His nickname, 'MacRobertson', gave the race its title. His aim in promoting the event was to stimulate the growth of aviation in Britain and Australia and he made just two stipulations; the race should be international and every means of control should be employed to avoid an accident. Air disasters tended to put people off flying, and as he was trying to promote it this stipulation was quite natural, but one wonders if he had the 'Pineapple Air Derby' in mind of seven years before.

Preparation for the 17,700 km (11,000 mile) race went ahead with great vigour, but the difficulties were enormous. Entering an aircraft was expensive and often meant finding sponsors, while engineers were needed to design and fit such modifications as more powerful engines, long-range fuel tanks and extra radio and navigation equipment. Planning the distribution supplies of fuel and spares down the route was also a mammoth task.

The race was to be divided into a speed section with a £10,000 first prize and a handicap section with a £2,000 prize. No

Right: Lyle Shelton's ex-Second World-War Grumman Bearcat undergoing maintainance before an 'Unlimited' air race.

one entrant could win both. Only one section could be won by any pilot, this division taking care of the wide differences in competing aircraft. Control points were established along the race route at Baghdad, Allahabad, Singapore and Darwin, with checkpoints at intermediate aerodromes. There were twenty entrants for the start at the RAF airfield at Mildenhall, Suffolk, and twelve of them eventually reached Melbourne.

After the event was over, it was agreed to have been the greatest single race in history, but the dramas, tensions and arguments that took place before the first competitor took off nearly stopped it on more than one occasion. Perhaps the most dramatic aspect of the race was the story of the de Havilland Comet *Grosvenor House*, the eventual winner. Geoffrey de Havilland, realising that no suitable British aircraft was available, announced

45

nine months before the start that his firm would build a limited number of machines specifically for this event, quoting a fixed price far below the actual cost of building them.

This colossal gamble paid off, for three Comets were ordered, built and delivered. These were flown by Jim and Amy Mollison, both already famous record-breakers, Charles Scott and Tom Campbell Black, and Cathcart Jones and Ken Waller. The race was won by Scott and Campbell Black in their signal red *Grosvenor House* in 70 hours 54 minutes flying time. This gave them the coveted speed prize and though they came first in both sections they could not claim both prizes. Less than a day behind them, to come second in both sections and win the handicap prize, was KLM's big twin-engined Douglas DC-2 airliner.

Black was later killed in an aircraft accident *en route* to the start of a race in South Africa. Moll and Parmentier, the pilots of the DC-2, found themselves the most famous men in Holland on their return. Moll lived on into the 1970s and was decorated by the British for his wartime achievements, while Parmentier was killed when his KLM Constellation airliner flew into high ground near Prestwick airport in Scotland in 1948 as a result of a printing error on his chart.

In 1936 a similar race was organized to Johannesburg to celebrate the Empire

Right: Air racing pilots must round the pylons with incredible precision. Cutting inside brings an automatic time penalty. *Below*: A Mustang banks steeply to round a pylon with a skill of which von Richthofen himself would have been proud.

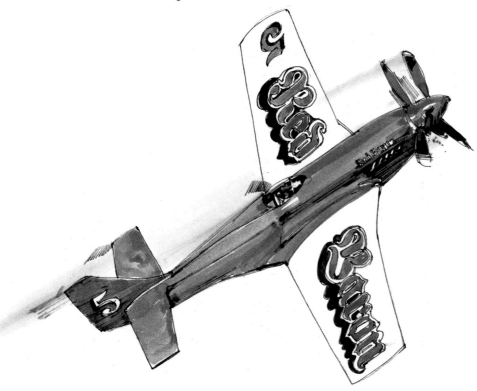

Exhibition. There were fourteen entries, including one or two from the earlier England – Australia race. The eventual winner from the nine actual starters was a graceful little Vega Gull, flown by Charles Scott of Comet fame and Giles Guthrie, later to become Chairman of BOAC (British Overseas Airways Corporation). None of the others finished.

Later, in 1953, a race was run from England to Christchurch, New Zealand, for their centenary celebrations. With both speed and handicap sections it resembled the 1934 event, but spice was added to the entry in the form of three four-engined transport aircraft and five Canberra jet bombers. Despite these attractions the race aroused little public interest.

The *Daily Mail*, recalling its extremely generous sponsorships of early aviation events, ran repeats of two of them when its 50th anniversary came up, organizing with the Royal Aero Club two very memorable races. The first was held between the Arc de Triomphe in Paris and Marble Arch in London to commemorate Blériot's winning the *Daily Mail's* cross-Channel prize in 1909. The second route led from the Post Office Tower in London to the top of the Empire State Building in New York, in memory of Alcock and Brown's momentous Atlantic crossing in 1919 for a *Daily Mail* prize of £10,000. Divided into

Above: **Even jet aircraft compete in 'Unlimited' races.**

Below: **A DC-7 airliner goes racing.**

several sections to give everyone a fair chance, both events were highly successful in terms of public interest. No holds were barred, except for flagrant breaking of the law, and the proceedings were carried through with great dash and flair. Excitement – especially in the London-Paris event – was terrific, as seconds were lopped off each dash. The winner's time 'Arch-to-Arc' was just 40 minutes 44 seconds, using two motorcycles, two helicopters and a Hunter jet fighter, enabling the commanding officer of No 65 Squadron, Squadron-Leader Maughan, to hand the RAF Benevolent Fund his winner's cheque for £5,000.

All sorts of records were broken during the course of the race. The British European Airways team, using public transport, found that a Parisian taxi driver, when roused, could make the Arc from Le Bourget airport in a mere 13 minutes, while a lady team member found her route included a short-cut through a gentlemen's public convenience!

The trans-Atlantic race was on a much grander scale, but turned out to be just as exciting. Competitors went to unbelievable lengths to beat each other. Clement Freud, the well-known television personality, unable to hire a fire engine to get him through New York's traffic in double-quick time, made do with an ambulance. Another competitor joined a scheduled airliner at London Airport through the cargo hatch at the end of the main runway to save time, while a famous racing driver got lost in the Empire State Building when he got out on the wrong floor! Fastest time to New York, at 6 hours 11 minutes 57 seconds, was put up by an RAF Harrier 'jump-jet', and it is no exaggeration to say that the subsequent blaze of publicity when it landed vertically in downtown New York helped to persuade the authorities to let the US Marines buy the type in significant quantities. Fastest time of all in the other direction was 5 hours 11 minutes 22 seconds by a Royal Navy Phantom jet – and this almost ten years before Concorde started flying on a similar route.

Two more races of this kind have since been held, the 1969 London-Sydney race, the bicentenary of the discovery of Australia, and the 1971 London–Victoria race to British Colombia for that Province's bicentenary. For the moment it seems that they will be the last events of their kind, for the changing economic and political conditions have conspired to make long-distance races extremely difficult to launch. A projected London-Perth, Australia race in 1980 came to nothing and we are still waiting for the greatest of them all – a 'Round-the-World' air race.

The winner of the 1969 *Daily Mail* Transatlantic Air Race, a Harrier, lands at St Pancras railway station!

ATTACK AIRCRAFT
Airborne Artillery

Germany's Hannover CL.III was designed and built by a company that specialized in producing railway trains! This did nothing to detract from its excellent handling characteristics and formidable firepower.

Attack aircraft are very exciting and versatile machines. They often combine the roles of fighter and bomber, although their primary task is to attack ground targets. Unlike ordinary bombers they usually work in close cooperation with troops on the ground and are often called in to blast any individual targets that are holding up the forward movement of soldiers and tanks. The idea of using aircraft as 'flying artillery' is certainly not new; even by the end of the First World War (1914-8) aircraft had been widely used against machine-gun positions and enemy reinforcements lurking behind the immediate scene of battle.

At the very beginning of the war, pilots took off armed with such crude weapons as steel darts and rained them down on the unfortunate troops below, but before long they had hand-thrown bombs and fixed machine-guns. This provided a spray of bullets and metal fragments that proved very effective against troops unlucky enough to be caught out in the open. This method of attack became known as strafing, a term derived from

the German word meaning 'punish', but it was unpopular with pilots because their aircraft were slow-moving targets within easy firing range of any soldier on the ground. Rifle fire remains a threat in modern times, for even very fast American aircraft flying over Vietnam in the 1960s were occasionally shot down by rifle fire from the ground!

'Furniture Van'

One of the earliest examples of ground strafing came in July 1916 when a patrol of British F.2B fighters could find no airborne targets during the Battle of the Somme and so switched to supporting ground troops. The Bristol F.2B had a Vickers machine-gun mounted on the nose and a Lewis in the rear cockpit, and since their standard ammunition had just been interspersed with a new type of fiery bullet known as a 'tracer', they were able to watch their fire disperse startled groups of infantry and cavalry. The French firm of Nieuport produced several fighter types during the First World War, among them the Bébé (Baby) – so called because of its tiny proportions –

which became a popular aircraft for the close support of advancing troops. Then the Germans entered the field with a number of very sound designs, specially built to take ground fire as they flew at low altitude over enemy positions.

The Junkers J.1 for example, had an armoured engine and featured a very advanced all-metal construction, being armed with two fixed forward-firing machine-guns and a third for the observer in the rear cockpit. Besides attacking the enemy lines and reporting troop movements it was also used to drop food and ammunition to isolated frontline soldiers. Its size and angular shape quickly earned it the affectionate nickname of *Möbelwagen*, meaning 'furniture van'. At the peak of their operational employment there were nearly 200 J.1s in action at the battlefront.

After the First World War fighter-bombers, as they were now called, were developed in France, Britain and the USA, while the Soviet Union's activities remained shrouded in secrecy. Germany began to redevelop her air force under the guise of improving her civilian airline, Luft Hansa, and placed great importance on attack aircraft. By the time the Luftwaffe's existence was made public in the late thirties it had a fighter-bomber force which was heavily committed to the concept of 'dive-bombing'. In 1941 the Nazis began to invade Russia, the assault being known as 'Operation Barbarossa'. They destroyed many Soviet planes on the ground and for the whole summer of that year enjoyed complete air superiority. The Russians retaliated with local night bombing attacks using the Soviet air force's family of

A Blackburn Ripon biplane unleashes a torpedo in a typical low-level sweep. Torpedo-armed aircraft are the scourge of enemy shipping.

Though virtually obsolete at the outbreak of the Second World War in 1939, the tough little Henschel Hs 123 served with distinction until late 1944.

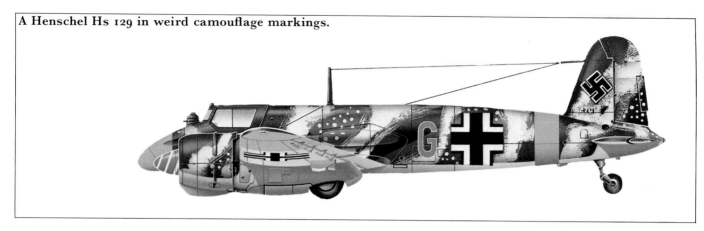

A Henschel Hs 129 in weird camouflage markings.

Polikarpov R-5s and R-Zs. They had been used in the Spanish Civil War (1936–9) and during the subsequent war against Finland, but by 1941 they were only really suitable for night operations. The R-Z carried eight bombs underwing and would fly to the front line to pick out the enemy's open fires and other lights as targets. The engine noise of the planes was so curious that the Germans referred to them as 'sewing machines'.

The Luftwaffe's principal ground-attack type between 1940–2 was the infamous Ju 87 Stuka. It has been described by some people as an ugly aeroplane, but it would perhaps be more accurate to call it functional. With its W-shaped wings, big fixed undercarriage and angular tailsurfaces; the Stuka was readily recognizable in flight, as its pilots were to discover to their cost, for although the Stuka could withstand heavy damage from ground anti-aircraft fire, it was something of a sitting duck for RAF fighters, whose eight-gun armament and superior handling signalled almost instant destruction for the German aircraft. The only situation where Stukas could demonstrate their real ability was one in which the Luftwaffe enjoyed complete control of the air. In these conditions the Stuka knew no peer, for it could then engage in the task for which it had been designed from the outset – dive-bombing. The pilot of a dive bomber locates his target and then dives straight at it almost vertically. At a predetermined height he releases his aircraft's bombs and pulls out of the high-speed dive with little or no margin for error. The falling bombs meanwhile continue on the same course as the original dive and explode with considerable accuracy and violence on their target. For the people who found themselves the targets of such attacks the experience must have been terrifying. The Stukas would form up in the sky in a long staggered line and then the leader's aircraft would roll over onto its back and enter a near-vertical dive, followed by the rest of the aircraft in

Blasting enemy armoured vehicles out on the battlefield was the Henschel Hs 129's *forte*. The version illustrated below was equipped with a fearsome 75 mm cannon.

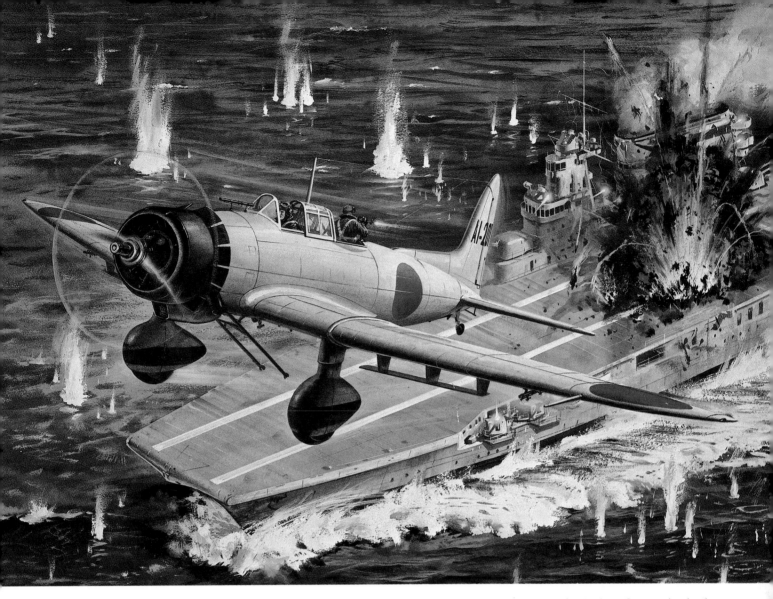

Japan's Aichi D3A *Val* was a superb dive-domber. Here an American aircraft-carrier is the victim of a particularly accurate attack. It is not generally known that Germany's Heinkel company contributed to its design.

the pack. This meant that bombs were hitting the target area with only seconds between each explosion, while the sirens fitted to the Stukas produced an unearthly screaming howl as they dived which their pilots delighted in calling 'the trombones of Jericho'. Dive-bombing will forever be associated with the Ju 87 as the word 'Stuka' is directly derived from the German term meaning 'dive-bombing aircraft'.

Obsolete

Although Stukas stole the limelight, the Nazis began to wish they had kept the old Henschel Hs 123 in production, rather than withdrawing it from frontline service in 1940 after the conflicts in Poland and France. It was finally recalled for the fight against Russia and once again proved itself to be a tough and versatile performer, despite its antiquated biplane wing configuration, fixed undercarriage and fat radial engine. When one Luftwaffe commander suggested in no uncertain terms that production should be started again immediately it was only then discovered that all the necessary tools and con-

struction jigs had been destroyed as obsolete. There was no alternative but press back into service existing Hs 123s that had found their way into other roles.

'Whispering Death'

In 1940, as the Stukas and Henschel 123s were bombing and gunning down troops and vehicles in France, Holland and Belgium, the British were attempting to destroy vital bridges and other 'bottleneck' targets. It took another four years before the RAF and USAAF were able to alter the balance totally in their favour. One of the aircraft that helped turn the tables was the Bristol Beaufighter — a twin-engined fighter, torpedo bomber and attack aircraft which was a potent night-fighter and became the major shipbuster of the RAF. A two-seater, it was armed with eight air-to-ground rockets, plenty of bombs, or a torpedo mounted under the centre of its fuselage. It had a formidable nose armament consisting of four 20 mm cannon, carried machine guns in its wings and earned the nickname of 'Whispering Death' when attacking the Japanese in Burma. This was because of the muffled

growl from its two 1,770 hp Bristol Hercules radial engines.

The Beaufighter was not the RAF's only successful attack aircraft of the war, for the de Havilland Mosquitos they operated on various fronts are among the true 'greats' of air warfare. The Mk.VI fighter-bomber version was capable of carrying a pair of high-explosive (HE) bombs underwing, as well as a nose armament of cannon. This was the most widely-used version of the ubiquitous Mosquito and went on to serve with RAF Coastal Command, when it was equipped with rockets for strikes against shipping. A later model was equipped with a powerful 57 mm gun for coastal attacks, some 27 being built. De Havilland must have been keen on calling their aircraft after insects as the new model was to be called the Tse-Tse, after the notorious African cattle fly! But it was with its rockets that the ground-attack 'Mossie' version scored its greatest victories.

Rockets had a slight advantage over bullets in that once the pilot was within range he could fire them and peel off, avoiding some of the ground fire he was certain to encounter during his attack.

Some Northrop P-61 Black Widows were equipped with this upper-fuselage gun turret for ground-attack.

There were two types of rocket, armour-piercing and HE. HE rockets had the same effect on a target as a big cannon shell, enabling one aircraft to put an explosive force equivalent to a cruiser's broadside into targets as small as a house or a coastal freighter. Camera-gun film from the latter months of the war show big German ships disintegrating in a flurry of spray and smoke when hit by rockets fired from aircraft. Armour-piercing rockets, on the other hand, were very effective against tanks and other armoured vehicles, as well as concrete emplacements and similarly tough targets.

Razor Blades

Other weapons employed by attack aircraft during the Second World War were of course machine-guns and cannon. Cannon which fire small exploding shells are normally belt-fed, but some of the heavier calibres used a drum or box magazine. They were often used against other aircraft but were also very effective against ground targets. By the middle of the war the Germans, Russians and British had found that cannon shells with hardened casings could penetrate the softer armour on the top of tanks and other armoured vehicles. There is a story that when Field Marshal Rommel reported that his tanks were being destroyed by aircraft using American armour-piercing cannon shells, Luftwaffe chief Hermann Goering replied that the Americans could only make razor blades. Rommel produced a cannon shell from his pocket and said bitterly, 'Well I wish we had razor blades like this'. In fact the Germans were quick to learn and soon fitted their aircraft with some awesomely heavy cannon which could penetrate even the thick armour of the Soviet tanks operating on the Eastern Front. Cannon attacks, like dive-bomb-

One of the Second World War's strangest oddities was the *Mistel/Misletoe* combination. The fighter on top steered the pilotless Ju 88 to its target.

ing, required the pilot to aim his aircraft as a whole as he closed in towards the target.

'Tin Opener'

The most famous names in the RAF's armoury between 1939 and 1945 were, of course, Hawker Hurricanes and Supermarine Spitfires; but while the latter type remained an interceptor, the slower Hurricane found itself relegated to ground-attack work. Versions used in this role included the Mk.IID – known as the 'tin opener' because of its Vickers 40 mm cannon. The tactics were simple. The Hurricane pilot spotted his target, 'aimed' with the tracer-loaded machine-guns in the wings, and then, when in range, opened up with the 40 mm cannon. In addition to this, rocket-armed versions of the Hurricane saw action in North Africa and the Far East.

Another Hawker product – the Typhoon – became the foremost ground attack aircraft of the RAF. It was modified to carry heavier and heavier weapon-

A hefty Curtiss Helldiver dive-bomber revs its engine on the deck of a US Navy aircraft-carrier.

Above: **At least 36,000 Ilyushin I1-2 Stormoviks were built, making this almost certainly the most-produced aircraft in history. Three gigantic factories turned out no less than 1,200 Stormoviks a month.**

Douglas Dauntless dive-bombers sank more Japanese shipping than any other Allied weapon, turning the tide of the war in the Pacific. Note the perforated dive-brakes protruding above the wings.

loads, starting with two 112 kg (250 lb) bombs and finally carrying two 450 kg (1,000 lb) bombs. During sweeps across the English Channel before D-Day, Typhoons destroyed an average of 150 railway locomotives a month with rockets and bombs. However, it was in 1944 during the air battle over Falaise in France that they finally established their reputation when in one attack alone they destroyed no less than 137 tanks!

On the seas too, Great Britain had a sizeable quantity of reliable carrier-based strike aircraft, spearheaded by the Fairey Swordfish and the Fairey Barracuda. The Barracuda was a three-seater torpedo carrier and dive-bomber, and it was in this latter role that it hit the headlines when a group of them attacked the legendary battleship *Tirpitz*, caught sheltering in a Norwegian fjord. Barracudas frequently served alongside the ageing Fairey Swordfish biplanes, the latter type being a legacy from a somewhat more glamorous era of aviation. Yet the 'Stringbag', as it was popularly known, outlasted a number of more advanced carrierborne aircraft designed to replace it and went on to establish a reputation with the pilots of the Fleet Air Arm similar to that enjoyed by the Spitfire and Hurricane with the pilots of the RAF.

The 'Stringbag' was held together by a maze of struts and bracing wires which were jokingly said to produce the note of Middle C when in flight. If the note changed the pilot was in big trouble! The old Swordfish scored numerous triumphs throughout the Second World War, notably the torpedo attack on the famous German battleship *Bismarck* and anti-

A Junkers Ju 87 Stuka.

shipping operations from the island of Malta, which sank an average of 50,800 tonnes (50,000 tons) of enemy shipping a month over a six-month period. 'Stringbags' were ideal aircraft for operation from the cramped decks of carriers because of their low take-off and landing speeds. They were able to land safely on decks which were pitching between twenty and thirty degrees, even by night.

Shark's Teeth

While the Swordfish was hitting German and Italian shipping in the Mediterranean, the RAF was fighting a grim war in North Africa. Among the numerous attack types they used were the American-built Curtiss P-40 Tomahawk and Kittyhawk. Characterized by their distinctive 'chin' radiator intakes, these aircraft also fought in the Far East, flown by the Australian and New Zealand air forces, as well as by the RAF and USAAF.

The American Curtiss company boasted another fine product in the SB2C Helldiver, used in both antishipping strikes and for attacking ground targets. The Helldiver is best known for the part it played in naval actions against Japanese land forces during the 'island-hopping' campaign in the Pacific. It could be armed with rockets in place of the more usual 450 kg (1,000 lb) bomb-load and operated with great success from the aircraft carriers of the US Navy, being fitted with the standard arrestor-hook gear beneath its rear fuselage and having folding wings to help save precious space onboard ship.

The battle for the Pacific islands provided a challenge for many types of combat aircraft, especially the chunky little Douglas Dauntless, one of the vital team of American torpedo strike and dive-bomber aircraft that crippled Japanese naval forces at Coral Sea and Midway and saw extensive service during the Solomons campaign. A two-seater radial-engined monoplane, the Dauntless could carry a 450 kg (1,000 lb) bomb under its belly on a special crutch which swung the projectile clear of the propeller blades during dive-bombing attacks. A total of nearly 6,000 Dauntlesses had been built by the end of the Second World War.

The Grumman Avenger TBF became the US Navy's standard torpedo bomber, but it was not ordered until 8 April 1940. It was a large and powerfully-armed aircraft with a crew of three (pilot, rear gunner and bombardier/ventral gunner). The first prototype took off on its maiden flight in August 1941 and deliveries reached the US Navy in January 1942. It was in action at the Battle of Midway in June of that year, and despite this rapid development the Avenger proved an outstanding aircraft and was still in service fifteen years after being taken on strength. The aircraft was also supplied to the Royal Navy and was, somewhat ironically, used by the Japanese armed forces after the war.

Hellcat

Yet another successful Grumman to see action during the Second World War was the F6F Hellcat. Like the Avenger it was pressed into active service very quickly – only 14 months after the prototype made its first flight the production models were in action. Hellcats proved themselves to be excellent bombers and were also capable of taking on enemy fighters and bombers. The Hellcat could carry up to 900 kg (2,000 lb) of bombs under its wing centresection, with rocket rails under the wings, while later marks had cannon in place of the machine-guns.

Vought F4U Corsairs release their bombs in a low-level attack. Characterized by its distinctive W-shaped wing configuration, the Corsair was co-designed by Igor Sikorsky (the famous helicopter manufacturer).

No account of the air war in the Pacific can pass without mentioning the Vought F4U Corsair. Strictly speaking, the Corsair was a straightforward dogfighter, and in this role it could boast an eleven-to-one 'kill' ratio against the Japanese, but it had other claims to fame – including that of being the last piston-engined fighter to serve with the American armed forces and the longest in production (eleven years). It was beautiful to look at, with W-shaped wings not unlike those of the Stuka but far more graceful. It became the first American aircraft to exceed 640 km/hr (400 mph) in level flight when the experimental prototype reached just over that speed in tests in 1940. Trials out at sea however showed that its long nose and high landing speed did not make it an ideal aircraft for operation from aircraft carriers and it was more effective with land-based US Marine Corps units. It could carry two 450 kg (1,000 lb) bombs or eight underwing rockets. Postwar models were able to carry as much as 1,800 kg (4,000 lb) of bombs. The Royal Navy operated Corsairs from *HMS Victorious* and after the war they were used by the French in Indo-China and Algeria and in support of the Anglo-French landings at Suez.

The success of types such as the Corsair and Avenger was equalled by the important work of the Republic P-47 Thunderbolt, which operated mainly in Europe. A radial-engined rather dumpy-looking aircraft, the P-47 was armed with eight machine-guns in the leading edges of its wings. It had been intended to serve as a fighter but with strengthened wings it could carry a formidable variety of bombs and by the end of 1943 the reservations originally felt about its performance had evaporated. The USAAF received 15,660 Thunderbolts,

Above: **Known to the Allies as** *Baka*, **Japanese for 'fool', the Yokosuka Ohka was purpose-built for** *Kamikaze* **suicide attacks.**

Below: **The carrier-based Douglas Skyray, a dual-purpose interceptor and attack aircraft, which first flew in 1951.**

Above: A Republic F-105 Thundercheif of the USAF unleashes two salvos of unguided missiles at a ground target during the southeast Asian conflict in the 1960s. The Thundercheif (known affectionately as the 'Thud' by those who flew it), bore the brunt of responsibility for this type of attack during the Vietnam War. It was powered by a single Pratt & Whitney J75 turbojet engine.

The Douglas Invader served with great success throughout the Second World War and went on to fight in both Korea and Vietnam.

of which less than one percent were lost in battle. This exceptionally low combat rate was due to their superbly rugged build. Thunderbolts were important in the USAAF and RAF attacks on transport and communications in Italy in 1943–5, when the Allies attempted to isolate the Germans from supplies coming in from the north. Earlier models of the Thunderbolt had a cockpit canopy not unlike that of the Hurricane, but a clear bubble canopy offering virtually unlimited visibility in all directions was introduced, as a good view is absolutely essential in air-to-air combat.

Among the truly classic attack aircraft to be brought into action during the Second World War, the Soviet Ilyushin Il-2 is one of the best. Known almost universally as the *Shturmovik* from the initials BSh which stood for *Bronirovanii Shturmovik* or 'armoured attacker', the Il-2 lived up to its name. Its liquid-cooled inline engine and cockpit area were completely enclosed in thick layers of armoured protection which has been likened to a bathtub. The weight of the armour accounted for fifteen percent of the aircraft's total weight, combat-ready.

A Dassault Mirage III of the Israeli air force strafes an Egyptian MiG-15 during the conflict of 1967.

The *Shturmovik* was produced in both single- and two-seater guises, the two-seater version being equipped with a defensive machine-gun. Like the 'tin opener' Hurricane it mounted cannon which were very effective against enemy armour. The Soviet air force evolved a tactic known as the 'circle of death' in which *Shturmoviks* would locate a target and then circle it in a loose formation which allowed an aircraft to put in an attack as the others were coming into position. In this way the target was always under fire. The Il-2 was instrumental in swinging the balance of power during the Battle of Stalingrad and the massive tank battle at Kursk. At Kursk the Il-2 was right in the thick of the action with cannon and special anti-tank bombs and by the close of the war the USSR had built around 35,000 examples and claimed with some justification that it was one of the war-winning weapons of the Eastern Front.

The Il-2 may have enjoyed a rather heroic reputation but the little U-2 bi-plane, which later became known as the Po-2, played an important part in Soviet history. It operated as a night-bomber,

harassing enemy positions, and during the great Soviet offensives against the Nazis worked closely with troops in the front line. The Po-2 even operated in close support of street fighting and was in action in the Battle of Berlin as late as 1945. Besides ground-attack work, the Po-2 was used for liaison and supply drops to partisans.

The successful Petlyakov Pe-2 aircraft began its service with one specification and ended as a very effective version of another type. It had been intended as a high-altitude twin-engined fighter and received the provisional designation VI-100 or *Vysotnil Istrebityel* (high-altitude fighter). However it proved to be an effective bomber and could carry a maximum bombload of 990 kg (2,200 lb). Its offensive armament was improved as the war progressed and Pe-2 pilots had the satisfaction of being able to outpace the standard German fighter operating in

1941, the Messerschmitt Bf 109E. It became a race to either uprate engines or increase the armament as the Germans produced faster Bf 109F and G fighters. At the close of hostilities the Pe-2 went into action against German convoys evacuating the Baltic and Prussian coasts.

Japan's army and navy had separate air forces and one of their constant problems was an intense rivalry bordering on hatred. Pearl Harbor might have been a naval triumph, but the army had conquered the vast areas that made up Japan's newly-acquired sphere of in-

fluence. An important aircraft in the Japanese naval success was the Aichi D3A (codenamed *Val* by the Allies). The D3A was a low-wing, all-metal dive bomber. Like the Dauntless its main bombload was slung on a crutch which swung forward during the attack dive to clear the propeller blades. Two more bombs were carried under the wings. Among the actions featuring the *Val* were the first wave assault on Pearl Harbor, and, in April 1942, the sinking of the old British carrier *Hermes* and the cruisers *Cornwall* and *Dorsetshire*. At the close of the war the D3A was used in a single-seater special attack or suicide role.

Kamikaze

The Yokosuka D4Y Suisei (known to the Allies as *Judy*) was an interesting departure from the conventional approach to carrierborne, dive-bomber design. Instead of a slow-flying aircraft with an air-cooled engine, the D4Y had an imported German Daimler-Benz which bestowed a top speed of around 560 km/h 350 mph. It went into action aboard the *Soryu* at the Battle of Midway in late 1942. Carrier losses forced the Japanese to base their bombers ashore and finally the D4Y was demoted to suicide missions. In this role it was packed with 3,883 kg (1,765 lb) of high explosive and fitted with small assisted take-off rockets. This single-seater version was not built in large numbers.

One Yokosuka *Kamikaze* type which was built in some numbers however was the MXY-7 Ohka or 'Cherry Blossom'. Whereas most suicide attack aircraft had been converted types or obsolete marks, the Ohka is unique as the world's only purpose-built suicide type to see action. It was less of an aircraft than a flying bomb, since it had only stubby little wings and crude controls. The pilot was carried by a 'mother' aircraft, usually a converted bomber, to within gliding range of his target and then released. His

small machine was so hard to locate on radar or hit with anti-aircraft fire that once he had lined himself up with the target of his choice, ideally an aircraft carrier or a battleship, the pilot would switch on the solid-fuel rocket motors and plough into the unfortunate target.

The Americans derided the Ohka as *Baka* (Japanese for 'fool') but the suicide pilots and their desperate tactics were unnerving for even the coolest crew member. In the earlier years of the war in the Pacific the Japanese had achieved their aims without resorting to the use of suicide pilots, one of their most effective aircraft at that time being the Nakajima B5N. Known to the Allies as *Kate*, the

An RAF technician loads some ammunition into a gun-pod, which is then attached to an attack aircraft.

B5N made its debut during the attack on Pearl Harbor and then ran up a score of victories that included sinking the US Navy carriers *Yorktown*, *Lexington*, *Wasp* and *Hornet*. *Kates* operated with either a 3,883 kg (1,765 lb) torpedo slung under its belly or two bombs mounted under their bellies. Defensive armament was two forward fitting machine-guns and two in a movable mounting in the rear.

Flying Bomb

As the war drew to a close in Europe, the Germans desperately began producing a series of much more radical weapons. The most unusual was the Fi 103 which became known to the world as the V-1, (from *Vergeltungswaffe* or 'revenge weapon' in Hitler's language). The V-1 was a pilotless jet-propelled aircraft, crammed with explosives and normally launched by catapulting up a ramp. Built by Fieseler, this fearsome weapon made more military and economic sense than the conventional manned aircraft, for the V-1 delivered the same weight of explosive at a fraction of the cost and took far less time to build. They also needed fewer skilled workers.

In Britain the V-1 was combatted by redeploying anti-aircraft (AA) guns to the coast and tasking fighters to intercept the 'doodlebugs' or 'buzz bombs' as they were known. The V-1s were a particular

This dramatic picture shows a McDonnell Douglas A-4 Skyhawk of the US Marine Corps firing a lethal air-to-ground missile. Skyhawks also serve with Argentina, Australia, Israel, New Zealand and Singapore.

trial for the population of south east England. Unlike manned aircraft, as Winston Churchill, the British Prime Minister, observed, there was no sense of satisfaction in downing a machine. Moreover the V-1 had its own uncanny engine note from its throbbing jet engine. When the jet cut out there was a lapse of a few seconds before the bomb plunged down to explode. V-1 launching sites along the French coast became priority targets for the RAF and after D-Day the Canadian armies were tasked to clear the coast as soon as possible. Here it is worth mentioning the Luftwaffe's incredibly versatile Junkers Ju 88. It began life as a bomber and became variously a fighter, reconnaissance aircraft and, finally, guided missile.

The Ju 88P-3 was intended for tank attacks and besides the extra armour plating mounted two 37 mm cannon in a 'gondola' offset to the port. The most fascinating version of the Ju 88 must be the *Mistel/Mistletoe*, a 'father-and-son'

combination. A fighter was carried on struts above a Ju 88 bomber and controlled the bomber by means of a linkage between the two aircraft. When they were within range of a target the bomber (laden with explosives) was cast off by the fighter and guided onto its target by means of radio control. The fighters 'up top' were always either Bf 109s or Fw 190s. Operational results varied but some successes were scored against Soviet-held bridges in the east.

When the war ended there were great hopes for a lasting peace, and while there have been no conflicts in Europe there has been continued fighting in some or other part of the world since 1945. The first major conflict was the Korean War (1950-3) which saw the first jet versus jet dogfights. The Americans deployed their Republic F-84 Thunderjet in both the interceptor and attack roles. American aircraft were also in action a little over ten years later when they were drawn into the Vietnam conflict. That war saw

a sizeable deployment of piston-engined ground-attack aircraft, one of the first of which was the Douglas Skyraider.

Close Shave

This sturdy old aircraft could fly slowly enough for the pilot to observe the terrain, but could also carry a mixed load of bombs, rockets or napalm, a highly-inflammable petroleum jelly. The longer the war lasted, the more experienced pilots became. One American watched a South Vietnamese Skyraider fly over his position and recalls his feeling of horror as the napalm canisters detached from the wings and seemed to fall straight towards the American lines. In fact they fell on the enemy tree line, but the heat from the blast could be felt by the soldiers, and more tellingly he could remember the pilot's smiling face as he looked down at him!

Napalm

Other operational planes used were

A dramatic view of the magnificent Panavia Tornado multirole combat aircraft. It was conceived from the outset as a collaborative programme involving Germany, Italy and the United Kingdom, countries that fought one another in the last war!

the North American Trojan (which performed a very similar role to the Skyraider), the A-4 Skyhawk and the F-4 Phantom, the latter two built by McDonnell Douglas. Skyhawks and Phantoms have also seen action in the Middle East, for Israel, during the Arab/Israeli conflict, as well as Indo-China. The Phantom has a bombload roughly similar to that of a wartime Lancaster bomber, which explains how the tonnages of HE weapons dropped in Vietnam reached such high figures. The slightly slower Skyhawk was perhaps a better aircraft for ground attack duties, but it carried a smaller bombload.

Some aircraft carried such armament as rockets, retarded bombs and napalm, and mounted multi-barrelled cannon whose rotating barrels could deliver an extraordinary volume of firepower. Like any other conflict of the Vietnam type, there was little opposition from the ground at the beginning, but by the end the enemy could deploy the very latest in manportable anti-aircraft missiles.

Television Cameras

The Republic F-105 Thunderchief, or 'Thud' to its pilots, was used over North Vietnam to put anti-aircraft guns out of action. The missions were known as 'flak suppression'. In this hazardous role it carried an electronic counter-measures (ECM pod) to jam the enemy's radar transmissions, thus confusing his homing missiles. 'Thud' itself carried special missiles which were designed to home in on the enemy's beams and follow them down to destroy their radar transmission centres. Thunderchiefs sometimes flew alongside Grumman A-6 Intruders, aircraft which had the rather bewildering ability to see in the dark. Equipped with highly-sophisticated infrared sensors and a low-light television camera the Intruder could monitor enemy troop and vehicle movements by night and attack with eighteen 225 kg (500 lb) bombs.

Africa

Africa is another continent which has seen constant wars and insurrection over the years. The Rhodesian and South African air forces have been in action on deep raids into neighbouring states, or in Rhodesia against insurgent groups in the bush. The interesting feature of these attacks has been the comparative vintage of the aircraft types used. The Rhodesians used aircraft of the 1950s such as Venoms, Hunters and Canberras, while the South Africans used the latest Mirage fighter-bombers. The Rhodesian air force team included Hunters which were called in to 'soften up' an area with bombs before the heliborne and parachute troops were inserted to comb the whole zone in search of enemy activity.

The extraordinary rotary-barrelled cannon around which the Fairchild A-10 'Warthog' is virtually built points out from the A-10's nose section.

The surface-to-air missile is dreaded by all attack aircraft.

Western Europe has been at peace since 1945, but its armies are still in a constant state of readiness. Among the aircraft available for immediate use in a wartime situation are two unusual and highly-specialized ground-attack types. One is the Harrier, now internationally famous for its vertical take-off and landing (VTOL) capability. This is, of course, an ideal aircraft for ground attack operations, as it can hide in wooded areas close to the battlefield and make strikes against ground forces at any time of the day or night, in any weather conditions, with no problems about finding nearby airfields with intact runways so air warfare takes on a new dimension.

Enter 'Warthog'

The second outstanding attack aircraft of the 1980s is the Fairchild A-10, known to its pilots as the 'Warthog', a twin-engined single-seater with an insatiable appetite for enemy tanks. The whole aircraft is built around the massive, *seven-barrelled*, 30 mm rotary gun which can split a tank or similar armoured vehicle into pieces with a single momentary burst. Four underwing pylons can take a total weapons load of 8,200 kg (16,000 lb). A-10s are usually painted overall matt green with yellow blotches for camouflage at low altitudes. They carry the very latest in ECM equipment in self-contained pods.

Since the Second World War ground attack weapons have improved dramatically. The basic principle of making an armoured thrust with air support may not have changed, but reaction times are faster and weapons can be delivered with frightening accuracy. Notable among the new munitions are certain types of napalm, the retarded bomb and the cluster bomb unit (CBU). Napalm is a thickened petroleum jelly which clings to the target when it burns. It also burns up the oxygen in the area which means that it is effective against bunkers and armoured vehicles. The retarded bomb has fins which reduce its speed on release so that the parent aircraft is safely beyond the target by the time it explodes. This allows fighter-bombers to drop at lower and consequently more accurate heights. The CBU is particularly effective against 'soft' targets or men in the open. It consists of an outer bomb casing which contains 'bomblets', usually filled with metal fragments. The CBU is dropped by the attacking aircraft at low level and explodes above the ground, scattering the 'bomblets' over a wide area. They either explode on contact or remain in the ground as an anti-personnel mine-field. An unusual, highly-specialized bomb is the 'dibber', which is designed to destroy airfields. After release from the parent aircraft it is slowed down by a parachute and then fired downwards by tiny rockets to penetrate the surface of an airfield. Once into the ground it explodes, creating a massive crater that prevents any enemy aircraft from using that part of the airfield until a great deal of time-consuming repair work has been carried out.

Programmed

The use of rockets against shipping has been covered earlier. Before they became the widely-used weapon for 'ship-busting' the primary method of destroying surface vessels was the torpedo. Torpedos were first launched from an aeroplane during the First World War and new ideas for delivering them were continually tried between the wars. By 1939 it had become a well-developed art, the most important torpedo actions being the Fleet Air Arm's attack on the Italian fleet at Taranto in 1940 and of course the Japanese attack on the US Navy at Pearl Harbor. Both these attacks crippled major fleets in the 'safety' of their own harbours.

Later, the famous battles at Coral Sea and Midway demonstrated the vulnerability of aircraft carriers and battleships to aerial attack. Since the war, aircraft have been fitted with much more sophis-

Harrier 'jump jets' concealed in a forest like this would be a difficult target for attacking strike aircraft.

ticated anti-shipping weapons which can be programmed so that once they have been dropped by the parent aircraft they will continue to hunt a ship wherever it goes until they have scored a direct hit.

Sensors

With the Royal Navy's aircraft carrier fleet now completely disbanded the remaining Buccaneer low-level strike aircraft have been deployed on land bases in Europe. Buccaneers have seen action in combat conditions during the South African foray into Angola. An interesting feature of the Buccaneer is its rotating underbelly bomb-bay, with room for four 450 kg (1,000 lb) HE bombs. Four further pylons on the aircraft's swept-back wings can each carry three bombs.

The Anglo-French Jaguar is the epitomy of the modern single-seater aircraft, with a dazzling low-level performance and a whole array of sensors mounted in its nosecone for operations by night. A laser rangefinder is a notable feature of the RAF version of this effective little aeroplane. Much further up the sophistication scale is the Panavia Tornado, produced as a joint effort by the aircraft industries of Germany, Italy and Great Britain. It has a variable geometry wing configuration, computer controlled to swing the wings right forward to create a wide span for slow-speed landings on unprepared airstrips, and swing them back again right along the fuselage sides to streamline the aircraft for supersonic flight below the enemy radar screen.

Swing wings are not unique to Western powers, for the Soviet Union has long recognized the value of a variable-geometry configuration. Their swing wing MiG-27 totes a six-barrel 23 mm cannon and a variety of other weapons and would be bound to play a major part in any future conflict over European soil.

BOMBERS
Scourge of the Cities

famous raid on 4 June 1918 involved dozens of Breguet 14s in an attack on massed German infantry. In the course of only a few hours, more than 7,200 bombs were dropped and the enemy force of several thousand virtually wiped out. By the end of the war, over 8,000 Breguet 14s had been built and many of them continued in service for another decade. Unfortunately for the French their range of big heavy bombers, including the famous Farman Goliaths, arrived just too late to see service. However, the Goliath was to become the standard French night bomber for many years.

Just as the Voisin had been the only purpose-built bomber on the western

The de Havilland (Airco) DH.9 first flew in July 1917 and was operated with great success by the RFC.

Bombs were dropped from a fixed-wing aircraft for the first time in 1910 by the US Army Signal Corps at an air display in San Francisco. They were first dropped in anger just a year later by an Italian pilot called Giulio Gavotti as he flew his flimsy Rumpler Taube observation machine over Turkish positions in Libya. Although the very same positions had suffered a heavy naval bombardment just a few days before, there was an immediate uproar in the correspondence columns of the world's press about the four modified 2 kg (4.4 lb) grenades Gavotti had rained down on the Turks. In those days there were still a few lingering conventions about how war ought to be conducted and Gavotti was roundly condemned on all sides for his 'unethical' actions. Nonetheless, the Italians were unrepentant. They not only continued to bomb the Turks in North Africa, but also dropped purpose-built aerial bombs from airships during fighting in the Balkans in 1912. In those early days aircrew simply threw their bombs over the side, but a few ingenious pilots wired them up along their aeroplane's fuselage or under the wings then cut the wire to let them drop.

Airship Attacks

Germany, meanwhile, followed the Italian lead and began to practise bombing from Zeppelin and Schutte-Lanz airships. Most military theorists thought simply in terms of attacking enemy ground positions around the battlefield, but others had even then realized the possibilities of long-range missions to

The earliest method of aerial bombing was crude to say the least and often resulted in missing the target by a wide margin.

bomb the enemy's factories and cities. So it was that on 6 August 1914 – just three days after the outbreak of the First World War – a German army airship attacked the Belgian city of Liège with several 250 kg (550 lb) bombs. Although it was hit by the world's first anti-aircraft fire in the process, the airship managed to crash-land back at its base.

Clearly the war was not destined to be an 'ethical' conflict because, on 14 August, French aircraft conducted the first fixed-wing bombing mission of the war against Germany's Zeppelin sheds. The aircraft used on this raid were 70 hp Voisin pushers, which were pathetically slow with their maximum speed of just over 80 km/hr (50 mph), but were steel-framed and therefore very strong. For the first year of the war they operated in groups as strategic day-bombers, carrying about 60 kg (130 lb) of ordnance in addition to their two crew members. Over 2,000 Voisins of all variants were built during the First World War, and the British and Italians also used them right up to the Armistice in November 1918.

By 1917 however, the French had found themselves a fine bomber in the Breguet 14, a 300 hp two-seater biplane. This was originally designed for reconnaissance duties, but as a long-range day or night bomber it could carry a sizeable load of bombs beneath its lower wing on missions lasting almost three hours. One

front at the outbreak of war, the Russian *Ilya Mourometz* was its opposite number on the east. Looking something like a garden shed with massive biplane wings and a fixed undercarriage of either wheels or skis, this was also one of the world's first four-engined heavy bombers. The *Ilya Mourometz* was designed in 1912 by Igor Sikorsky (later of helicopter fame) and was powered by two 200 hp engines and two of 135 hp. It was undoubtedly the best warplane in the world at that time.

Pinpoint Accuracy

During the First World War about 80 *Ilya Mourometz* bombers were built with a variety of engines, eventually giving a top speed of 120 km/hr (75 mph). They could carry more than 680 kg (1,500 lb) of bombs and deliver them with pinpoint accuracy using very effective bombsights of Russian design. Moreover, the *Ilya Mourometz* could fly well out of range of ground fire and had up to seven flexible machine-guns as defence against fighters. As a result, in over 400 operational sorties between February 1915 and the Revolution which withdrew Russia from the war in October 1917, only one *Ilya Mourometz* was lost in combat with enemy fighters – and even this took three of its assailants down with it!

In comparison with these Russian machines, Britain's long-range bombers at the outbreak of war were mere improvisations. In fact, the first British strategic bombing raid – against Zeppelin sheds in October 1914 – was undertaken by a pair of diminutive single-seater Sopwith Tabloids, each of which carried a negligible bombload. These were later replaced by slightly larger machines in the shape of newly-modified Avro 504 trainers. During an attack on a Zeppelin factory 160 km (100 miles) inside Germany in November 1914, three of these 504s managed to virtually destroy an airship under construction and cause a massive explosion in a neighbouring gas works.

Clearly convinced by the usefulness of this and similar raids the British Admiralty, whose RNAS was then largely responsible for long-range bombing, soon put out a tender to the country's planemakers for an aircraft able to deliver up to six of its big new 50 kg (110 lb) bombs. Frederick Handley Page promptly delivered just such a design, only to be told by the Admiralty to build something even bigger – in fact to 'build a bloody paralyser of an aeroplane!' By December 1915 Handley Page had done just that. His O/100 was a twin-engined biplane with the typical strut and fabric construction of the time, but it could carry a very impressive load of bombs on missions lasting almost eight hours.

With their crew of four manning up to five defensive machine-guns, the first of 46 'Bloody Paralyzers' (as they were predictably nicknamed) became operational in 1916 as day bombers. Unfortunately, their slow speed made them too vulnerable by daylight, so in appalling conditions they commenced bombing operations by night deep into Germany. Exposed to the elements in their open cockpits, the crews endured intense cold – protected only by electrically-heated flying suits that rarely worked. Of course many O/100s were shot down during these night raids, despite their armour-plated engines and fuel tanks, but their losses were by no means as high as among the smaller contemporary DH.4s, which were often sent out un-

A giant of the First World War, the Handley Page O/400 was powered by a pair of 360 hp Rolls-Royce inline engines.

escorted during the daytime.

When the Royal Flying Corps formed their Strategic Bomber Wing in October 1917, it was equipped with both these types in addition to the general-purpose FE.2 'pusher'. By late 1917 however, the first of over 250 Handley Page O/400s had begun to bear the brunt of the Wing's heavy-bombing duties. These were in essence modified O/100s with two 360 hp engines giving them a top speed of almost 160 km/hr. They had the ability to carry an even heavier bomb-load than their predecessors, toted up to five .303 machine-guns and carried a crew of four or five. With a flight endurance time of up to eight hours, the O/400s were well able to bomb the enemy's homeland, and in countless night missions before the war ended they did just that to great effect. On one occasion, the night of 14 September 1918, a formation of 40 undertook an early form of 'area bombing' in the Saas industrial region, laying waste to vast areas with the biggest bombs ever carried aloft.

Had the war gone on beyond that November of 1918, even more formidable British heavy bombers would have come into use, including the Handley

Loading was made considerably easier with the addition of winching gear inside their bomb-bays.

Page V/1500. This formidable aircraft had been built in secret with the intention of bombing Berlin from bases in the south of England. It was able to take-off at a total weight approaching 14,865 kg (30,000 lb) – more than twice that of the O/400. On its four engines, the V/1500 could fly at almost 160 km/hr (100 mph) and had a maximum range of around 1,600 km (1,000 miles) carrying two of the latest 1,500 kg (3,300 lb) 'blockbuster' bombs. A truly stunning air weapon, the V/1500 arrived just too late to see action in the First World War. So, too, did the twin-engined Vickers Vimy, a modified example of which made the first fixed-wing crossing of the Atlantic in the hands of Alcock and Brown.

Enter Italy

Italy, meanwhile, centred itself on the war against Austro-Hungary in May 1915, by which time she had what was perhaps the best-trained air force in the world. Although most of Italy's serving aircraft were outdated French types, an exception was her range of skeletal-looking Caproni Ca3 biplanes. Along with Russia's *Ilya Mourometz* these were among the first large bombers ever built and they gave Italy an early lead in the field of heavy bombing. On their three 100 hp engines (one driving a 'pusher' propeller between the two fuselage booms), these peculiar machines could

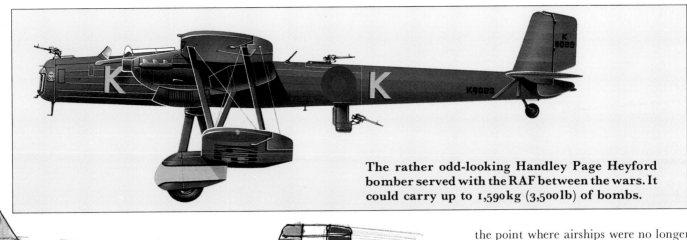

The rather odd-looking Handley Page Heyford bomber served with the RAF between the wars. It could carry up to 1,590 kg (3,500 lb) of bombs.

Italy's Ca 46. Note the gunner's positions in the nose and behind the upper wing.

carry a 450 kg (1,100 lb) bombload. The most successful variant of the series was the Ca 32, which entered service in 1916 and was armed with four machine-guns, operated by gunners at front and rear. In such exposed machines many unsung Italian heroes braved the extreme conditions to fly across the Alps and then face enemy fighters over Austria before releasing their underslung bombs and flying hopefully for home.

However, with the introduction of Caproni's latest bombers in 1917 the quality of their lives must have improved considerably. These were the Ca 4 series of triplanes with huge 30 m (100 ft) wings, five tailfins, three hefty Fiat engines and fabric-covered airframes. In action these spectacular machines soon

proved too vulnerable for daylight missions, so they were confined thereafter to night bombing across the Adriatic. Finally, just before the war came to an end, large numbers of triple-engined Ca 5 biplanes began to enter service. These aircraft could defend themselves with three well-positioned machine-guns and were the finest Italian bombers of the first war. They flew by night or day and even served on occasion as torpedo bombers.

Enemy Fighters

Like the other warring nations, Germany opened hostilities in 1914 with a wide variety of aircraft types – some of which were used to drop the occasional bomb on enemy targets. In the long-range bombing role she at first relied on huge hydrogen-filled airships, a field in which she had a substantial lead thanks largely to the efforts of Count Ferdinand von Zeppelin. His first airships were just as fast as contemporary fixed-wing aircraft, were higher flying, were capable of much greater endurance and could carry a far greater weaponload. Before long however, enemy fighters developed to

the point where airships were no longer safe in hostile skies, and so the need for fixed-wing strategic bombers became much more pressing.

As a result, in 1916 both the Fiedrich-shafen G series and Gotha G series of twin-engined 'heavies' entered service. The Friedrichshafen G.IIs which entered service that year could carry a 450 kg (1,000 lb) bombload and two machine-guns for self defence. Nonetheless they were rather poor performers, so the later G.III model of 1917 came as a great improvement. This was the main production variant, some 300 examples being built, and it could carry more than twice the bombload of its predecessor, flying missions lasting up to five hours. With four machine-guns for its three crew members to use in their defence, this type was a mainstay of Germany's heavy bomber units for the final two years of the First World War.

Railway Raid

So too were the later Gotha G.IVs and G.Vs, which could only carry a bomb-load of around 450 kg (1,000 lb) – but could deliver it from the relatively safe height of 6,100 m (20,000 ft). In addition, they had one machine-gun in a front station and another behind the wings which could fire both upwards and down behind the tail to fend off enemy fighters. When Gothas began both day and night raids on London in May 1917, many residents were heard to long for the 'good old days' of the Zeppelin raids. And no wonder, because during an attack in broad daylight on 13 June of that year a formation of fourteen Gothas coolly circled the city in full view before dropping over 100 bombs near Liverpool Street Station – killing more people (162) and causing more serious injuries (438) than all the airship raids put together. As if this were not bad enough, the efforts of a sizeable pack of British fighters were insufficient to prevent all the Gothas from returning to their base completely unscathed.

The delicate balance of power was redressed in the course of time however, for the Gothas were gradually outnumbered by improved anti-aircraft guns, capable of firing much higher, and new British fighters (notably Sopwith Pups, Sopwith Camels, and the superb SE.5a). By the time Gothas were demoted to night-bombing, though, the Germans had begun to introduce their R-class bombers, made by various companies but generally known as Zeppelin Staaken 'Giants'. The first R-class bombers were fitted with the same 260 hp engines used by the Gotha G series, but these proved inadequate to power the nine-tonne aircraft. By 1916 the more refined R.III model had appeared with a most extraordinary engine configuration. Two engines were placed back-to-front in each wing to drive single 'pusher' propellers, and another two were placed side-by-side driving a single propeller in the nose. This too proved unsuccessful, but in mid-1917 production began of the new operational variant, the R.VI. This could fly at over 130 km/hr (80 mph) for up to ten hours at a time.

Eighteen Wheels

With a total weight of over 11,250 kg (25,000 lb), the R.VI was a giant of an aeroplane, and needed an eighteen-wheeled undercarriage to support it on landing! The R.VI's crew of seven were seated in an enclosed cabin and had four machine-guns with which to deter British fighters that ventured too close. The Zeppelin Staaken also had a novel internal bomb-bay, with rows of bombs slung up inside ready to be released by a single lever in the cockpit. The eighteen R.VIs built were truly remarkable machines, able to carry the largest bomb of the war – one which weighed 990 kg (2,200 lb). They operated at first on the Eastern Front and then began night raids on London and Paris early in 1918 without suffering a single loss. However, when the defences of these cities were improved in the summer of that year, R.VIs and other heavy bombers were

Above: **Poland produced her own bomber aircraft in 1936, the PZLP-37 Los (Elk). Nazi onslaughts on Polish airfields quickly reduced their usefulness.**

transferred to the low-level strike role against installations just behind the enemy lines. Such missions soon showed how vulnerable large aircraft with a slow top speed could be, for the Zeppelin Staakens took a heavy pounding from enemy anti-aircraft fire.

Smaller Bombers

In the light of this bitter experience, smaller bomber aircraft were sent into action. These included German Halberstadt CLs, LVG C.IIs and AEG G.IV biplanes. To the single-engined LVG C.II went the distinction of becoming the first aeroplane to drop bombs on London, while the twin-engined AEG types proved particularly suitable for attacks on enemy lines and had a top speed of over 160 km/hr (100 mph). Despite their relatively lightweight bombload of just 350 kg (770 lb) and their rather short range, these agile aircraft were well able to penetrate hotly-contested airspace, drop their bombs and then return safely to base. They did this by virtue of their high speed and good manoeuvrability, though the AEG's four-men crews were often forced to resort to their three machine-guns for extra protection.

Many lessons were learnt during these and other types of bombing raids, and new hardware was developed to make bomber aircraft more efficient. Chief amongst these developments were highly accurate bombsights, long-range radio navigation equipment, oxygen masks for

A CRDA Cant Z.1007 Alcione triple-engined bomber pictured during a daylight raid on the Mediterranean island of Malta.

the crews to use during high-altitude raids, and special underslung racks for holding a number of bombs for simultaneous or individual release. In addition, a wide variety of bombs were developed for use against different types of target.

After the First World War, Russia in particular was quick to improve her bomber forces when her warplane industry was re-established in 1924, seven years after the Revolution. A design team lead by Andrei Tupolev came up with two outstanding types of bomber

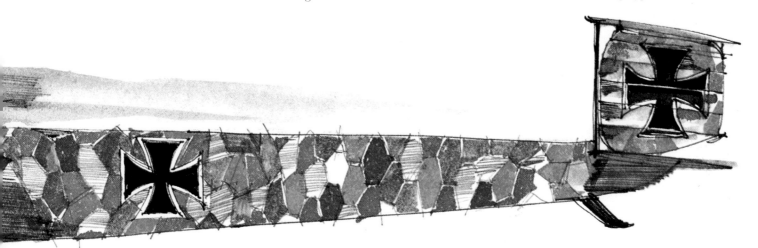

Germany's mighty Zeppelin-Stakken R.VI. Note the 'push-and-pull' arrangement of the engines, two being fitted back-to-back in each streamlined nacelle.

aircraft; namely the ANT-4 (known to the military as the TB-1) and the TB-3. The ANT-4 was a majestic twin-engined monoplane built entirely of metal, and it set the style for Soviet bombers right through the forties. It had a crew of six, carried over 3,000 kg (6,600 lb) of bombs and was in concept a lumbering monster of an aeroplane simply bristling with defensive machine-guns. In 1929 an ANT-4 hit the headlines by flying around the world in a series of long-distance stages. Two years later the type was flown with two small fighters mounted on its wings to test the theory that bombers were capable of carrying their own best defence with them.

Ten Machine-guns

This 'parasite fighter' idea was also tested on Tupolev's other major interwar bomber – the gigantic TB-3. This massive monoplane had a wingspan of 40 m (130 ft) and on occasion successfully launched *five* parasite fighters at once during airborne tests, but it is best remembered for its ability to carry a heavier bombload than any other aircraft of the interwar years. Capable of speeds up to 290 km/hr (180 mph) on its four engines (which could be reached in flight by catwalks *inside* the wings), the TB-3 carried a crew of six in open cockpits and sported no less than ten machine-guns for all-round defence. Despite their big fixed undercarriage units and rather old-fashioned general appearance, the 800 or so TB-3s built from 1930 onwards undoubtedly number among the most outstanding warplanes of their time and established a trend towards sheer size that was to become the hallmark of all heavy bombers in the future.

TB-3s went on to establish a number of commendable 'firsts' in the history of aviation, including the first aircraft landing at the North Pole (a ski-equipped example) and the first airlift of a battle tank. They were widely used for dropping paratroops and were still in service at the outbreak of the Second World War. Unfortunately, by then they were easy prey for the latest German fighters, so they were quickly relegated to transport duties.

Nightmares

The declaration of war in September 1939 was followed almost immediately by the first air-raid warning. The citizens of London ran to their air raid shelters and wondered if they were to become victims of the air warfare nightmares that scaremongers had predicted in the 1930s. Among these stories was one that predicted the saturation of urban areas with gas bombs which would leave toxic vapours hanging in the streets for days and kill the entire population in a matter of hours. In practice the Second World War began with only modest air raids, mostly directed against vital military targets. Luftwaffe bombing of Warsaw and Rotterdam, for example, were linked to German land operations.

'Operation Punishment'

As the war progressed, bombing was to become an end in itself and was directed increasingly against urban areas, the aim being to demoralize the enemy population at home. Luftwaffe bombers attacked Belgrade in 1941 at Hitler's command after the Yugoslavs had rebelled against their pro-German government. 'Operation Punishment' as it was called was an act of calculated savagery, but it was nothing compared to the massive fire and explosive raids which were to become the German's own nightly experience. For while the USAAF directed daylight raids against industrial targets in Germany, the RAF flew by night to hit the cities. RAF tactics reflected the inadequacy of the bomb-sights and aiming equipment of the time, and also the fact that bombers were very vulnerable to fighter and anti-aircraft fire by the light of day.

The USAAF had believed that their heavily-armed bombers could fly unescorted over Germany, but in 1943 the Luftwaffe put up fighters along the route

The full fury of a daylight bombing raid by Consolidated Liberators of the USAAF is well illustrated.

taken by these aircraft. They hit them hard both on their way in and when they returned, the resultant American losses being very heavy indeed. It was only when they received assistance from long-range escort fighters that the USAAF's bombers were able to roam relatively safely over the German airspace. Luftwaffe pilots had already discovered the vulnerability of bombers in daylight when they themselves attacked the British Isles in 1940-1.

The Battle of Britain was the

The Vickers Armstrongs Wellington was one of the mainstays of RAF Bomber Command throughout the Second World War. Illustrated here is the Wellington B.IC version.

Above: **Lying flat on his stomach, an RAF bomb-aimer peers through his elaborate sighting mechanism to ensure a direct-hit on the target. In his hand is the bomb release button.**
Right: **An RAF pilot and co-pilot set out on a raid.**

Germans' attempt to destroy the RAF in preparation for an invasion, but the Luftwaffe suffered unacceptably high losses during these attacks, so when they became involved in fighting Russia they called a halt to their daily raids on Britain. The RAF survived mainly by dint of their outstanding courage and dogfighting ability, but also because the Luftwaffe switched their attacks to targets other than airfields and gave the

RAF pilots breathing time to recover from an almost daily pounding in the air. The Luftwaffe's assault on cities such as London, Coventry, Plymouth, Southampton and Swansea in the winter of 1940 came as a direct result of raids on Berlin by the RAF. In turn, these rather modest attacks had only been ordered after a lone German bomber accidentally dumped its bombs on houses in London's East End. In Churchill's words the Germans had sown the wind and now they reaped the whirlwind.

Harvest of Death

This harvest of death grew to the point where the RAF were able to put up to 1,000 bombers at a time into the air over Cologne. It was Bomber Command's greatest triumph and by 1944 no city in Germany was left undamaged, many having had their centres reduced to vast areas of rubble. British tactics for a night raid included equipping their aircraft

A group of North American B-25 Mitchells of the USAAF pounding at the heart of a German city.

with a deadly mix of HE (high explosive) and incendiary (fire) bombs, plus mines fitted with delayed-action fuses. RAF bombers would split open houses with the HEs and then mix in an increasing volume of incendiaries, packed with magnesium, a chemical whose fire is almost impossible to extinguish. Mixed in

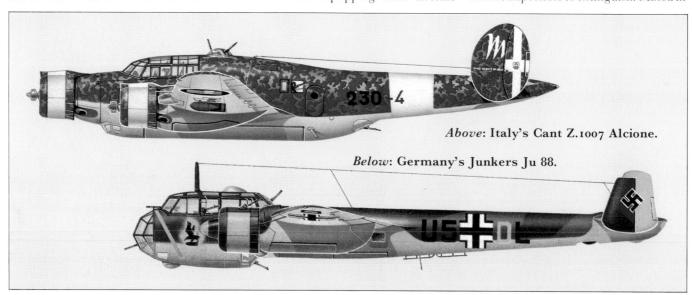

Above: Italy's Cant Z.1007 Alcione.

Below: Germany's Junkers Ju 88.

with the incendiaries were the delayed-action mines, timed to explode soon after the raid was over, killing rescue workers and firemen caught out in the open. Delayed-action mines also disrupted road traffic, as they had first to be located and then made safe before life in the shattered city could return to normality.

'Fire Storms'

If all this seems inhuman remember that in those days the end justified the means and the bombing campaign seemed to be one sure way of hastening an end to the war. The most terrifying form of mass bombing was the 'fire storm'. This was achieved by mixing HE and incendiary bombs, but instead of causing scattered fires throughout the target area, the whole city caught alight. Hamburg and Dresden were horrifying examples, but a more awesome 'fire storm' was one which engulfed Tokyo. The USAAF in the Pacific conflict had concentrated on daylight raids and attempted to bomb from great heights, thus avoiding enemy fighter attacks, but the results were not very impressive. In a dramatic change of tactics the Americans not only switched to night raids, but flew low down with a bombload made up entirely of incendiaries. The Japanese, who had almost no night-fighter defence and whose cities were built of light

inflammable materials, suffered the heaviest losses ever inflicted upon a population in any war in history. There are no accurate figures available for the number of dead, because in some areas the heat was so intense that nothing remained to be identified as human.

The final round of the bombing war came in 1945 when Germany brought into service the first jet bombers and Japan became the only nation in history to suffer an atomic bomb attack. German operations were of considerable technical interest, but did nothing to stop the war from grinding to its inevitable conclusion, while the atomic bomb gave Japan an excuse to get out of the war. It was such a horrifying weapon that a nation who made war a religion found that they had met their match and could bow out without losing face. Bombers had rendered unnecessary the bloodbath that would have followed an invasion of the Japanese mainland.

Fast and Agile

Bombers, however, are not just massive four-engined aircraft which penetrate enemy air space and flatten whole areas of houses and factories. That is the work of strategic bombers. Tactical or medium bombers, on the other hand can work very closely with frontline troops, and are usually twin-engined machines

which attack troop concentrations, road and rail links and frontline airfields. They are usually faster and more agile than their heavy bomber counterparts, and can even be pressed into service as fighters or attack aircraft. Such aircraft were Britain's de Havilland Mosquito and Bristol Blenheim and Germany's Junkers Ju 88 and Dornier Do 17.

Faster than Fighters

The Blenheim made headlines when it entered service with the RAF in 1937. Though it was a bomber it was nearly 65 km/hr (40 mph) faster than contemporary fighters! It served with all commands of the RAF (Bomber, Fighter, Coastal, Army Co-operation and Training), but by 1940 it was becoming outdated. In the early months of the war Blenheims were one of the mainstays of the RAF, attacking German forces in France in 1940 and then during the night raids on London serving as a radar-equipped fighter. The versatile Ju 88, on the other hand, underwent numerous modifications to serve as a ground-attack aircraft, medium- or high-altitude bomber and radar-equipped night fighter and had been one of the bombers deployed by the Luftwaffe during the Battle of Britain. Dornier's Do 17 was another notable German medium bomber of the Second World War. It was

Colourful nose markings were a feature of bomber aircraft during the Second World War. This is a B-25 Mitchell of the USAAF.

Pictured here being loaded with bombs before a raid is one of the RAF's massive Short Stirlings.

intended as a civilian airliner, but when hostilities started it began a distinguished career with the Luftwaffe. Because of its slim fuselage, the Do 17 became known as the 'Flying Pencil' or 'Eversharp'. A progressive development of the Do 17, the Do 217, was another medium bomber which changed roles as time went by. With a 'solid' rather than glazed nose section and fitted with a comprehensive radar system it worked as a night fighter, while in a bomber role it sometimes served as a 'mother' aircraft for the glider and rocket bombs used against Allied shipping in the Mediterranean. An unusual feature of early Do 217s was their long tail sections, which contained an umbrella-style airbrake built in four sections and used during dive-bombing attacks.

The Luftwaffe's most famous medium bomber, though, was the Heinkel He 111. During the Battle of Britain it was easily recognized from the ground by the note from its two Junkers Jumo engines as it flew over enemy cities by night. A vast variety of types were built during the war; some even being used for torpedo attacks, and others as the

launching platform for jet-propelled V-1 flying bombs. The He 111 was also occasionally used for troop carrying, but this is not so unusual as it sounds, because the type had begun its prewar career as an airliner with Luft Hansa.

Flying Fortress

While Europe was deeply embroiled in war the United States was trying to keep clear, but was also taking a very friendly interest in the safety of the British Isles and supplied many aircraft under a lease/lend scheme. During the last few years of peace they had had time to develop the various weapons that went on to stand them in good stead when they finally joined the conflict in 1941. One of these was the Boeing B-17 Flying Fortress, first loaned to the RAF in 1940 to give the Americans some idea of its performance in action. The Flying Fortress was to become the main equipment of the USAAF strategic bomber squadrons based in England, and a source of terror to the people of Germany. Combat experience against Luftwaffe fighters led to an increase in the number of machine-guns it carried, with some aircraft being

fitted with as many as 30 on different points around the airframe. Consequently, attacking a 'box' of B-17s took considerable nerve, but German fighter pilots were ruthless enemies and the Fortress crews welcomed the fighter escorts that later became essential to keep marauding Luftwaffe Bf 109s and Fw 190s at bay.

The air war against Germany is popularly regarded as an exclusively Anglo-American operation. True, these two countries certainly bore the brunt of the effort, but it is a little known fact that the USSR was in action over Germany from as early as August 1941, when a group of Ilyushin Il-4 bombers under Colonel Preobrazhensky made a raid on Berlin. Though air attacks became harder as the Germans pushed relentlessly eastwards, the Russian air force continued to hit targets in Germany and her allies throughout the war. The Il-4 had already seen action against Finland during the Winter War of 1939-40, and remained in service even after the Second World War.

A somewhat reluctant foe of the Russians was the Italian expeditionary

76

force. Sent in on the express orders of Mussolini, these unhappy soldiers faced an enemy armed with superior weapons and in far greater numbers. Among the aircraft available to the Italians at that time was the Savoia-Marchetti S.M.81 Pipistrello (meaning Bat). This bomber created a vogue in Italian aircraft design for installing three engines. By the time Italy entered the war she had about 100 Pipistrellos in frontline service, but despite their early successes in an anti-shipping role against British convoys they proved vulnerable to fighter attack due to their low speed and were relegated to troop carrying after operations in Africa, Greece and Russia. The earlier Savoia-Marchetti Sparviero (Hawk) remained in service with the Italians until as late as 1952. In common with a number of Luftwaffe bombers it had begun life as an airliner and worked as a torpedo bomber, reconnaissance and close-support attack aircraft.

Japan

Japan was the most belligerent ally of the Germans and Italians, their bomber force being particularly suitable for long-range missions. Their force of Mitsubishi G3M medium bombers made headlines when they attacked the Royal Navy's prize battleships *Prince of Wales* and *Repulse* off the Malayan coast and sunk both ships with dramatic efficiency. These aircraft had earlier seen action in China, but they suffered heavy losses when flying unescorted. Improvised versions of the G3M (codenamed *Nell* by the Allies) were used as personnel transports, but they had room for only ten troops and were used only in small numbers. Another bomber which was pressed into service in a transport role was the Mitsubishi Ki-21 (codenamed *Sally*). The *Sally* was used as an assault aircraft for transporting troops to attack Okinawa in 1945, but these were sitting ducks for American fighters and only one reached its targets. Previously, Ki-21s had served throughout the war against China but suffered badly in Burma at the hands of RAF Hurricane fighters.

Countless Raids

The Japanese bomber which comes to mind more readily than any other is the G4M, or 'Betty'. As well as carrying out countless conventional bombing raids, these aircraft were the most common 'mother' aircraft for the deadly Ohka *Kamikaze* attack aircraft, ferrying them to within close range of their targets and releasing them with uncanny precision. However the G4M was only really effective when there were no enemy fighters around. Under attack it had a nasty way of catching fire, leading American pilots to nickname it 'the one-shot lighter'.

Facing a long night raid over enemy territory is an awesome prospect, even with good aircraft, but it became the regular fare of young crewmen serving with RAF Bomber Command. The distinction of launching the first aerial raid of the war against Germany rests with the twin-engined Armstrong Whitworth Whitley, for on 19 March 1940 a group of these aircraft, accompanied by six Handley Page Hampden medium bombers, dealt the Germans a nasty blow. But in 1942 the type was withdrawn from front-line service as it was by then outdated by larger types like the four-engined Avro Lancaster and Handley Page Halifax 'heavies'.

Another twin-engined British bomber, the Vickers Wellington, soldiered on into the war long after the Whitley had been

Above: **A Boeing B-17 Flying Fortress, the USAAF's primary daylight bomber of the Second World War.**

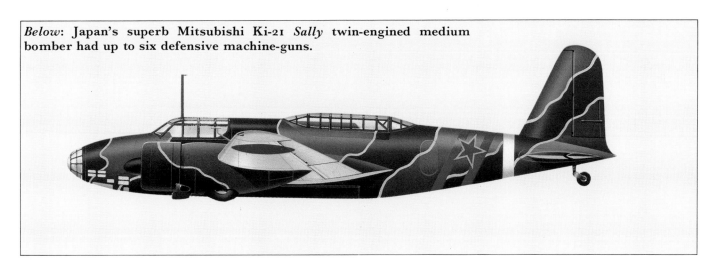

Below: **Japan's superb Mitsubishi Ki-21 *Sally* twin-engined medium bomber had up to six defensive machine-guns.**

withdrawn. Known as the 'Wimpey' (after J. Wellington Wimpey – friend of the popular cartoon character 'Popeye') it featured a novel 'basketwork' airframe which could withstand very heavy battle damage. It was used for a variety of tasks during the Second World War, including triggering magnetic mines out at sea using a huge loop slung under the airframe which generated a powerful magnetic field. Later, during a raid on Emden, a Wellington also dropped the first 1,800 kg (4,000 lb) 'blockbuster' bomb.

One of their more interesting features were the special fairings fitted around their exhaust pipes to conceal the flames that constantly spluttered from their engines. These fairings helped to ensure that the aircraft were not spotted by enemy night-fighters.

water behind the dam, cleverly avoiding most of the Germans' anti-aircraft fire. As history now records in its most hallowed pages, these raids were a great success and helped make the Lancaster the legend it is today. They carried heavier and heavier bombloads as the Second World War progressed, cul-

The mighty Boeing B-52 Stratofortress, powered by eight underwing turbojet engines, was responsible for carpet-bombing southeast Asia.

Bomber Command also had four-engined 'heavies', not least of these being the Short Stirling – the first of the RAF's three long-range wartime bombers. Readily recognizable by its stately lines and high undercarriage (including twin tail wheels) the Stirling was unfortunately hampered during its period of operational service by the relatively small size of its bomb-bay cells and its poor performance at high altitudes. This forced its pilots to fly at a lower height than normal, bringing the Stirling well within range of enemy anti-aircraft fire. The other two bombers which were to share the full weight of the RAF's campaign against Germany were the Handley Page Halifax and the Avro Lancaster. Production of the Halifax totalled 6,176 aircraft of seven main variants.

Dambusters

Lancasters are of course best remembered for the part they played in the destruction of the Mohne and Eder dams in 1943. The vast quantities of water held behind these dams were essential to German industry and were therefore very heavily guarded. Anti-aircraft batteries provided an umbrella of overhead cover, while huge underwater steel nets would stop torpedoes dropped from enemy aircraft from hitting the wall of the dam at any point along its length. The RAF's solution to this daunting problem was characteristically ingenious. In an unprecedented operation led by Barnes Wallis the brilliant aeronautical designer and inventor, a special spinning bomb was developed that could literally bounce along the surface of the water, skip over the rows of torpedo nets and explode on impact against the dam's inner wall.

The Lancaster aircraft that delivered these bombs flew very low across the

The Boeing B-50 Superfortress was a refined version of the B-29 Superfortress which dropped atomic bombs on Hiroshima and Nagasaki.

minating in the awesome 9,900 kg (22,000 lb) 'Grand Slam' which was designed to fall at supersonic speed, enter the ground nose-first on impact and then explode to create massive shock waves that would destroy bridges and other vital targets even if the bombs themselves 'missed'.

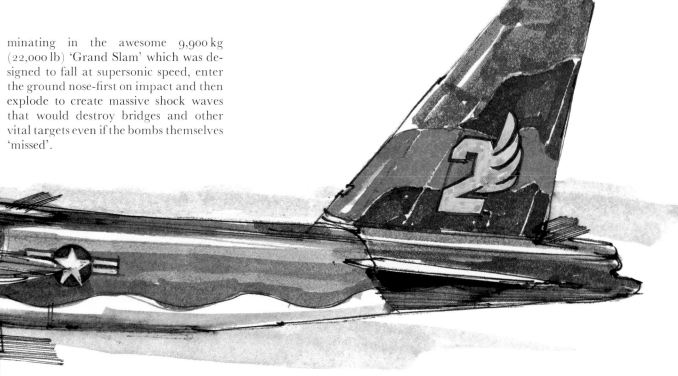

Pathfinders

A crucial part of the RAF night bomber campaign against Germany were the 'Pathfinders'. Post-raid photographic reconnaissance flights had revealed that many bombers had missed their target by huge margins. Navigation under stress was blamed and so the 'Pathfinder' system was evolved. Small numbers of de Havilland Mosquitos or heavy bombers equipped with navigation aids like Oboe (which allowed the aircrew to 'see' the ground even through cloud cover) would drop flares over the target to provide a beacon for the following waves of bombers to aim at. As more bombs were added to the fires caused by the first wave of the raid the target became obvious to subsequent waves of attacking aircraft.

Daylight Raid

The USAAF in England and Italy deployed a well balanced mix of heavy and medium bombers during the second war. The 'mediums' hit targets in France, Belgium and Holland with relentless precision while the 'heavies' hammered at the heart of Germany. Side by side with the B-17 Flying Fortresses, four-engined Consolidated B-24 Liberators attacked targets in the *Reich*. The Liberator was a more angular-looking aircraft than the B-17 and German fighter pilots found that under attack it caught fire quicker than the more streamlined Flying Fortress. However, Liberators claim the distinction of being chosen for the raid on the vital Rumanian oil wells at Ploesti. This dramatic long-range raid across enemy-held southern Europe in broad daylight hit the German economy at one of its most vulnerable points. Many USAAF air-

craft were shot down, but the loss of oil proved critical to the German war effort. Liberators played a vital part in the Pacific theatre too, where their long range was of particular value to the USAAF.

Another famous 'medium' of the war was the North American Mitchell. This was the bomber used in the dramatic and almost suicidal raid on Tokyo from the USS *Hornet* in 1942. The raid did little damage to the city but was excellent for morale and persuaded the Japanese to expand further eastwards and so become entangled in the Battle of Midway. The Mitchell saw service in numerous variants, one modificating being a 'solid' rather than glazed nose fitted with a

Below: **Vulcans bear camouflaged uppersurfaces for their low-level bombing role. In the 1960s they were white for high-altitude missions.**

Above: **Vulcans were a cornerstone of Britain's 'V-bomber' nuclear deterrent force of the 1960s. Here the crew practice a 'scramble'.**

The graceful FB-111B indicates that lumbering giants are gone forever.

massive 75 mm cannon. This proved to be an excellent weapon for attacks on enemy shipping and some 405 aircraft were thus equipped. Mitchells were still in service into the mid-sixties with various South American air arms.

Atomic Bombs

But of all the bombers that went into action in the Second World War, the mighty Boeing B-29 Superfortress stands unique. Not only was it the aircraft which dropped the atomic bombs on Hiroshima and Nagasaki in August 1945, but after the war it was copied almost exactly by the USSR. Because they had the benefit of pressured accommodation for their crews, the Superfortress could fly so high that Japanese fighters had great difficulty reaching an attacking position before the big American aircraft had flown away.

Boeing has had the distinction of supplying the USAF with heavy bombers for the last four decades, starting with the B-17 Flying Fortress, following up with the B-29 Superfortress, which in turn gave way to the jet-powered B-47 Stratojet and B-52 Stratofortress. The six-engined B-47 was the first sweptwing bomber to be built in quantity for any air force. It served with the USAF in the 1950s and 1960s and was used for a variety of tasks, including trials with 'stand-off' bombs – large missiles that can be unleashed many hundreds of kilometres from their targets and literally fly across to their impact points while the 'parent' bomber returns to safety.

As for the B-52 Stratofortress, this of course the massive eight-engined giant that played such a vital part in the USAF's campaign against Communist forces in southeast Asia in the sixties. With its awesome ability to bomb targets accurately even through heavy cloud cover and saturate whole areas of jungle in a manner reminiscent of the 'fire storms' that engulfed key Japanese cities in the later stages of the second war, the B-52 became one of the most feared weapons in the Western arsenal. Capable of carrying up to 32,000 kg (70,000 lb) of bombs, the first Stratofortress entered service in the early 1950s and are now enjoying a new lease of life. They are 'mother planes' for the latest Air-launched Cruise-Missiles (ALCMs), prompting the grim remark from some present-day pilots that they now fly the planes their fathers flew. ALCMs are pre-programmed, pilotless 'mini-aircraft' that can be released a tremendous distance from their targets and proceed to fly an erratic course to shake off enemy interception before striking the planned impact point and detonating their nuclear charge.

Reprieve

The age of massed bomber fleets has now long passed but, as the war in Vietnam so dramatically demonstrated, there can still be a use for the heavy bomber. A single big bomber can do in one mission that it takes faster but smaller strike aircraft numerous risky missions over enemy territory to complete. In general though, it is potent devices like the ALCM that have heralded the end of conventional bombers – though, somewhat ironically, it is these new missiles that have given such aircraft as the B-52 a last-minute reprieve, for they now serve as aerial launching platforms for the little ALCM as we have seen.

FIGHTERS
1913-45
Warfare Grows Wings

Aircraft were first used in warfare when early aviators were sent up to observe the movements of the enemy. It was not very long before the other side realized that the advantages gained from reconnaissance missions of this kind were great. It was necessary, therefore, to find a way of preventing any information reaching the enemy ground forces. Soon after this realization, aircraft on surveillance missions found themselves coming under attack from enemy two-seater aircraft in which the observer carried a hand-aimed rifle or pistol.

As early as 1910, there were aircraft in the United States and France which had borne men with rifles and within a couple of years there were three types of machine-gun and one shell-firing automatic cannon which could be fired from aircraft with a fair degree of success. Pilots of the First World War, however, were understandably suspicious of early experiments with aircraft armament. The only shooting most of them had done was to take pot-shots at small kites and other training targets with rifles that were too long and which did little but shoot up their own fuselage and wing structures and endanger innocent bystanders. Because of this, aircraft were used mainly in a passive role at the beginning of the war.

By 1915, warfare had taken on a new dimension, with the air forces of both sides doing their utmost to shoot each other out of the skies using machine-guns attached to their aircraft.

It was the French who took the lead in

The diving Spad XIII of American ace Captain Eddie Rickenbacker.

developing the fighter as we understand it today with the formation of their *Escadrilles de Chasse* to protect reconnaissance aircraft and bombers. These squadrons were made up mainly of monoplanes of various types including the Morane-Saulnier type N, first used as fighters in the spring of 1915 and introduced to the front line by one of the pioneers of air warfare, Eugen Gilbert. Gilbert's aircraft was fitted with an 8 mm Hotchkiss machine-gun on top of the

A Farman F.40 biplane of First World War vintage, armed with ten Le Prieur rockets for air-to-air combat.

forward fuselage so that the stream of bullets could fire straight through the arc of the propeller blades.

This brought about one of the first problems with the use of machine-guns in aircraft, for a bullet could quite easily knock off one of the blades of the propeller and the resulting imbalance often ripped the engine off its mountings. Several methods were experimented with in an effort to get round this problem. Pairs of guns were fitted on struts to fire past the propeller or were attached to

Garros finally came up with a successful method. In March 1915, he rejoined his squadron after months of secretive experiments with a Morane-Saulnier type L monoplane fitted with steel bullet deflectors on its propeller blades. This was originally the idea of Raymond Saulnier but was further developed by Garros.

On 1 April 1915, Roland Garros succeeded in shooting down an enemy aircraft, but the idea was not taken up by the French authorities. As if to make the

and the trigger of the aeroplane's Parabellum machine-gun. The mechanism was timed so that the gun fired once every three or four revolutions of the propeller.

This synchronization gear worked so well that Allied pilots stood very little chance against the attacking Fokker Eindeckers which were equipped with it, despite the fact that aircraft such as the Fokker E.I (first of the Eindecker family) had a top speed of only 130 km/hr (80 mph). The Germans inflicted such

A German Fokker Triplane attacks an RFC Bristol F.2B in a typical dogfight between 1914–18.

inclined mountings overhead or diagonally at the sides of the fuselage, but this made aiming very difficult and it was more often by luck than by skill that a hit was made. One ingenious individual in France even tried fixing an extra machine-gun on struts *in front* of the propeller!

Eventually it became clear that the only sure way of knowing where the machine-gun was pointing was to have the gun straight in front of the pilot and to aim the whole aircraft at the target. It was from this realization that designers began to think in terms of developing a machine-gun which could fire through the propeller arc without hitting the blades. A Frenchman named Roland

matter worse, on 18 April Garros' aircraft was hit by an enemy bullet fired by a rifleman defending Courtrai railway station which fractured the petrol pipe on Garros' machine. He landed safely but before he could set fire to his aircraft it was captured by the Germans. They discovered that he had a machine-gun which could fire through the propeller arc and the system was shown to inventor and aircraft designer Anthony Fokker. Within 48 hours he had improved the deflector system still further by adding an interrupter gear to prevent bullets hitting the propeller blades. This synchronizing mechanism consisted of a simple linkage of cams and pushrods between the oil-pump drive of the engine

heavy casualties on British and French squadrons that the six months or so that this slaughter lasted become known as the 'Fokker scourge'. The E.I was not a particularly impressive aircraft in itself and was first used only in the escort role, but its superior armament now made up for its basic deficiencies. Its ultimate version was the E.III, which had an increased wingspan and twin machine-guns. The extra weight of this second gun severely affected the performance of the aeroplane but the greater firepower still took a dreadful toll of Allied airmen.

In January 1916, when two of Germany's best-known pilots, Oswald Boelcke and Max Immelmann, had each scored eight confirmed kills, they became

with his opponent directly below him.

Despite doing their utmost to outwit their enemies, pilots hated to see a plane go down in flames. These were the days of the 'gentleman' pilots, and a few bullets meant certain death for the luckless victim because no parachutes were carried at this time. The official reason for not carrying parachutes was that they were too unreliable, but many thought the real reason was that the authorities were afraid that if the pilots had the luxury of a parachute it would discourage them from taking aggressive action. This meant that many brave men were forced to endure the terrible and painful fate of burning to death.

Despite this horror, aerial combat at this time was an extremely sporting affair, with pilots overflying enemy airfields and dropping messages to their counterparts. Challenges were issued for personal duels in the air and most of these

Three Bristol Bulldog biplanes climb away from their home airfield.

the first airmen to be awarded Germany's highest decoration – the *Order Pour le Merité*. It did not take the Germans very long to realize the great morale boost this could give to their pilots and so the 'ace' system was instigated. Eight kills remained the standard for eligibility to ace pilot status, until later that year when so many enemy aircraft were being shot down that they had to double the target figure to sixteen before ace status was given.

Tactics

Air combat was fast becoming an art and pilots were beginning to work out serious battle strategies. A favourite tactic was to fly up behind an enemy to a position offering safety from his machine-gun fire. Height was an important factor here because then the pilot could take advantage of any cloud cover or glare from the sun and dive on his opponent to gain extra speed. When the enemy was equipped with a rear gun, the best position to be in was behind and slightly below his tail.

Manoeuvrability was a great advantage, in attack (to be able to get onto the enemy's tail) and defensively (to be able to get out of the enemy's gunsights). Germany's Max Immelmann was probably one of the best exponents of air combat. One of his favourite tricks if he found himself with an enemy on his tail, was to pull up as if to loop and then execute a half-roll to shake off his bemused opponent. This manoeuvre is still known today as the 'Immelmann turn' in honour of a great pilot.

Sensitive Controls

The British meanwhile were still trying to figure out a way of preventing their pilots shooting off their own propellers. It was their temporary solution to this problem that brought about the development of the DH.2 and FE.8, both of which helped put an end to the 'Fokker scourge'. These aircraft were single-seaters with 'pusher' propellers *behind* the fuselage and their guns up front. The sensitive controls of the DH.2 caused some handling problems for the British pilots initially, but eventually these were overcome and the type became recognized as a highly robust and very manoeuvrable dogfighter.

The French solution to the problem of propeller blades getting in the way of the guns was to mount the gun on the centre section of their biplanes' upper wing, pointing at a slightly upward angle. This meant that the stream of bullets missed the arc of the propeller blades altogether. Their Nieuport series of fighters employed this configuration with great success and were widely used by a number of Allied air forces, being flown by some of the leading aces of the First World War. In the British examples, however, the standard French machine-gun mounting was replaced by the Foster mount, which allowed the gun to be pulled down into the cockpit for a change of ammunition drums. Albert Hall, the famous British fighter ace, used to pull his gun back and attack his opponents by pointing it straight up and firing into the enemy's underbelly, whose pilot must have thought himself to be in a safe position

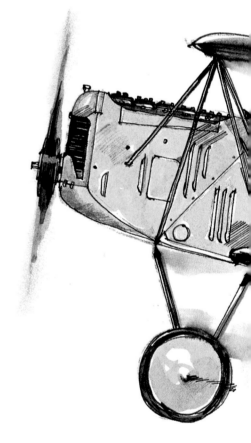

challenges were accepted because, as they saw it, their honour was at stake. The most successful aces were those who personalized the art of combat, and all these pilots had their favourite tricks for catching the enemy unawares. A favourite technique employed by Albert Ball was to allow his opponent to get onto his tail, then when he had been lulled into a false sense of security and was about to fire, he would go into a short dive and then come up underneath while the German was still sighting his guns. Ball was awarded the Victoria Cross and scored 44 kills before his luck finally ran our and he himself failed to return from a mission.

The first British fighter to be equipped with synchronized guns was the Bristol Scout, which appeared over France in March 1916. In May of that year these guns were fitted to the Sopwith 1½ Strutter, a two-seater fighter with the pilot in the front cockpit and an observer/gunner in the rear. Although this aircraft was originally designed as a bomber and was therefore too stable to be an ideal dogfighter, its two machine-guns made it an extremely effective performer. Enemy pilots attacking from an angle where they thought they were safe found themselves flying into a steady stream of bullets from the observer/gunner's position.

Another revolutionary Sopwith design to appear in 1916 was the Sopwith Triplane. Having three wings improved the pilot's visibility because each wing was narrower and shorter than those of a biplane. This configuration also made the Triplane more manoeuvrable and it

power aeroengines were able to deliver. Probably the most successful of the new breed of engines was the Hispano-Suiza V8, which powered the French Spad VII. This entered service in the summer of 1916. One Spad VII was flown by the leading French ace, René Paul Fonck, and for a while helped swing the balance of power on the battlefront back into the Allies' favour. The Fokker biplanes developed to replace the Eindeckers were disappointing, but the Halberstadt D.II and D.III did much to stop the Allied domination.

'The Red Baron'

Perhaps the most outstanding fighter of this period was Germany's Albatros, with its characteristic 'fishtail' tail surfaces. The Albatros D.I, which came into service in August 1916, was not as fast as the Spad V.II or as manoeuvrable as the Nieuport but it possessed a somewhat

superior rate of climb and it had far greater firepower. This was the end of the Allies' latest run of success, for on 17 September Boelcke in the Fokker D.III that he had chosen as his personal aircraft, led his best 'pupils' on their first operation. One star 'pupil', Baron Manfred von Richthofen (flying an Albatros D.II) scored his first victory that day, shooting down an FE.2b.

During the Battle of the Somme Britain's Royal Flying Corps (RFC) lost a total of 782 aircraft, many of them shot down by the fighters under Boelcke's command. It was during this battle that Richthofen (known as 'The Red Baron' because his aeroplane was painted blood red) had one of his most significant victories. On November 23, flying his Albatros D.II, he shot down Major L G Hawker, VC after a long and gallant battle.

The Germans, however, also suffered

Germany's superb Fokker D.VII. This particularly striking example bears the characteristic dazzle of bold patterns in bright colours. This trend was first established by Baron Manfred von Richthofen (the 'Red Baron') who had the idea of bringing back the traditions of the medieval knights.

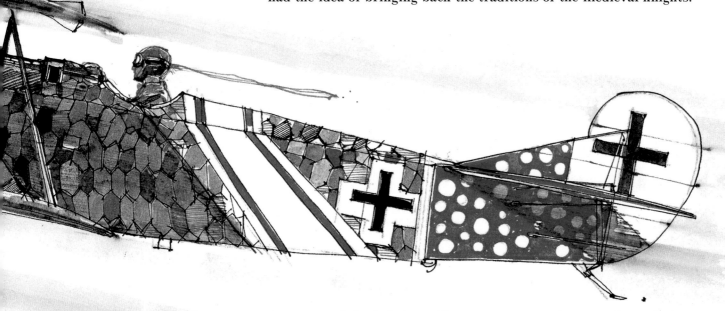

A group of British fighter pilots use maps to plan a combat mission.

became known as an outstanding combat aircraft. Its most remarkable achievement was when serving with No 10 Naval Squadron, commanded by a brave Canadian Flight Sub-Lieutenant, Raymond Collishaw, who shot down a total of 87 enemy aircraft with the type. Many pilots in this squadron were Canadians and belonged to what was known as the 'Black Flight', their Sopwith Triplanes being appropriately titled *Black Death, Black Maria, Black Prince, Black Roger* and *Black Sheep.*

One of the biggest advances to be made around this time was in the horse-

the loss of one of their best flyers when Oswald Boelcke collided with one of his own squadron and was killed outright while pursuing a British aircraft. His squadron, *Jasta 2*, was renamed *Jasta Boelcke* to honour this great man's memory. By the end of the war *Jasta Boelcke* had lost four commanders and 26 pilots but had notched up an incredible tally of 336 acknowledged victories. It must be remembered however, that because the Allies were on the offensive, most of their aircraft were employed in spotting for artillery and involved in photo reconnaissance missions. The Germans, on the other hand, were on the defensive and their main task was to shoot down Allied aircraft. For this reason it was small wonder that 'The Red Baron' and the other *Jasta* pilots were able to build up their scores so quickly.

Coat of Arms

When the Germans withdrew to the Hindenburg line in 1917 they had the added advantage of high ground for better observation. Good equipment, good training and an abundance of targets which were relatively easy prey boosted the German score to four times that of the RFC. It was at this period of the war, while facing the RFC across the Hindenburg line, that Richthofen had all the aircraft in his squadron painted in brilliant colours, totally contrary to German army regulations.

Richthofen himself kept his machine red, with his personal crest and coat of arms emblazoned across the fuselage sides in the highly-individualistic style of the medieval knights. The introduction of the blood red aircraft of 'The Red Baron' was a masterstroke of publicity, but Richthofen's capers ended once and for all the age of chivalry in air warfare. 'The Red Baron' was a ruthless hunter and as a bizarre hobby used panels of fabric from his victims' aircraft as wallpaper.

With the entry of the United States into the war in 1917 it became necessary for the Germans to try for a quick victory. To increase their score rate still further *Jastas* 4, 6, 10 and 11 bonded together into a formidable force which came to be known as the 'Richthofen

Above: **This picture of an early fighter aircraft's cockpit shows how basic the flying instruments were.**

Circus'. The RFC meanwhile had also begun to hunt in packs. The first mass dogfights took place toward the end of April when Richthofen's four *Jastas* met a British offensive patrol of Sopwith Triplanes, SE.5s and FE.2bs. The British lost six aircraft and the Germans lost five. Despite setting off to a rather slow start the British aircraft industry made startling progress during the First World War and in the last eighteen months of hostilities produced some of the best fighters of the whole conflict.

The most famous of these was the Sopwith Camel, which entered service in July 1917. On 25 March 1918 Captain John Trollope of 43 Squadron, flying a Camel, set a new record by shooting down six enemy aircraft in one day. By the summer of 1918 the Camel had reached its fighting peak. In terms of manoeuvrability, only the Fokker Dr.1 triplane could equal the Camel in a dogfight. Even the Fokker D.VII, generally acknowledged as the finest German fighter of the First World War, though possessing a good climbing performance, could not stop the Camel pilots amassing more and more victories. Sopwith Camels were the first single-seat fighters to fly at night and two Camels scored the first victory on night combat by shooting down a Gotha bomber in January 1918. With the increasing variety of uses to which fighters were being employed, a 2F.1 version of the Camel was developed for launching from ships. This model had

Below: **The Fiat CR.42 Falco was virtually obsolete by the time it made its maiden flight.**

An RFC Sopwith Camel, reckoned by many to be the greatest fighter aircraft of all time, downs a German Albatros biplane. The Sopwith aircraft was nicknamed the Camel by those who flew her because of the humped cover enclosing the breeches of her twin Vickers machine-guns. This nickname was officially adopted soon after.

a shorter wingspan and a detachable rear fuselage to save valuable space on the confined decks.

Another very successful British fighter to reach its peak towards the end of the war was the Bristol Fighter. On 5 April 1917 six Bristol Fighters were attacked by Richthofen's *Jasta* and four were shot down. It took the RFC quite a few more losses before they realized that the fault lay with their pilots' tactics and not with the actual aircraft. Once pilots had learned to aim the aircraft as a whole at the target, using the synchronized Vickers machine-gun, rather than relying on the observer's gun, it quickly developed into a very effective combat machine. It was such a success, in fact, that when the United States entered the war in 1917 they placed ambitiously large orders to equip their fighter squadrons with the type. Unfortunately, they tried to redesign the aircraft in order to accommodate their own 400 hp Liberty engine and this idea (implemented by the American company Curtiss and others) hindered production, with only

27 examples finally being built.

It was in 1918 that an Air Ministry was established in Britain to amalgamate the RFC and the RNAS (Royal Naval Air Service) into a new body called the Royal Air Force. Despite this branch of the armed services' vast potential and the number of enemy aircraft that were being destroyed over the battlefields of France, neither the army generals nor the government of the day considered military aviation to be of vital significance in the conflict. As far as they were concerned the 'real' war was being fought on the ground.

Recognition

It was not until the Second World War and the drama of the Battle of Britain that the true importance of aircraft in combat became widely recognized. The interwar years saw little progress in either fighter tactics or techniques in Europe, as there were no battles in which to try out new ideas, but there was what could only be called a revolution in technology. The average horsepower

delivered by aeroengines increased to four times that of the units fitted to the fighters of the First World War, and of course reliability and performance improved considerably. Ingenious new methods of constructing airframes were developed, with light yet strong structures of welded steel tube which eliminated the need for internal bracing cables and struts. Although most of the interwar fighters had traditional structures, with frames made of steel or aluminium instead of wood, the outer covering was still almost always made of fabric.

Following the Armistice in November 1918, Britain and France were swept with a wave of anti-war feeling and there was a rapid run-down of military strength. In Britain the Sopwith Snipe and the Bristol Fighter formed the backbone of the remaining force. Between April 1920 and October 1922, the Sopwith Snipe was the RAF's only home-defence fighter and it remained their major type until the mid-1920s. In 1923, a very small expansion programme was authorised, fifty-two squadrons being allocated to air defence. The Gloster Grebe and Hawker Woodcock replaced the Snipe, although they were merely developments of the same type of aircraft, having fabric-covered wooden fuselages, wooden propellers with twin Vickers machine-guns mounted in front of the pilot's cockpit.

Then came the Gloster Gamecock and Bristol Bulldog, but the principles of construction were similar, even though the Bulldog remained in service until as late as 1936. In 1925 the League of Nations began to examine various methods of implementing a general disarmament. But for years countries argued with each other over the degree of disarmament, no-one wanting to leave themselves totally defenceless. Eventually, in May 1934, the Disarmament Conference broke up without achieving anything, for it was clear that no country was willing to agree to a complete and

to mount a cannon which could fire through the hub of the propeller.

Prize

Meanwhile, a series of events that did more for the development of fighters in the interwar years than anything else were the regular contests for the coveted Schneider Trophy. This prize went to the fastest aircraft over a measured course, and many fighters of the Second World War were partly inspired by the speed merchants of the late 1920s. As aircraft became more sophisticated, so too did the art of flying them. Whereas at the start of the First World War pilots were going into combat with less than twenty hours flying time behind them, by 1939 at least 150 hours flying training was required.

In the United States aircraft production in the military field had got off to a very slow start. It was not until 1924 that

The Gloster Gladiator was the RAF's last biplane fighter, as Spitfire and Hurricane monoplanes were already on the drawing board when it first flew. Most 'Gladbags' were armed with four .303 Browning machine-guns.

A Supermarine Spitfire in fierce combat with a twin-engined Messerschmitt Me 110.

common solution. This was particularly so since Adolf Hitler had now come into power in Germany and it was evident that he was determined to rebuild his armed forces and begin a campaign of aggression.

By the mid-1930s, light alloy stressed-skin structures were revolutionizing aircraft design. This new form of construction was particularly suitable for fighters because it made possible higher standards of streamlining, which greatly improved the speed at which an aircraft could move through the air. Speed to a fighter aircraft is particularly important. So by 1935 a new kind of fighter had emerged on paper, if not yet in the air – a 1,000 hp monoplane with stressed-skin construction, a retractable landing gear, flaps to help reduce landing speeds, an enclosed cockpit, variable-pitch propeller and armed with a much more deadly selection of weapons. Aeroengine development was led by the French, with the Hispano-Suiza company introducing engines with geared propeller drives able

a fighter of any consequence appeared in that country. This was the PW-8, first of the Curtiss single-seat fighters which resulted in the famous Hawk series. Curtiss biplane fighters served with the US Navy up to the mid-1930s and it was only when it became apparent that the biplane could not be developed any further that the Curtiss-Wright Corporation decided to design a monoplane single-seat fighter. Boeing also began building excellent military aircraft, their greatest achievement during the interwar year's being their classic P-12/F4B family of biplane fighters.

With the black clouds of war gathering over Europe, the major powers were beginning to equip themselves with more modern and effective fighting aircraft. The French, under the direction of Emile Dewoitine, were developing a low-wing monoplane fighter to meet the requirements of their government's 1930 defence specifications. The result was the all-metal Dewoitine D 500 series. The D 501 model especially attracted a great

deal of attention because of its 20 mm Moteur cannon which fired through the propeller shaft. The first Russian single-seat fighter to appear in large numbers was the Grigorovich I-2 biplane. Later came the tough little Polikarpov I-15, a biplane whose upper wing was gull-shaped to provide the pilot with excellent forward visibility. This aircraft first saw combat in the Spanish Civil War (1936–9).

Great Britain was caught unawares to a certain extent at the beginning of the Second World War, despite the fact that when two British ministers visited Germany in 1935 they reported that Hitler's air force rearmament programme had progressed further and faster than anyone believed possible. The British Government continued in their naïve belief that if they did not rearm then nobody else would and wasted a good deal of valuable time before placing orders for Hawker Hurricanes and Supermarine Spitfires. Because of this, when war broke out in September 1939

the balance of power, in terms of modern aircraft, was about four to one in favour of the Germans. This is not altogether surprising, since the Nazis had been preparing for war for some years. Most of the Allies' knowledge of fighter tactics gained during the First World War had been forgotten, but the Germans had an opportunity to brush up on these techniques during the Spanish Civil War. Strangely enough, one of the techniques they 'discovered' was one that Oswald Boelcke had perfected during the First World War, namely that two fighters flying side-by-side could cover each other effectively from enemy air attacks. The only difference was that Boelcke's Albatros biplanes usually flew quite close together, whereas Luftwaffe pilots practicing the same technique in the Second World War tended to hold a fairly loose formation. It was becoming apparent that dogfighting techniques were not going to be much different from those of the Great War, except that combat would take place over a wider area of airspace as a result of the higher speeds involved. The 'side-by-side' principle was later extended to four aircraft working in pairs, with highly-efficient radio

Below: A typical scene in an RAF operations room, from which fighters were guided to targets.

Above: Group Captain Douglas Bader became one of the great fighter pilots, despite having no legs.

telephones making it possible for pilots to remain in constant communication both with each other and with their ground controllers.

Spanish Civil War

One of the aircraft which was given an invaluable testing under combat conditions during the Spanish Civil War was the Messerschmitt Bf 109, without doubt one of the greatest single-seat fighters in aviation history. It was certainly produced in greater numbers than any other fighter at any time, one estimate for the quantity built between 1936–45 being as high as 33,000 aircraft – nearly two thirds of Germany's total output of single-seat fighters.

Spitfire

By the end of the 1930s Britain's principal fighter aircraft were the Hawker Fury and the Gloster Gladiator biplanes, the latter entering service in 1937. Both were obsolete compared to the sleek new monoplane fighters with which other nations were equipping their air forces. All this changed with the arrival of the Hawker Hurricane and what is probably the most famous aircraft ever built, the Supermarine Spitfire. Inspired by the Supermarine S.6B racing seaplane which won the Schneider Trophy for Britain in 1931, the Spitfire had been designed by the brilliant R J Mitchell – one of the few people who took the German threat seriously. The other fighter always associated with the RAF during the Second World War was the Hawker Hurricane, which first flew in 1935 and entered service two years later.

At the start of the Second World War, although the numbers of aircraft were not exactly equal on both sides, all the major powers were at least equipping themselves with single-seat monoplane fighters of the very latest breed. In France some Dewoitine D 500s and D 501s were still in service but these were now giving way to the Morane-Saulnier 406 and the Bloch 151 and 152 all-metal low-wing monoplanes.

Zero

Across the Atlantic two thirds of the United States' fighter strength in the first half of the Second World War was made up of just two types; the Bell Airacobra and the superb, bulbous-nosed Curtiss P-40 Warhawk/Kittyhawk series. The Airacobra went on to enter service with the RAF in October 1941 and was unusual in that its engine was situated *behind* the pilot, with its driveshaft to the propeller running forwards between his feet. The Curtiss P-40, on the other hand, was a more or less conventional aeroplane and performed steadily with the USAAF in the Pacific theatre against the

Japanese. It was not an outstanding machine by the standards of the Spitfire and Hurricane but it proved adaptable to many different battle environments and was available in very large numbers as some 14,000 examples were built during the course of the war.

Across the Pacific Ocean, Japan was also building up her air force. In mid-1937, the first Japanese low-wing monoplane fighter with an enclosed cockpit entered service, the Nakajima Ki-27 (codenamed *Nate* by the Allies). This was the main Japanese fighter until it was replaced by the Nakajima Ki-43 (codenamed *Oscar*) at the end of 1942. *Oscars* were one of Japan's most widely-produced fighter aircraft, with nearly 5,800 examples being built before the war ended. But the finest Japanese fighter of the war and the one that Japan built in the largest numbers, was the Mitsubishi A6M Zero. This tough little aircraft had superb handling characterstics and a

long range, and saw extensive service both from shore bases and from the decks of Imperial Navy aircraft carriers in the Pacific.

When Germany invaded Poland in 1939 the Polish air force was ready for them. The Luftwaffe's plan was to destroy the Polish fighters on their airfields before they even had chance to leave the ground, and this they did with great success. This took the Poles by surprise, and in the ensuing battle their ageing PZL fighters were no match for the Luftwaffe's Messerschmitt Bf 109s. Although the Poles fought courageously to a man they were soon crushed by the German onslaught. In response to the unprovoked attack on Poland, Britain declared war on Nazi Germany.

RAF fighter pilots wait to go into action during the Battle of Britain.

Radar Stations

German fighter production at this time had reached its peak but Britain's re-equipment programme was still in its early stages and was not due to be completed until at least 1942. The total number of aircraft available to the RAF was still only about half the number then in service with the Luftwaffe. This major deficiency was to some extent put to rights when R A Watson-Watt of the National Physics Laboratory developed an effective system of early warning to allow the RAF's fighters to get into the air quicker and intercept enemy intruders on their way across the English Channel. A chain of coastal radar stations was set up in the south of

The Kawasaki Ki-45 Toryu (codenamed *Nick* by the Allies) was originally intended for use as a long-range escort for Japanese bombers. It was later used as a night-fighter and attack aircraft.

England which could detect aircraft up to 160 km (100 miles) away, indicate how many aircraft were coming across, and calculate their course and speed. This radar system, plus effective radio communications, enabled close control of all aerial conflicts to be maintained from a series of ground stations.

When the Nazis attacked Holland, Belgium and Luxembourg, the only aircraft able to put up any resistance to the hard-hitting *blitzkrieg* tactics employed by the Germans were the seven RAF squadrons of Hurricanes at that time based in France. These were assisted by what was left of the French air force with their Morane-Saulnier 406s and Dewoitine D 520s. But this was not enough to stop the Germans sweeping through Holland and Belgium and into France, and it soon became clear that more fighters were needed to counteract the air support the Luftwaffe was giving to its troops

on the ground. The RAF's Air Chief Marshall Dowding, however, realized that he would need all his aircraft for the decisive air battle that would soon be fought over Britain, and refused to send the necessary reinforcements, on the grounds that he would be throwing these aircraft away in a battle that was already lost.

RAF Hurricanes had reasonable success against the Luftwaffe's Stuka dive bombers at first, but when the German aircraft began flying in large formations with twin-engined Messerschmitt Bf 110s as escorts, the British pilots knew they had met their match. On more than one occasion a pack of eight Hurricanes found themselves confronted by as many as sixty Stukas, complete with their escort of thirty or more Bf 110s and Bf 109s. The Nazis forced the Allies back to the English Channel and on 27 May 1940 the evacuation of Dunkirk began.

By this time Britain had lost something like a quarter of its whole fighter force.

It was during the evacuation of Dunkirk that Messerschmitt Bf 109s met Spitfires for the first time, and for the first time the Messerschmitt pilots found themselves equalled in capability.

With the Allies pushed out of western Europe only Britain remained unconquered, but the German chiefs-of-staff realized that before they could invade Britain they must have complete air supremacy. Hitler issued an order to the Luftwaffe: 'The Luftwaffe is to overcome the British air force with all the means at its disposal, and as soon as possible'. Luftwaffe chief Hermann Goering reckoned it would take two weeks, but he could never have guessed at that time that victory would elude him. This was the start of the Battle of Britain.

'Eagle Day'

The Luftwaffe began to amass its aircraft on the other side of the Channel. There were three *Luftflotten* (air fleets), the main ones being under the command of General Kesselring in northern Germany, Holland, Belgium and northern France, and Field Marshal Sperrle in north and west France. Luftwaffe aircraft from these bases could pose a threat to the whole of southern England by day, and by night they would be able to reach even further to threaten the industrial north and certain parts of Scotland. There was also a smaller force based in Denmark and Norway. Of the 3,000 aircraft available for the Battle of Britain about 1,100 of them were fighters, mostly Messerschmitt Bf 109Es.

In the ten weeks following the evacuation of Dunkirk, Britain had virtually doubled her fighter strength of Spitfires

Australia possessed a tough and outstandingly manoeuvrable fighter in the Commonwealth Boomerang, designed and flown in a matter of months.

Five Macchi M.C.200 Saetta fighters of the Regia Aeronautica over Malta during the Second World War.

and Hurricanes. The RAF had lost nearly 300 pilots over France and the Low Countries and could not have hoped to supply the men necessary to fly the aircraft of 60 new squadrons that had been formed. As a result, pilots from the Commonwealth countries were brought in alongside American volunteers and escapees from Poland, Czechoslovakia, France, Belgium and Holland.

The German air offensive began on 13 August 1940, known as 'Eagle Day'. The Luftwaffe launched a total of 1,485 sorties against various targets in Britain. The Germans lost 45 aircraft and Fighter Command only thirteen. On 15 August, the most intense attack of the Battle of Britain took place. The idea was for the Luftwaffe to concentrate its entire effort on knocking out the RAF's fighters, but the balance remained in the British favour. Fighter Command were losing aircraft and pilots quicker than they could be replaced but the Luftwaffe were losing even more, so, although the RAF were being steadily worn down, they were winning the battle. The Germans had not been prepared for a prolonged fight, as the reason for the struggle in the air had simply been to make 'Operation Sea Lion' (the German codename for the invasion of Britain) as troublefree as possible.

Hitler now began to look towards London and took the decision to bomb Britain's capital for three reasons. Firstly, to bring about even bigger air battles, and therefore still greater wastage of RAF Fighter Command's resources. Secondly, to undermine and disrupt the British government and terrorize their people into submission. And thirdly, to carry out an act of revenge against Churchill, who had ordered the bombing of Berlin after some bombs had been accidentally dropped by the Luftwaffe on the East End of London.

While Hurricanes and Spitfires were extremely effective during the day, the Germans had developed a radio-beam system to guide bombers onto their targets by night. To protect Britain against night bombers the RAF had already brought special night-fighter aircraft into service, the first squadron of highly-modified Bristol Blenheims being delivered in July 1939. The night-fighter

Characterized by its distinctive twin-tailed layout, the Lockheed P-38 Lightning played a big part in the fighting in North Africa, north west Europe and the Pacific. It served with both the USAAF and the RAF.

Another view of the Macchi M.C.200 Saetta (Italian for 'lightning'). Saettas were powered by 870 hp Fiat A74RC38 14-cylinder radials and were usually armed with two machine-guns fixed atop the engine cowling.

crews gradually learned the difficult art of interception in pitch darkness and they were extremely effective during what became known as the 'Night Blitz'. London survived the concentration of attacks by the Luftwaffe, while Britain's aircraft factories took their chance to replenish the RAF's flagging supply of fighters.

Meanwhile the other European Axis power, Itàly, had entered the war. She was not nearly as well prepared for action as Germany and Japan. Her Fiat CR.32 and CR.42 biplanes constituted about two-thirds of the Italian air force's single-seat fighter strength. The CR.42 Falco (meaning Falcon) served as an escort aircraft and night-fighter, later being joined in their duties by monoplane aircraft powered by engines of German design.

In the early stages of the war in North Africa, the Middle East and the Mediterranean, most of the fighting that took place between the RAF and the Italian air force was between biplane fighters, with the Gloster Gladiator quickly gaining air supremacy for Britain. It was a supremacy that they managed to hold on to even when the Luftwaffe arrived to help the Italians. In fact the Luftwaffe seemed to be suffering on all fronts, for any attempt by them to rebuild their forces after they had been so severely depleted in the Battle of Britain were quickly used up by the invasion of Russia.

Adolf Hitler's decision to attack Russia at this point in the war was a huge mistake, because all it did was to stretch his limited resources along another very long and unnecessary battlefront. In the early months of the invasion, the Russians had to rely on fighters such as the wooden Lavochkin LaGG-3 and the Mikoyan MiG-1/ MiG-3 series. The sleek MiGs were very fast but had little else in their favour and were eventually relegated to the reconnaissance role. The LaGG-3 was strong but not very manoeuvrable and was usually employed to escort ground-attack aircraft on strafing missions. Neither of these aircraft stood much chance against the Luftwaffe's Bf 109s, but probably the most promising of Russia's fighters was the new Yak-1. This aircraft had a fuselage formed of welded steel tubes covered with fabric-faced plywood and was notable for its graceful lines and its lightweight construction. Along with such aircraft as the Spitfire, the Yak-1 ranks with the best fighters of the war.

Soviet Fighters

Another significant Russian aircraft made its first appearance in combat

Russia's Mikoyan MiG-3.

during the Battle of Stalingrad in October 1942. This was the Lavochkin La-5. It gave an extremely good account of itself in combat against the Bf 109 and apart from its rate-of-climb was a better all-round performer than the German fighter. The La-7 model improved still further on the La-5's combat performance, while the Yak-9 was another Soviet fighter to appear around the time of the Battle of Stalingrad. It was very light and easy to handle and was built by the thousand for the Red air force. In fact, of the whole series of Yak fighters over 37,000 of the various types were produced during the Second World War.

Meanwhile the Germans had brought the superb Focke-Wulf Fw 190 into service to help the Messerschmitt Bf 109 keep the RAF's Spitfires and Hurricanes at bay during dogfights. This purposeful-looking aircraft boasted the best all-round fighting capabilities in terms of speed and manoeuvrability at both low and high altitudes, possessed pleasant handling characteristics and was an excellent machine-gun and bomb platform. Other aircraft may have had the edge over it in one of these qualities, but overall it had less faults than any other.

Enormous Losses

On 7 December 1941 the Japanese attacked Pearl Harbor with 353 dive bomber and torpedo aircraft. The attack was totally unexpected and was intended to destroy the US Pacific Fleet before it could interfere with Japan's plans for military expansion. Fighters based on six Japanese aircraft carriers played an important part in the raid by strafing American aircraft while they sat helpless on the ground, preventing them from taking-off and intercepting the dive-bombers which were playing havoc with the US Navy ships moored in the harbour. Only a few American fighters managed to get into the air, but with the help of anti-aircraft fire they succeeded in shooting down 29 Japanese aircraft. The American losses, however, were enormous. Over 300 aircraft were destroyed, mostly on the ground. Five battleships and three destroyers were sunk and many others badly damaged, and nearly 2,500 men were killed.

'Sleeping Giant'

This came as a heavy blow to the United States Navy but it was not as decisive as the Japanese had hoped. It had one effect even more significant than that on the balance of sea power, for it brought the American people into the war, totally committed and united. Perhaps only a shock of this magnitude could have achieved such a result. Perhaps one disillusioned Imperial Navy commander summed up the conse-

quences of the Pearl Harbor raid better than anyone when he said, 'Gentlemen, we have succeeded only in awakening a sleeping giant'.

The RAF suffered a crushing defeat by the Japanese at the same time when their bases in Malaya were completely destroyed. Britain and America both learned from these attacks the importance of aircraft carriers as a main striking force. By 1941 the Japanese single-seat carrier fighter the Mitsubishi A5M4 (codenamed *Claude*) was obsolete and was being replaced by the famous Zero, the last of the *Claudes* being used as *Kamikaze* suicide aircraft. The Zero dominated the air over the Pacific until early 1943, but the Japanese had other notable fighters. One which was encountered in virtually all battle areas in the Pacific theatre was the Kawasaki Ki-61 Hien (known to the Allies as *Tony*). It was particularly prominent around the vital parts of Rabaul and in the Battle of Leyte Gulf.

On the American side the standard US Navy fighter type during the conflict in the Pacific was the Grumman F4F Wildcat. Like all maritime carrier-borne aircraft, this stubby little machine had folding wings to save space on the confined decks of aircraft carriers. Although the Wildcat was slower and less manoeuvrable than the Zero, it was faster in a dive and was an extremely rugged aeroplane, with armour plating around the pilot's seat to give him extra protection from enemy gunfire. To force a conclusion to the conflict in the Pacific, Wildcats helped Grumman F6F Hellcats and Curtiss P-40 Warhawks. One of the most successful American fighters in service at this time though was the Vought F4U Corsair. It earned itself a legendary reputation during the war in the Pacific and in addition to daytime combat was successfully adapted to night-fighting. In

spite of its weight it was more than a match for most Japanese fighters.

Midway

Following the battles of the Coral Sea and Midway which halted the Japanese expansion in the Pacific, the Allies turned their efforts to the defeat of Germany. To this end the Americans joined the RAF in persistent raids on the *Reich* from bases in England. To escort their bombers the USAAF introduced the twin-tailed Lockheed P-38 Lightning. Known to the Japanese as the 'Fork-tailed Devil', the Lightning was the epitomy of the long-range fighter. Nearly 10,000 examples of all versions were built and they were responsible for destroying more enemy aircraft in the Pacific than any other fighter. The Lightning enjoyed just as much success in all other theatres

The Grumman F6F Hellcat was a snarling, aggressive fighter aircraft of the US Navy. It turned the tide of the Pacific war.

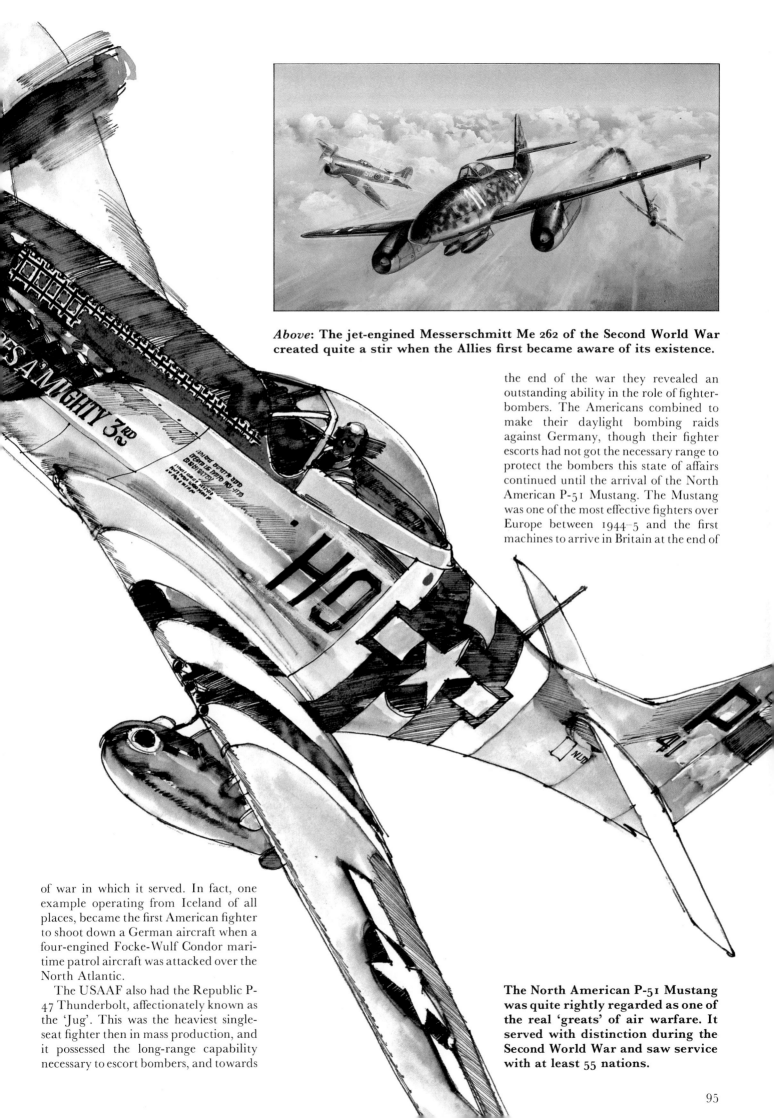

Above: The jet-engined Messerschmitt Me 262 of the Second World War created quite a stir when the Allies first became aware of its existence.

the end of the war they revealed an outstanding ability in the role of fighter-bombers. The Americans combined to make their daylight bombing raids against Germany, though their fighter escorts had not got the necessary range to protect the bombers this state of affairs continued until the arrival of the North American P-51 Mustang. The Mustang was one of the most effective fighters over Europe between 1944–5 and the first machines to arrive in Britain at the end of

of war in which it served. In fact, one example operating from Iceland of all places, became the first American fighter to shoot down a German aircraft when a four-engined Focke-Wulf Condor maritime patrol aircraft was attacked over the North Atlantic.

The USAAF also had the Republic P-47 Thunderbolt, affectionately known as the 'Jug'. This was the heaviest single-seat fighter then in mass production, and it possessed the long-range capability necessary to escort bombers, and towards

The North American P-51 Mustang was quite rightly regarded as one of the real 'greats' of air warfare. It served with distinction during the Second World War and saw service with at least 55 nations.

1941 were almost as fast as the best fighters then in operational service.

Speeds were continuing to rise as each new variant of the principal fighters of the time were introduced. As a logical development of this progression, the first jet-propelled fighter in the world went into service in 1944. This was the sleek Messerschmitt Me 262, powered by a pair of Junkers Jumo 004B turbojet engines, one situated under each wing in streamlined pods. The first jet fighter to be used in action however was Britain's Gloster Meteor, also powered by a pair of wing-mounted turbojet engines, this time Rolls-Royce Wellands. On 4 August 1944 the pilot of a Meteor managed to bring down a V-1 flying bomb by manoeuvring alongside it and tipping it over with his wingtip.

Although the Me 262 and the Meteor were very revolutionary aircraft by the standards of the day, by far the most radical fighter of the Second World War was the Messerschmitt Me 163 Komet. This was powered by a rocket engine and sacrificed everything to the ability to climb up to Allied bomber formations and blast them apart. Even its undercarriage unit was jettisoned on take-off to save weight, the Komet landing on a special skid set into its underbelly.

Underground Factories

The ambitious plans the Luftwaffe chiefs had for this tiny little fighter were never realized however, for by the time it entered service in late 1944 defeat was staring the Nazis in the face. Production of Komets, as with all other new German aircraft, was being continually interrupted by relentless Allied air strikes, despite the fact that they were being built in special underground factories. To make matters worse, the few Komets in operational service were gaining a bad reputation for bursting into flames on landing.

But despite these shortcomings, the Me 163 had a truly phenomenal performance. Though its rocket motor had an unquenchable thirst for fuel and restricted the flight duration to a mere ten minutes, the Komet could take-off and climb to 9,140 m (30,000 ft) in just two-and-a-half minutes! After making a few high-speed attacks on the enemy's bombers, the Me 163's fuel supply would run out and the little aircraft would glide down to a bumpy landing on its skid.

By this time not even the launching of the deadly new V-2 rockets against comparatively vulnerable targets in both Britain and Belgium could stop the Allied onslaught. Those piston-engined Luftwaffe aircraft that were still operational towards the last few days of the war were forced to remain helpless on the ground because of an acute lack of fuel. The end of Hitler's plan for world domination was finally in sight, while many thousands of kilometres away the Japanese continued to throw away their valuable fighters in desperate *Kamikaze* suicide attacks until the Americans put an end to all these atrocities by dropping atomic bombs on Hiroshima and Nagasaki in August 1945.

One of the most exciting warplanes ever built was the little rocket-propelled Messerschmitt Me 163 Komet. Due to the radical nature of its design, the Komet did not enter service until the closing stages of the war, despite the fact that it had made its first powered flight as early as 1941.

FIGHTERS
1946-80
The Shapes
of Air Supremacy

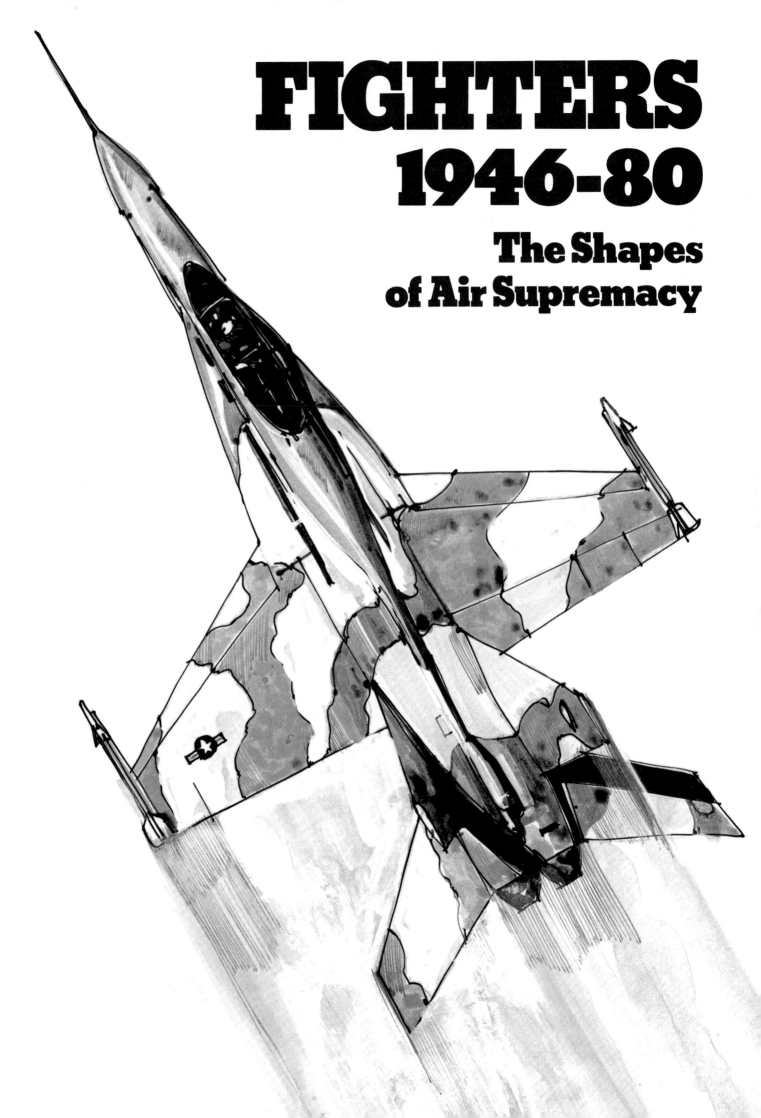

After the end of the Second World War in 1945, the development of piston-engined fighters virtually stopped, because the aircraft industry considered that only the jet was worth evolving. At this time only Britain and the USA had jet fighter construction programmes underway. The Russians were desperately keen to catch up with them, but they were in no position to do so until their designers could learn from German aeronautics experts and materials they had captured at the end of the war. The French were similarly keen but their aircraft industry had been shattered by the war and was in desperate need of reconstruction.

Right from the start, the British and American fighter designers went in different directions. British designers considered that the jet engine was short of power, especially at take-off and when flying at low speeds. They tried hard to keep power losses to a minimum by using the shortest possible air-intake and jet exhaust ducts. The de Havilland company managed to achieve this with their neat little Vampire by mounting the tail surfaces on twin booms extended back from the wings. This meant that there was no need for the jet exhaust to travel the length of a conventional fuselage before rushing into the outside air to propel the aircraft forward.

Carrier Landings

Although the early Vampire fighters had even less power than some of today's jet trainer aircraft, they comfortably exceeded 800 km/hr (500 mph) in level flight. Overseas air forces liked the Vampire because of its small size, and the fact that it was fairly cheap and simple to operate. Eventually it was operated by a dozen major air forces in Europe and the Commonwealth, and built under licence in several countries. It was also developed into a two-seat night fighter, for which purpose the cockpit of the piston-engined wartime Mosquito was grafted onto the existing Vampire fuselage.

Vampires were also adapted for naval use, being fitted with an arrester hook to permit landings on aircraft-carrier decks. In fact, the Vampire was the first jet aircraft to be successfully operated from one of these vessels. Although the Vampire was popular immediately after

the Second World War, its limited performance meant that as a straightforward fighter it was always outrun by its competitor, the twin jet Gloster Meteor, whether as a single-seat day interceptor or as a radar-equipped two-seat night fighter. Eventually de Havilland produced the Venom, which retained the Vampire's general layout but had a thinner wing and was therefore faster. Sadly, it came too late to cash in properly on the Vampire's popularity with overseas customers.

The Americans meanwhile had decided to go for simplicity of layout. Their Lockheed F-80 Shooting Star was the first of their postwar jet fighters, and like Britain's Vampire it was exported to a large number of countries and was developed into a two-seater radar-equipped night fighter, known as the F-94 Starfire. Also like the Vampire, it formed the basis for an even more widely-used advanced jet trainer aircraft when its days as a frontline fighter were over. The Shooting Star, with its curve-tipped wings and tailfin, was reminiscent

of a piston-engined design but that did not stop it performing well by the standards of the day. It had a maximum speed at sea-level of 930 km/hr (658 mph) and a combat ceiling of 14,700 m (44,000 ft). It achieved this performance mainly by dint of its single rather chubby Allison J33 engine.

Despite the Shooting Star's success American designers were quicker than their British counterparts to realize that the future lay with the slimmer and potentially far more powerful types of jet engine that were now becoming widely available. It was the much more compact Allison J35 which powered the next major American fighter, the Republic F-84 Thunderjet. There could have been nothing much simpler than the Thunderjet. Basically, the fuselage was a slender

A MiG-15 of the People's Republic of China air force.

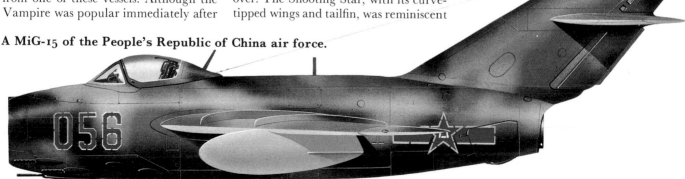

A de Havilland Vampire starting up its Goblin jet engine at night. Note the characteristic twin tail.

tube with a circular air-intake in the extreme nose and a straight wing that was so little tapered that it looked almost like a length of plank. Its only traditional feature was the tailfin, which retained the Republic company's familiar outline and promoted it almost to the status of a trademark.

The Republic F-84 Thunderjet was only marginally faster than the Shooting Star, for the limitations of the straight wing were now becoming apparent. The F-84's main virtue was its ability to carry heavy loads of bombs and rockets, and in the end it came to be regarded much more as a low-level strike aircraft than as a serious dogfighter. It was the first aircraft to be fitted with an in-flight refuelling probe as a standard production item. This enabled it to be flown from the USA to NATO bases in Europe without an intermediate landing.

'Sound Barrier'

In the 1940s high maximum speed still seemed the greatest virtue of the fighter aircraft. Jet engines had given maximum speeds an almost instant boost from the 720 km/hr (450 mph) of the best wartime piston-engined fighters right up to about 960 km/hr (600 mph). Beyond that, it

Right: **The F-86D version of the superb North American Sabre is easily distinguished by the bulbous radar nose above its engine air intake. The aircraft illustrated here is on an attack mission.**

quickly became plain that the very strong air resistance that is felt as the speed of sound is approached meant that further big advances in performance could only be gained by an enormous increase in power, or by adopting new designs to delay the onset of this sudden rise in air resistance – the so-called 'sound barrier'. The answer was simple, at least in theory. Various German wartime designs had already shown that by sweeping the wings back from the fuselage the rise in air resistance could be considerably delayed. The more the wings were swept back, the greater the potential gain in speed. Sadly, more sweep angle also meant more difficulties in construction and the aerodynamic problems of achieving the necessary stability and control, but all the major fighter

design teams now set about overcoming these problems.

The British followed a painful process of development through several cautious stages, with both the Hawker and Supermarine companies easing their way towards a production sweptwing fighter via a series of more conventional designs. The Americans were more fortunate in that the design team at North American Aviation, which had developed the famous Mustang fighter in wartime, achieved success yet again, and with remarkable speed, when they produced a jet-engined fighter which was right first time. The North American design team

99

did not quite start from scratch, but used as a basis a straight-winged single-engined fighter they were already designing for the USAF. This was fitted with a new wing swept back at 35 degrees, and the result was the classic F-86 Sabre.

The Sabre first flew in late 1947, barely eighteen months after the Thunderjet, and less than a year after that it stamped its name on the record books with a new World Air Speed Record of 1,047 km/hr (671 mph). This was a remarkable figure for a single-engined aircraft of only 5,200 lb thrust, the engine in question being the General Electric J47. The Sabre looked deceptively simple, but was the result of a lot of work on high-speed stability and control. It was this as much as superior American aircrew and training which made the Sabre such an effective fighter in the Korean War (1950–3) when it so consistently outflew the Russian-built MiG-15 of similar performance. There was only one thing which let down the Sabre in air-to-air combat — its rather meagre armament of six machine-guns rather than larger and more deadly cannon.

The MiG-15 was the Russians' first effective jet fighter. Their first attempts to build such an aircraft had relied on the use of one or two small German-built jet engines of wartime origin slung under the noses of piston-engined fighter airframes. Then in 1947 the British government agreed to sell the Russians a small number of their new Rolls-Royce Derwent and Nene jet engines.

Above left: **A Gloster Javelin armed with underwing air-to-air missiles.** *Centre*: **A Convair F-102 Delta Dagger showing off its sleek delta-winged shape.** *Above right*: **A Gloster Meteor with two underwing fuel tanks.** *Below*: **The extraordinary McDonnell XF-85 Goblin fighter was designed to be carried by USAF bombers and released to defend them when enemy fighters approached, but never saw service.**

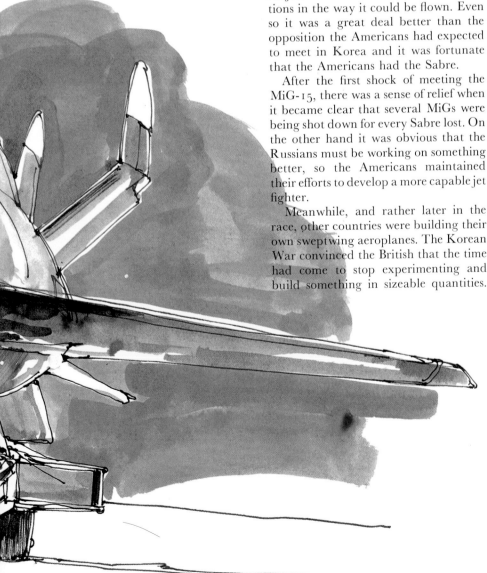

The Russians were so delighted with the Nene that they copied it and put it straight into production without any form of licence. Its fairly modest but reliable thrust was sufficient for the MiG designers to take advantage of the German aerodynamic knowledge which they already had, and the result was a simple little fighter with a circular air-intake in the nose, a big swept tailfin and a wing swept back at an angle of 35 degrees like the Sabre's. Its performance was good, though its control systems were somewhat primitive and made it subject to some uncomfortable restrictions in the way it could be flown. Even so it was a great deal better than the opposition the Americans had expected to meet in Korea and it was fortunate that the Americans had the Sabre.

After the first shock of meeting the MiG-15, there was a sense of relief when it became clear that several MiGs were being shot down for every Sabre lost. On the other hand it was obvious that the Russians must be working on something better, so the Americans maintained their efforts to develop a more capable jet fighter.

Meanwhile, and rather later in the race, other countries were building their own sweptwing aeroplanes. The Korean War convinced the British that the time had come to stop experimenting and build something in sizeable quantities.

Despite the haste with which the decision was taken, the result was the excellent Hawker Hunter. This was produced in large numbers and proved very adaptable and it was sold to many countries overseas. Although it had a family resemblance to the earlier Hawker experimental fighters, the Hunter was actually an all-new design intended to take full advantage of the new and very powerful Rolls-Royce Avon engine of 6,500 lb thrust.

The Avon was ultimately developed to produce 10,000 lb thrust, but despite this power advantage over the Sabre, the Hunter was not that much faster. One Hunter prototype briefly held the World Air Speed Record at 1,169 km/hr (728 mph) in 1953, but that was achieved with the use of reheat – an apparatus that was never fitted to standard production Hunters. This involved spraying 'neat' fuel into the engine's jet pipe at high pressure during flight to boost forward speed. However, the Hawker aircraft made its name on the strength of its superb flying qualities and the robustness of its airframe in low-level operations, but it showed yet again that a new design approach was needed to achieve the next logical goal – that of building a fighter that could reach supersonic speeds in level flight rather than in a dive.

Marcel Dassault

The French had begun their postwar efforts with a series of peculiar-looking prototypes, some so odd that it was a wonder they flew at all. Eventually Marcel Dassault, the brilliant French aircraft designer, came up with a series of simple, logical designs. When his Ouragan jet first flew in 1949, it looked for all the world like a French version of the F-84 Thunderjet. With its straight wing and air-intake in the extreme nose there was nothing obviously clever about the Ouragan, yet its potential soon began to make itself clear.

The Ouragan was ordered by the air arms of France, India and Israel and proved its worth mostly as a ground-attack fighter in operational service. Its

with the Sea Vampire, it was the Americans who began to produce specialized seagoing designs. Chance Vought and Grumman, the traditional suppliers of fighters to the US Navy, were beaten into the jet age by the young firm of McDonnell who flew their twin-engined FH-1 jet before the end of the Second World War, and made the first US Navy jet fighter carrier landing in July 1946. Their Banshee was a bigger, much more powerful and faster development of the FH-1, and was built in far larger numbers to become the first jet fighter widely used by the US Navy. It was a solid and workmanlike design but it was rather big and heavy, and certainly not the ideal choice for dogfighting with nimble little MiG-15s. Not that this mattered too much because it was really intended to patrol the fleet and shoot down attacking enemy strike aircraft.

Pilot's Ideal

It was left to the more experienced design teams at Grumman and Chance Vought to produce something closer to a fighter pilot's ideal. Grumman's fighter was the F9F Panther. It first flew in late 1947 and was a compact straight-wing design built around what was essentially a British engine, the Rolls-Royce Nene, which the Pratt & Whitney company built under licence as the J42. The Panther proved popular with its pilots and over 1,000 were built. It was the mainstay of the US Navy's fighter strength in Korea, where it performed very well. Despite its straight wing it was capable of speeds up to 990 km/hr (620 mph) and was therefore not at too much of a disadvantage when engaged in combat with Russian MiG-15s.

To close the margin still further, Grumman developed a sweptwing version, the F9F-7 Cougar, which first flew in 1951 and had a maximum speed that was approaching 1,200 km/hr (700 mph). Cougars were not the first swept-wing fighter to enter regular US Navy service, however, for that honour goes to the odd-looking Chance Vought Cutlass. To meet all the conflicting needs of carrierborne operation, not least the requirement for close packing in an aircraft carrier's limited underdeck hangar space, Chance Vought chose an unusual layout that dispensed with the need for a tail and had two engines situated side-by-side, with a vertical tailfin and rudder on each swept

real importance, however, was that like North American (one of the United States' major aircraft manufacturers, who developed the sweptwing Sabre from an earlier straight-winged design), Dassault used the Ouragan as a base for a 30 degree sweptwing, more powerful aircraft, the Mystère. This sleek-looking machine was successful from the outset. A Mystère II version was eventually followed by the faster Mystère IV with yet more wing sweep, and Dassault moved beyond that to create a whole new series of fighters known as the Mirage family.

Compared with the USA, Britain, Russia and France, it might not seem logical to think of Sweden as a country likely to produce a fighter in advance of its time. But during the Second World War Sweden had adopted a policy of building her own combat aircraft. Because she was neutral during the war, Sweden had the opportunity to build up her own aviation industry uninterrupted by the pressures of warfare.

Once the war was over, the Swedes took out a licence to build de Havilland's Ghost engine and bought British Vampires for their air force to fly until their own fighter was ready. It flew less than a year after the Sabre and was designated Saab J29, though it soon gained the affectionate nickname of '*Tunnan*' (or 'Barrel') because of its unusual plump fuselage shape. This did not detract from its performance, however, and it gave the Swedish air force a 1,040 km/hr (650 mph) sweptwing fighter before even the RAF had one.

The advent of the jet engine did not stop the disagreement between those who thought that carrierborne fighters should be adapted from land-based aircraft, which was the official British view, and those who preferred to see their navies writing their own specifications, as the Americans had tended to do. As land-based jet fighters became faster, and as their wings became more swept back, so their landing speeds became higher and their low speed handling more tricky, thus increasing the difficulties for pilots.

Although the Royal Navy pioneered the handling of jet fighters on carriers

The 'Black Arrows' formation display team show off the classic lines of the superb Hawker Hunter. Powered by one Rolls-Royce Avon turbojet engine, the Hunter was exported all over the world over a period of many years.

A typical control centre.

fighter bore no real resemblance to the F-86 Sabre; its fuselage was flat-bottomed with the wing and tailplane mounted low down. The wings were swept back at 45 degrees and were very thin to minimize air resistance. Power for this impressive addition to the USAF's fighter strength was provided by Pratt & Whitney's new 10,000 lb-thrust J57, complete with re-heat apparatus. Super Sabres were not merely capable of easing just past the dreaded 'sound barrier', for they could exceed Mach 1 by a considerable margin and delighted their pilots with surprisingly docile handling characteristics as they passed from subsonic to supersonic speeds.

The speed of sound varies with temperature. It is around 1,215 km/hr (760 mph) at sea-level, where the surrounding air is most dense. As an aeroplane flies higher and the air gets colder, so Mach 1 is reached at a lower speed. The assumption was that the Super Sabre would take over from the older F-86 Sabre and do the same job, but as we shall see things did not quite work out that way.

'Century Series'

It was a pleasant stroke of coincidence that the USAF's fighter numbering system resulted in the Super Sabre being designated F-100, for as the first truly level-supersonic fighter it ushered in what became known as the 'century series' of combat aircraft, some of which were to boast an even better performance. The two-seater F-101, from McDonnell, was extremely large and heavy for a fighter and was powered by *two* J57 engines to suit its long-range interceptor role. Convair's F-102 Delta Dagger, on the other hand, was a short-range interceptor with a thin, very highly swept delta wing and a single J57. This was followed by the F-106 Delta Dart, a highly developed version of the F-102, but powered by the even larger and more powerful Pratt & Whitney J75 engine.

wing. It was a bold effort and indeed the Cutlass was built in some numbers, but it did not serve with any real success. Chance Vought had to wait a little while longer before they re-established themselves as serious fighter-builders for the US Navy.

All fighter designs up to about 1950, even those with swept wings, found the rise in air resistance towards Mach 1 (the speed of sound) so great that they could only achieve supersonic speeds in a dive. It was clear that more power alone would hardly be enough to take a fighter up the performance slope and onto the plateau beyond. Thinner, more highly-swept wings and new fuselage shapes to reduce air resistance would also be needed. The first close approach to achieving supersonic speeds in level flight came with the aeroplane which represented the Douglas company's first attempt to get into the US Navy fighter-building business.

Hitherto known mainly for their at-tack aircraft designs, Douglas designed a comparatively small delta-shaped wing/fuselage structure around a powerful engine and flew it early in 1951. This tidy little machine was the F4D Skyray – a name that went well with the shape of the aircraft. The second prototype raised the World Air Speed Record to 1,213 km/hr (754 mph) in 1953, coming very close in the process towards achieving Mach 1 in level flight. In the event, confusion over engines (the Skyray was one of several victims of the failure of the Westinghouse J40, which was to have been the US Navy's principal jet engine) and changes in requirements meant that the Skyray never achieved any major impact on the world fighter scene.

Breakthrough

The real breakthrough in the struggle for level-supersonic performance came in May 1953 with the first flight of the North American F-100 Super Sabre. Despite its name, this impressive new

A Dassault Super Mystère of l'Armee de l'Air (French air force).

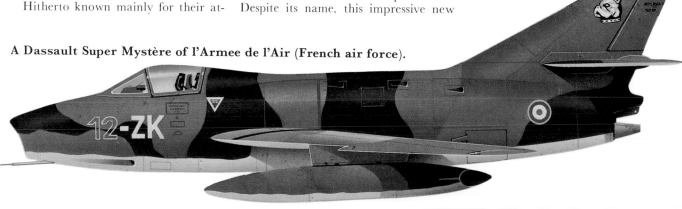

Above: This weird 'ghost' effect is caused by the Lightning firing its twin Aden cannon. *Right*: The English Electric Lightning was the mainstay of Britain's air defence network throughout the 1960s. It was also exported to Saudi Arabia and Kuwait. In this dramatic painting we can clearly see the Lightning's twin Firestreak missiles and the nose air-intake, complete with its conical fairing.

The Lockheed company took a somewhat different view of the situation and decided that most of the 'century series' fighters were too big, heavy and expensive to be fighters in the old-fashioned sense of the word and to a large extent they were right. At this period in aircraft development it was felt that fighters needed to be fast, but not necessarily manoeuvrable, because air-to-air missiles would do all the manoeuvring that was needed in a combat situation. In fact, many fighter projects were well on the way to becoming nothing more than mere missile platforms.

Lockheed's answer to this situation was both daring and ambitious. They took a moderately powerful engine, installed it in a long needle of a fuselage with an extremely clever air-intake system, and added almost grotesquely short *straight* wings. As long as the wings were small and thin enough, they said, they did not need to be swept to reduce drag. Straight wings were lighter and easier to

make, and handling was simpler too. The result of all this thinking was the extraordinary F-104 Starfighter.

The thinking was good but not quite good enough. Though it was smaller and lighter than the other 'century series' fighters, the Starfighter proved limited by its tiny wing area – or perhaps by its small engine, for in reality it needed a bit more of both. It did not make the natural dogfighter Lockheed had dreamt of, but it did point the way to something better. In operational service, though, Starfighters had a spectacular career. They performed well in the low-level attack role but earned themselves a bad reputation in a seemingly endless series of accidents. The Luftwaffe alone lost well over 150 of their Starfighter fleet. One terrifying story to emerge from this stream of accidents concerns a Luftwaffe Starfighter taking-off from a military base in Germany. Traffic lights at the end of the main runway warned the drivers of air force support vans that an

aircraft was about to take-off, but one driver ignored this warning and drove straight across. At that very moment a Starfighter was hurtling up the runway at top speed. The needlenosed jet scythed through the van at right angles with fearful violence, literally chopping the vehicle in half. Yet the Starfighter was virtually undamaged and proceeded to continue its take-off run, complete a circuit of the airfield and land safely.

Meanwhile, other countries were also working away at the task of developing fighters capable of supersonic speeds in level flight. At about the same time that the Super Sabre first flew, in 1953, another important first flight must have taken place on the other side of the 'Iron Curtain'. The MiG design team had not rested on their laurels with the MiG-15,

A MiG-21 of the Indian air force in unusual camouflage markings.

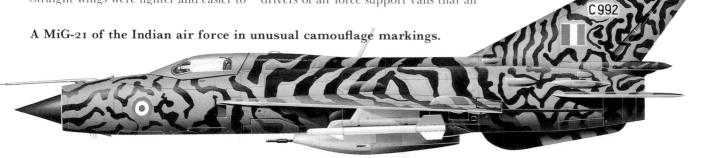

A McDonnell Douglas F-4E Phantom of the Heyl Ha'Avir (Israeli Defence Force – Air Force).

for they went on to build the MiG-17, a development with more power, a longer fuselage and a more highly-swept wing. Then they started work on their level-supersonic project, the MiG-19.

Because they had yet to develop a single large and powerful engine, the MiG designers had to use two smaller units side-by-side to obtain the power they needed. They installed them in as slender a fuselage as they could manage, and mounted this on a mid-set wing and tailplane, the wing being heavily swept and rather more slender than that of the Super Sabre. As with the MiG-15, the MiG-19's flying controls and other systems were slightly less sophisticated than the American fighter's, but unlike their ancestors, the MiG-15 and F-86 Sabre, the MiG-19 and the Super Sabre were not destined to meet in combat. Despite this, the MiG-19 was still a power to be reckoned with and by 1955 the Soviet air force was equipped with a fighter that would do close to 1,600 km/hr (1,000 mph) in level flight, and that in turn was an impetus to developments in other nations.

Mirage III

After a great deal of very careful thought, the British decided that they could do without a fighter of the MiG-19 and F-80 Sabre type. They accordingly cancelled what might have been a first-class aeroplane as well as a certain export winner, the P.1083 development of the Hawker Hunter with a thinner, more highly-swept wing and more power. The French on the other hand were deeply interested in such a concept. By 1955 they had flown yet another addition to the Dassault Mystère series, this time called the Super Mystère, which had 45 degrees of wing sweep and reheat. This was easily capable of attaining supersonic speeds in level flight, but that was not all.

Almost at the same time Dassault built a small twin-engined delta-winged fighter as an entry in a national light interceptor competition. When nothing came of this competition, Dassault took his entry, removed the two small engines and replaced them with a single, much more powerful, one – and so produced

the first Mirage III. This made its maiden flight in late 1956.

Marcel Dassault freely admits that the layout of this highly successful fighter owed a good deal to the influence of Britain's Fairey Delta 2 research plane, which in 1956 gained Britain's last-ever World Air Speed Record at 1,811 km/hr (1,132 mph). Plans for fighter versions of the Fairey Delta 2 were drawn up but they were scrapped when it was decided in 1957 that there would be no need for any further British fighters in the long-term future. As far as Britain's military planners were concerned at that time, the fighter aircraft would soon be obsolete, as they believed that long-range missiles would take over their role.

Apart from the classic single-seat dog-fighter, the Second World War had highlighted the need for a second type of fighter, with two seats and a full complement of radar guidance devices to seek and destroy raiding enemy bombers by night. Such an aircraft needed to be fairly big to carry its crew and equipment, for early radar sets were large and clumsy.

The application of jet engines to night fighters was slower than it was to day fighters, as it was felt that the higher landing speeds of the jet-propelled aircraft would make night landings too difficult for regular operations. That feeling eventually passed and two-seat night fighter versions of the early day fighters began to appear. The Gloster Meteor, for example, was easily adapted, while the de Havilland Vampire and Venom proved somewhat less convert-

able. The Americans turned the F-80 Shooting Star into the F-94 Starfire, which ran through several versions to arrive at the F-94C with reheat, improved radar and all-rocket armament instead of machine-guns. Even before the days of guided missiles, the Americans were firmly convinced, at least for quite a time, that there was more chance of hitting a target with a cluster of unguided rockets than with a shower of bullets.

While these early adaptations filled the night-fighter need for a short time, military planners came to the conclusion that specialized types were needed to carry better radio equipment and operate in even worse conditions. This notion led to several large and impressive

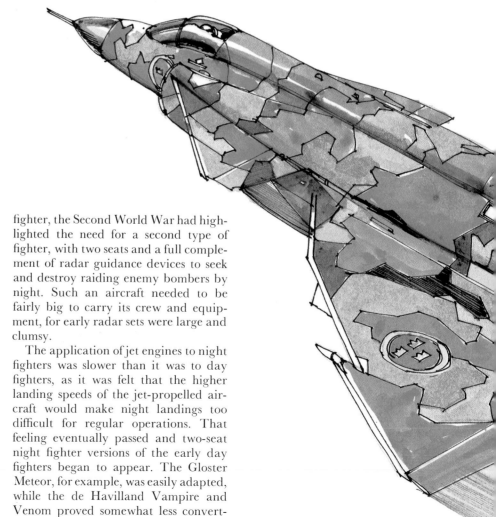

Above: **Sweden's Saab Draken features a unique double-delta fuselage/wing configuration.** *Below*: **The Saab Viggen is equally original in concept and has a superb performance.**

(though not always terribly good) night fighters. In British eyes at least the most successful was probably the Gloster Javelin, a twin-engined delta-winged aeroplane which carried its two-man crew and their complex radar equipment without difficulty and provided a good platform for some of the earliest air-to-air missiles. The Javelin got off to a rather unhappy start in terms of prototype accidents, and was never free from restrictions not normally imposed on fighters – looping it, for instance, was always strictly forbidden. It served well and yet passed on seemingly before the best had been extracted from it.

The same could be said of its nearest American equivalent, the Northrop F-89

Scorpion, and the big Avro Canada CF-100 Canuck. Re-development of the C-100 was as close an indication as any that Canada was ready to join the small and exclusive 'club' of genuine fighter-building nations. It was an essentially simple design with a straight wing and two engines set on either side of a cigar-like fuselage. It was introduced because the Canadian government felt in the late 1940s that nobody else would be able to design a fighter capable of operating in Canada's Arctic conditions, with below-zero temperatures and permanent darkness for much of the year.

The Avro Canada team showed that the Canadians could fulfil their own requirements without outside help, for even the engines were Canadian designed. The result was a very capable, long-range interceptor which was comparatively simple and safe to fly up to a maximum speed of 1,040 km/hr (650 mph). At one time the Canadians were working on an even more ambitious successor, the CF-105 Arrow, which had striking looks and was designed for Mach 2 (twice the speed of sound) performance. But it never saw operational service.

During the 1950s, governments became convinced fighters would need radar equipment, because enemy attacks were quite likely to arrive under cover of darkness and poor weather. This meant that if performance was still to be improved, some way would have to be found of making radar-equipped fighters smaller, since there was no question of making anything the size of the Gloster Javelin supersonic at reasonable cost. One obvious answer was to do away with the second crew member and arrange the systems so that the pilot, given proper aptitude and training, could do everything. This at once would make the aircraft smaller, lighter and more manoeuvrable. The first fighter designed to try this approach in a serious manner was a special version of the F-86 Sabre, the F-86D. This had radar installed in a prominent 'blister' above its nose air-intake, and its gun armament was replaced by rockets, as in the F-94C. This idea worked well enough to encourage the USAF to continue with it, and all the 'century series' fighters, even the hefty McDonnell F-101 Voodoo, were planned as single-seaters.

Mini Fighter

The 'smaller is better' way of thinking was perhaps inevitably distorted as military planners asked for more and more equipment to be carried. This led to a new generation of heavy, expensive, radar-equipped single-seat all-weather fighters. There was, however, a notable reaction to this trend when Teddy Petter, the designer of the superb Lightning jet interceptor, left the English Electric company and set out to produce a new kind of fighter half the size and a quarter the weight and cost.

By ruthlessly cutting out things which were previously regarded as essential he ended up with a fighter which had a wingspan of just 7m (22ft) and which weighed a maximum of 3,990 kg (8,800 lb). Contrasting this weight with the 11,340 kg (25,000 lb) of the Hawker Hunter, let alone the 18,600 kg (41,000 lb) of the Lightning, it becomes very clear why Petter thought he had the right answer to the 'heavy fighter' problem.

His new machine was called the Gnat and was built by the little Folland company, later to be absorbed by Hawker Siddeley. It took to the air for its maiden flight in May 1956 but, alas, things did not go quite as Petter had planned. His action to reverse the trend of size, weight and cost might itself have been welcome, but air forces still wanted their fighters to carry *some* kind of radar, and to lift *some* kind of bombload, just in case they were needed. The Gnat was simply too small to carry either. As a straightforward dogfighter, however, it promised better. It carried two large cannon, was small and therefore more difficult to see and hit, and was very manoeuvrable. The snag was that by the time it had flown, dogfighters needed level-supersonic performance and the Gnat did not have it. This is why it was not a great success for

Israel now has her own aircraft manufacturing industry and has proved her ability in this field by producing the sleek little single-engined IAI Kfir (Lion Cub) fighter.

the Indian air force in various conflicts with Pakistan. A two-seater training version proved totally successful with the RAF, however, and performed with faultless precision in the hands of the famous 'Red Arrows' aerobatic display team. The lesson of the Gnat was by no means forgotten, for it showed that fighters could actually gain from being smaller, but that it was possible to make them too small for full effectiveness.

The next moves came one on either side of the 'Iron Curtain'. In 1956 a new Russian fighter appeared at a Moscow air display having first flown the year before. It was a fairly small and obviously simple design with a single powerful engine, an air-intake in the extreme nose, a small delta wing and a conventional-looking tail. This was the MiG-21, and the most important point it made was that it had a larger and more powerful engine and was much faster than its predecessor, the MiG-19, although it was actually smaller and lighter overall. The Russians had decided there was a place in their armoury for a dogfighter in the true sense of the word, and it was a great success. The MiG-21 has been in production for some 25 years in a bewildering succession of versions, and was exported to dozens of countries, some very much Soviet-influenced and others neutral.

Exports

It was the attraction of this last point, that of earning sizeable exports, which led to a rather similar fighter emerging from the USA. Its starting point was of all things a training aircraft, the T-38 Talon, which Northrop was developing as an advanced jet trainer with level-supersonic ability for the USAF. Being a trainer rather than a radar and bomb-equipped fighter, the Talon had the advantage of being quite small.

Northrop designed it with two small (but reheated) engines and a thin, slender, straight wing. Long before the Talon first flew, the decision had been taken to remove one of the seats, use the space for a little extra fuel and equipment and make it into a proper fighter. At first the USAF was unimpressed, but export sales started to grow and it was clear that Northrop had come up with a sound idea. In the end they bought a large batch of the Northrop fighters, designated F-5, and used them to equip special squadrons which could simulate MiG-21 performance in combat practice with other USAF fighters.

While all this was going on, Dassault in France had settled on the same sort of formula for the Mirage III, though not through the same path of reasoning, and went on to achieve the same impressive results, with hundreds of export sales to eager customers wanting a supersonic fighter at a reasonable price.

A force of lightweight dogfighters is all very well if you have an all-weather force to back it up if the enemy does decide to attack at night and in solid cloud. So there was still a place for the big, sophisticated, expensive fighter. The only question was how it should be developed. Britain's standard equipment was to become the English Electric (later BAC) Lightning, an odd-looking aeroplane with two reheated Rolls-Royce Avon engines installed one above the other, the uppermost one being placed considerably further behind the other. The Lightning proved itself to be a first-class interceptor, but the RAF had it so single-mindedly designed in that direction that it proved more or less hopeless when the BAC tried adapting it for ground-attack. Its narrow fuselage and peculiar undercarriage layout made it difficult to find anywhere to hang bombs or rockets, and even the extra fuel tanks fitted later in its

Left: The General Dynamics F-16 uses reheat to achieve its swift climb. Note the wingtip-mounted air-to-air missiles. *Above*: This exciting sequence of pictures shows an F-16 unleashing one of its deadly missiles during a weapons testing mission at a desert firing range.

career had to be installed over rather than under its wings.

The Americans developed their Convair F-102 Delta Dagger and F-106 Delta Dart at about the same time as the Lightning, with the same object of producing a large, fast, well-armed all-weather interceptor whose main task was to knock down incoming enemy bombers rather than to mix it with other fighters.

As mentioned earlier, the British had decided that after the Lightning, ground-to-air missiles would take over. The USAF showed signs of thinking the same way. It spent a lot of money on large, long-range missiles which at one time were even accorded proper fighter designations, like Boeing's F-99 Bomarc. Fortunately the US Navy did not agree, and through the McDonnell design team they came up with a new fighter so good that everyone had to take notice.

Phantom

McDonnell must have learned a lot from their large and rather clumsy F-101 Voodoo. Their new fighter – the Phan-

tom, as it became known – needed to be almost as big, for the equipment. But compared with the Voodoo this latest design had newer engines, much more wing area and more of almost everything else. When it first appeared in 1958, the ugly Phantom did not *look* like an obvious winner. Flight testing quickly proved that it was, however, with a string of speed and time-to-height records. The Phantom turned out to be so good that in the end even the USAF had to join the US Navy and buy it – a complete turnabout from the more usual practice. Then other countries began to buy it, quite simply because there was nothing else as capable. Great Britain bought it for both the RAF (to replace the Lightning) and the Royal Navy (to replace the Sea Vixen) and over 5,000 Phantoms were eventually built – an astonishing total for a big and expensive fighter.

While the Phantom filled an important gap in the armouries of Great Britain and several other 'western' nations, some either preferred to or had to go their own way. The French, with their highly in-

dividualistic defence outlook and one eye always firmly on valuable export orders, followed up their Mirage delta-winged series with the more adaptable Mirage F1, which returned to a thin, moderately swept wing and conventional tail unit for better manoeuvrability and landing performance. Despite a couple of big two-seater fighter prototypes, Dassault and the French air force have so far stayed faithful to the idea of a single-seat all-weather fighter. So too have the Swedes, who built on the experience they gained with their original Saab J29 'Tunnan' by developing the two-seat J32 Lansen, and then progressed to the impressive Draken and Viggen ground-attack and all-weather fighter types.

Thunderbolt

Both the Draken (meaning Dragon) and the Viggen (Thunderbolt) feature highly original configurations. The Draken is a 'double-delta', in that the streamlined air-intakes which flank its forward fuselage sides spread out to form part of the slim delta wings which pro-

Left: McDonnell Douglas' F-18 Hornet is the latest carrierborne air superiority fighter and attack aircraft. Below left: The Soviet Union's MiG-23 Flogger is a formidable fighter aircraft. Right: F-16 cockpit.

trude from them at slightly sharper angle. This configuration improves the aircraft's streamlining considerably, and yet provides the extra internal capacity for fuel and electronic equipment. The Swedes have made a great success of the Draken, though their stalwartly neutral outlook has, perhaps inevitably, lost them some valuable export sales.

Like the Draken, the Saab Viggen has one seat and one engine, but its layout is even more unusual in that it is one of the very few successful 'canard' aeroplanes, (with the tailplane *forward* of the wing). Saab would actually prefer the Viggen's flying surfaces to be thought of as two sets of wings, though the technical arguments along these lines are rather involved. The main benefit of this highly unconventional layout as demonstrated by the Viggen is that it gives very good short take-off and landing (STOL) performance, enabling the aircraft to operate safely from emergency airstrips formed by short stretches of Sweden's road system. The 'canard' configuration also bestows excellent manoeuvrability in combat conditions.

Sukhoi

No such financial limitations applied to the Russians when they decided it would be worth having a lightweight 'pure' fighter like the MiG-21. They were also able to decide that alongside it they would deploy one bigger, heavier

single-engined type, and one even bigger twin-engined fighter for long-range interception equipped with heavier (and therefore more destructive) air-to-air missiles. Both of these types were designed by a relatively new Russian design bureau, that of Sukhoi. The single-engined fighter, known first as the Su-9 and later developed into the Su-11 (but known in the strange NATO codename system for Russian aircraft as *Fishpot*), is about half as heavy again as the MiG-21 (*Fishbed*) and can therefore carry heavier air-to-air missiles and better radar equipment.

The same applies, but even more so, to the big twin-engined Su-15 *Flagon*. This hefty fighter is very much in the Phantom class where size and weight is concerned, for it carries a heavy missile armament and has an estimated maximum level speed of around Mach 2. It is clear that the Russians felt it worthwhile to develop a range of fighter designs, all suited to particular types of operation. At one time few other nations could have afforded such a luxury, but during the 1960s and early 1970s attitudes changed to a large extent. It was realized that because fighter design had evolved so strongly towards the heavy all-weather interceptor, a gap had opened up for a more pure breed of air-to-air dogfighter.

If the impact of the MiG-21 on the war in Vietnam and other areas of conflict made the Americans realize the need for

a smaller, more agile dogfighter than the Phantom, it did not mean they had to go precisely the same way as the Russians. In fact the Americans had been doing some hard new thinking about fighter design as a result of their combat experiences, and they realized that above all more power was needed. It was not needed to generate even more speed, as would always have been the case in past, but to enhance manoeuvrability in air-to-air combat conditions.

When a supersonic fighter turns tightly, it needs extra lift to pull it round the turn. This sets up so much extra air resistance that its speed very quickly drops below that of sound. The only way to avoid this, and to maintain any possible supersonic advantage, is to have enough power to overcome all that extra air resistance. In practical terms, that in turn means having at least as much thrust from the engine as the weight of the aircraft, and preferably more. Even the Phantom could not manage that, however – equipped for combat it has about two-thirds as much thrust as weight – though it is worth bearing in mind that the Phantom's basic design is over twenty years old. The Americans looked for ways of doing better, and came up with several answers.

The ball was set into motion when the US Navy issued a specification for a Phantom replacement. If the Phantom itself had been big, heavy, expensive yet extremely capable, the new fighter this specification produced was to be even more so. Grumman, who won the contract to build it, felt that a variable-sweep wing was the only way of meeting the US Navy's requirement for high (Mach 2.2) maximum speed, low landing speed, long endurance and heavy bombload when used as a ground-attack machine.

A variable-sweep wing configuration enables a designer to give his aircraft the best of both worlds at the expense of a little extra weight and complication. The wings are mounted on pivots where they join the fuselage. Driven by hydraulic rams deep within the airframe, they are swept fully forward at right angles to the fuselage when slow-speed flight is required (presenting the maximum flap and wing area to the oncoming air on landing) and are drawn back along the fuselage sides for superb streamlining when high-speed flight is required. Also called for in the US Navy's specification was the most powerful airborne radar

system ever carried by anything other than a specialized early-warning aircraft, and new air-to-air missiles with a range of well over 200 km (125 miles).

The new fighter, the F-14 Tomcat, flew in late December 1970 and astonished everyone with its sheer complication. With its swing-wings, twin tailfins and two enormous engines (Pratt & Whitney TF30s of 21,000 lb thrust each) the Tomcat met the US Navy's tight specification to the letter, and proved that it was still possible to build a fighter which could do everything equally well.

If the fighter had to become more specialized, recent experience suggested to the Americans that it should move in the direction of air-to-air combat, so that air superiority could be achieved above battlefields, while more specialized ground attack aircraft like the brutish Fairchild A-10 hit targets below, such as tanks. Accordingly, the experienced designers of the McDonnell Douglas company began work on a new fighter intended quite simply to be a thoroughly capable dogfighting machine. They knew that to achieve this they needed more thrust than the total weight of the aircraft, so they elected to use two of the new Pratt & Whitney F100 engines in their design. They also relied on a comparatively simple fixed wing of modest sweep and generous area, together with a twin-finned tail layout not unlike that of the Grumman Tomcat.

This new McDonnell Douglas fighter, the F-15 Eagle, quickly proved to be an excellent design and quickly became just what its designers set out to make it – one of the world's best dogfighters. However, there were still worries at its size and cost. Though it was smaller and lighter than the F-14 Tomcat (yet even more powerful), it was still 20 m (60 ft) long and weighed up to 30 tonnes. The USAF bought the Eagle, but at the same time wondered if the job could not be done almost as well by something smaller and cheaper. They organized a design competition to find out, and the two most promising projects were built and tested against one another in a 'fly-off'. These two new fighters were the General Dynamics F-16 and the Northrop F-17.

The F-16 was powered by a single Pratt & Whitney F100 engine, in sharp contrast to the Eagle's two, while the air-intake was placed well back under a needle-sharp nosecone. The wing had a comparatively short span and a straight trailing edge but a sharply-swept leading edge, to give it almost a delta shape. Most important, the designers had decided to totally reject the usual system of operating the flying controls via a series of push-and-pull rods and opted instead for a sophisticated all-electronic control system nicknamed 'fly-by-wire'. This daring approach saved a lot of weight and, combined with various revolutionary aerodynamic devices, made the F-16

more manoeuvrable than any of its contemporaries. Its pilot has an unrestricted field of vision through the F-16's big one-piece cockpit canopy and reclines in a special tilted ejector seat, which helps stop the blood from rushing to his feet when pulling out of steep dives during dogfights. This had previously been a serious problem with high-performance fighters, as pilots frequently blacked-out at critical times during combat manoeuvres.

'Fly-by-Wire'

By contrast, the Northrop F-17 was a twin-engined design with a strong family resemblance to the earlier F-5 light fighter. It too had a semi-delta wing, but it featured twin tailfins in the manner of the F-14 Tomcat and F-15 Eagle. When flown against the F-16 in mock combat and other tests it proved to be an excellent fighter, but not quite as good as the General Dynamics design. The F-16 was chosen for the USAF shortly afterwards, and was also selected by the air arms of Belgium, Holland, Norway and Denmark.

There are proving to be many advantages to the USAF having this team of two high-performance fighters. The F-15 Eagle is more powerful, but the F-16 with its nimbleness and low initial cost, complements it perfectly. This fact was not lost on the US Navy, who called for a dogfighter of its own to fly alongside their impressive fleet of F-14 Tomcats. Northrop teamed up with McDonnell Douglas to suggest a developed version of the F-17, which was finally accepted by the military planners. This new naval fighter, so far the latest in America's armoury, is the F-18 Hornet.

While all this work was going on in the USA, Europe was also thinking about its next generation of fighters. The prolific French design team at Dassault returned to the delta wing configuration for their specialized high-performance fighter, the Mirage 2000. Like the other Mirage deltas, the 2000 is very compact and lightweight, and like the F-16 it features the latest in 'fly-by-wire' control systems.

Britain meanwhile is developing an ADV (Air Defence Version) of the Panavia Tornado, first designed on a multinational basis by Britain, Germany and Italy as an all-round strike aircraft. Another swing-wing, two-seater design with two compact engines, the Tornado ADV has much in common with America's F-14 Tomcat, although it is smaller and lighter.

V/STOL

Another British aircraft has captured the imagination of the public for rather different reasons. This is the Royal Navy's version of the extraordinary Hawker Siddeley Harrier 'jump-jet'. Known as the Sea Harrier, this subsonic V/STOL (Vertical Short Take-Off and Landing) aircraft will maintain fleet air cover now that Britain's *Ark Royal* and the other big aircraft carriers have been withdrawn from service in favour of the newer, smaller 'through-deck cruisers'.

Because the Sea Harrier has the high thrust needed for vertical take-off, it has just the kind of thrust-to-weight ratio that a modern fighter aircraft needs. It has the additional advantage, only re-

A two-seat shipboard multirole fighter, the Grumman F-14 is one of the West's latest warplanes.

cently discovered, of enabling its pilot to alter the position of the aircraft's swivelling exhaust nozzles (normally used only in the transition from vertical to horizontal flight and vice versa) during combat to make possible what can only be described as 'square-cornered' turns. This amazing technique, officially called 'vectoring in forward flight' but known to Harrier pilots as 'viffing', has introduced a whole new dimension in air combat.

In a dogfighting situation, for example, if a Harrier pilot finds himself being chased by a faster enemy aircraft, he can quickly swing the exhaust nozzles round to tighten his turn quite dramatically. The enemy plane does not of course have this advantage and flashes past his intended victim to place himself right in front of the Harrier's air-to-air missiles. Work is still going on in Britain and America (at the hands of McDonnell Douglas) to develop the Harrier still further along these lines.

Swing-Wings

On the other side of the 'Iron Curtain' the Russians decided that swing-wings were a good idea and adopted them for several new designs. One of them, the MiG-23S *Flogger*, was intended, at least partly, to replace the long-serving MiG-21. Like its forebear, the *Flogger* has a single, large and extremely powerful engine and is built in several versions, some of them clearly aimed at interception, others at ground-attack. Beyond the MiG-23S however, and the very fast but not very manoeuvrable MiG-25 *Foxbat*, it remains to be seen how the Soviets are going to answer the challenge of America's new generation of high-technology fighters.

As for the original British idea of phasing fighter aircraft out of service altogether and replacing them with long-range missiles, this still seems a long way off. It is a reassuring fact that, so far, no-one has developed a computer capable of replacing the human pilot.

FLYINGBOATS & FLOATPLANES
Wings on Water

ater has an attraction for aviators – it's soft! Not only that, but it constitutes an almost limitless surface for take-offs. It was these considerations that prompted some of aviation's pioneers to use floats for the landing gear of their early aircraft. The first recorded float-plane was the unusual biplane *Fabre Hydravion* which made an attempt at take-off on the harbour at La Mede near Marseilles in March 1910. After some trouble it became airborne and ushered in a new era in the story of aviation.

After that first attempt, flyingboats and floatplanes went on to play an increasingly important part in the aviation scene, only to disappear again virtually as quickly as they had arrived. Between the two world wars, flyingboats linked many parts of the British Empire, while many other countries made the long journeys to their colonies in the Far East by the same method. The United States, with her interests in South America and the important staging post and naval base of Hawaii under her control, developed her own flyingboat bearing the romantic name of *Clipper*.

U-boat Menace

The First World War was really the heyday of flyingboats and floatplanes. Many major warships carried their own float-equipped spotter aircraft which could be swung out on derricks or launched from a catapult on deck. These little machines would fly 'over the horizon' and scout ahead of their parent ship,

A float-equipped biplane takes off from a ship by means of a special trolley.

or spot the effect of gunfire on targets both ashore and at sea.

At this point we should describe the basic difference between a flyingboat and a floatplane. A flyingboat is an aeroplane whose whole lower fuselage is shaped like a boat to permit take-offs and landings on water. A floatplane, on the other hand, is a more or less conventional-looking aeroplane with a normal fuselage, but it has floats attached to its fuselage and wings by means of special struts or pylons.

The flyingboat deserves a special place

in aviation history, both in its peaceful role as an air-sea rescue machine and as the airborne hunter which did so much to reduce the menace of the Germans' U-boats. After the war, flyingboats lingered on for some years, but land-based jet airliners made the leisurely speed of the older types unsuitable for anything except nostalgic travel. Flyingboats and floatplanes lingered on in the lakes of Canada and the United States, and they continue to serve as forest fire 'water bombers' in such places as the south of France and North America.

This Felixstowe F.2A carries a striking pattern on its hull to help confuse enemy gunners. A number of flyingboats were painted like this during the First World War.

The 'water bomber' is a flyingboat which takes water within its fuselage by skimming along a nearby lake and then flies to the area of a forest fire and dumps its watery cargo. A big advantage of this type of flyingboat is that it can turn round far faster than any fire-fighting team based on the ground. The USSR and Japan have retained flyingboats for maritime patrol work and there are even plans in Japan to develop a passenger-carrying flyingboat service to link coastal communities in southern Asia.

£10,000

Before the First World War, aviation was regarded as a rich man's game or the pursuit of dreamers. In 1913 the *Daily Mail* newspaper offered a £10,000 prize for the first direct crossing of the Atlantic Ocean. Among those who decided to go for the prize was Rodman Wanamaker, who commissioned the American firm of Curtiss to build him a flyingboat. It appeared in 1914, had a crew of two and was given the patriotic title of *America*.

With the onset of the war in Europe, John Porte, one of the Curtiss team, returned to his native Britain to rejoin the Royal Naval Air Service (RNAS). He was to be linked with flyingboat design for the rest of the war. He suggested that the British authorities order Curtiss flyingboats and soon *Large America* and *Little America* machines appeared on the order of battle in the First World War. They were wooden aircraft with hulls shaped to deflect spray from the cockpit area on takeoff. *Little America*

A Luft Hansa Dornier Do 8-t Wal is pulled onto a special ramp.

was the name given to the smaller Curtiss H-4 type, but these were somewhat underpowered. The Curtiss H-12 *Large America* was armed with machine-guns and bombs and became the first American-built aircraft to destroy one of the enemy's planes in battle when it shot down a Zeppelin airship in May 1917.

Tough Odds

Flyingboat design was not the sole preserve of the British and the Americans, however, for the Austrians and Germans used them on the North Sea and Adriatic throughout the First World War. Among the more advanced designs was the Hansa-Brandenburg W.29. This monoplane came into operation at the end of the war and with its sleek fuselage and downward-facing tail surfaces was an unmistakable sight to the Germans on the North Sea coast. In August 1918, W.29s attacked and sank three Royal

Navy motorboats on patrol along the coastline. The odds were stacked in favour of the Germans, however, since there were fourteen aircraft against just three vessels.

British flyingboats usually operated out of the port of Felixstowe and when John Porte set to work to improve on Curtiss' designs his name was linked with that of the famous naval air station. John Porte's Felixstowe proved to be an excellent aircraft with its two pilots and up to seven Lewis machine-guns for self-defence. It had an impressive range too, with fuel for up to nine hours continuous flying. At the end of the war Felixstowes appeared in 'dazzle' markings to distinguish them from enemy aircraft and were finally declared obsolete in 1921, but not before they had had the distinction of becoming the first of a great line of British flyingboats.

The last years of the Felixstowes were

A majestic Boeing Clipper flyingboat of Pan American. Note the tailfins.

the formative years for various new sporting and civilian types. The Schneider Trophy had become a major international flying prize and the designers of Italy, Britain, France and the USA pitted themselves against one another to produce faster and faster racing floatplanes to compete for the trophy. Competition of this type was useful for the air forces of all four nations, as it gave their governments and aircraft designers the incentive to improve and update their designs.

During the First World War the Italian company of Macchi had already produced successful seaplanes such as the M.4 and M.5 and in 1926 they won the Schneider Trophy at Hampton Roads in the USA. Their entry was a sleek red racer known as the M.39. They had trouble in later competitions but in 1934 their MC.72 was a real record-breaker. Painted in the same national shade of red, it had two engines mounted in effect in tandem. The propellers rotated in opposite directions and so cancelled out what is known as 'torque effect' – the corkscrew twist that powerful engines would have had on the tiny airframe. The Schneider Trophy became a battle between the British and Italians and in the end the British won it with the beautifully streamlined series of S.5, S.6 and S.6B floatplanes designed by Reginald Mitchell. They were to provide the impetus that led to the Supermarine Spitfire fighter and in the early years of the Second World War a morale-boosting film was produced telling the story of the races and of the birth of the fabulous Spitfire.

These racers, however, were highly specialised types and the 1920s and 1930s were a time when no aircraft builder

airliners, crossing the Atlantic from east to west in August 1930 and in doing so setting a new world seaplane distance record. In 1932, a Wal flown by Wolfgang von Gronau made the first round-the-world trip. Transatlantic flights became the vogue in the early thirties and the Italians gave a delighted American audience a spectacular display when they flew 24 Savoia-Marchetti S.55s to the Chicago World Fair in 1933.

Welcome Boost

Three years earlier they had flown 12 of them across the Atlantic, but 24 was a triumph of organization and engine maintenance.

The newspaper headlines of the time portrayed it as the dawn of a new aviation age – but what they did not realize was that it pointed to the massed fleets of heavy bombers that would later roam over Europe on their flights of destruction. However, the flight was a welcome boost for the people of the United States, who were still recovering from the trauma of the Depression.

The American aviation industry had suffered too, but had still managed to design and build new types. Sikorsky's S-42 grew out of specifications laid down in the early thirties and first flew in 1934. Before long it had become an important addition to the Pan Am service operating between San Francisco, Hawaii and later New York, Bermuda and South

Above: The immense size of the Dornier Do X is apparent in this picture as King George V of Britain inspects her. *Below*: The huge Do X lifts off.

could afford the luxury of an uneconomical aircraft. Racers often had government backing and were flown by service crews, while commercial flyingboats had to pay for themselves. The German firm of Dornier produced a unique flyingboat in 1929 — the *twelve-engined* Do X, which made its first flight in October of that year carrying a ten-man crew, 150 passengers and nine stowaways! This was almost 'jumbo' capacity some 40 years before the world had heard of the term. Despite its size the Do X was not as economical as the Dornier Wal. This twin-engined aircraft pioneered many of the routes now regularly flown by jet

America. On short trips the S-42 carried up to 40 passengers, while a night version could carry up to fourteen in sleeping berths.

Part of the same fleet being operated by Pan Am in the 1930s was the Martin 130. It had been built to meet a similar specification to that which led to the S-42, but was, in fact, superior to the Sikorsky design. With better flight and sea-keeping performance than the S-42, the 130 was the first flyingboat to take the name *Clipper*. The *China Clipper*, *Philippine Clipper* and *Hawaii Clipper* were some of the hardest-working civilian flyingboats of the era and by 1940 the two surviving aircraft each had a total of 10,000 flying hours behind them. Travellers on the run down to Bermuda still recall the service as a combination of the comfort and style of an ocean-going passenger liner with the speed of an air service. Those were the days when pas-

sengers would choose a meal from a menu and know that it was freshly cooked for them in the aircraft galley. Indeed, both American and British passenger seaplanes carried fresh food, bought by their crews at each stop on the journey. The trip may have taken longer, but the experience was in some ways more pleasant than modern jet travel.

Pick-a-Back

By 1938 there was a grim feeling that

war was a matter of 'when' rather than 'if'. For the British and French, however, there was the consolation that they could expect the support of their colonial allies. Both nations had sea links to Africa and the Far East, and both had developed their airlines with commendable efficiency. The Short S.23 'C' Class, for example, flew almost 60 million kilometres (38 million miles) between Britain and her colonies between 1936 and 1947 – with some 42 aircraft — the Empire Class flyingboats. These were attractive four-engined aircraft capable of carrying 24 passengers by daytime or nineteen in sleeping berths. The 'C' Class also carried mail, which soon became a very important part of the flyingboat service.

In the late 1930s, the British even produced a special flyingboat and float-plane combination known as *Mercury* and *Maia*. Experimentally, the large

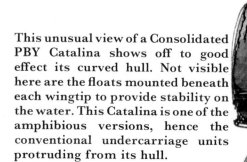

This unusual view of a Consolidated PBY Catalina shows off to good effect its curved hull. Not visible here are the floats mounted beneath each wingtip to provide stability on the water. This Catalina is one of the amphibious versions, hence the conventional undercarriage units protruding from its hull.

Russia's Beriev Be-2 of the Second World War.

When the war came Europe watched the USSR battle it out with Finland in the winter of 1939–40. It was an extraordinary contest, but despite the obvious imbalance, Finland fought well. Among the aircraft deployed by the USSR was the little Beriev MBR-2. This single-engined flyingboat had also worked as a commercial airliner though it was mainly used by the Russian navy for short-range reconnaissance work and air-sea rescue and was capable of carrying bombs or depth charges for anti-submarine work. Across the Atlantic, the United States watched the war and began to re-arm. Among their aircraft already in service was the Grumman Duck. This single-engined machine had its float faired in to the fuselage, which gave the curious impression of an aircraft with a large slipper tucked under its fuselage. The Duck might have looked quaint, but it served throughout the war in an aggressive role as a land-based scout with the US Marine Corps and Coast Guard.

four-engined *Maia* carried the smaller *Mercury* on its back and at a chosen altitude *Mercury* took off with a load of high-priority mail and flew on its way. This combination allowed the smaller aircraft to make record-breaking flights because it did not have to use any fuel to get airborne and could therefore carry more mail than a conventional aircraft. The Second World War put a stop to these flights and in-flight refuelling meant that an aircraft could be 'topped up' whilst airborne and so did away with the need for what had more formally been called the Short-Mayo Composite. This unusual creation never saw active service.

Japanese Giant

Among the many threats to the USA at this time was the growing military might of Japan. This nation had jumped into the twentieth century with enormous energy and though Europeans still thought that she couldn't really understand complex weapons, Japan possessed plenty of very effective military equipment and formidable armed forces. Besides putting a number of good fighter

The Supermarine Walrus was powered by a single 775 hp Pegasus radial.

types onto floats and so giving such aircraft as the Zero a new potency, the Japanese also developed two effective flyingboats. The giant Kawanishi H6K (codenamed *Mavis* by the Allies) had four engines and a maximum range of 6,700 km (4,200 miles), though it normally flew patrols over slightly shorter distances. It was used for maritime reconnaissance in the Pacific theatre, where it eventually proved easy prey for Allied fighters.

A much more difficult target for air attack was the beautiful Kawanishi H8K (codenamed *Emily*). This was the fastest flyingboat to serve during the war and had defensive armament of up to five 20 mm cannon and one 7.7 mm machine-gun, while a transport version could accommodate up to 64 passengers. At the other end of the Japanese armoury was the three-seater Aichi E13A (*Jake*). This was an important type if only because it supplied the final reconnaissance details of Pearl Harbor before the Japanese attack in December 1941. It also made the first contact at the famous battles of Coral Sea and Midway.

Severe Weather

The severe weather conditions in the Pacific, that the Japanese often had to contend with were often similar to those that the Italians faced in the Mediterranean. With their tradition of flyingboat and floatplane design, the Italians produced a winner for bad weather conditions in the triple-engined Cant Z.506 Arione (meaning Heron) which could take-off and land in the strongest of winds. It served with the Italians when they fought alongside the Germans and later helped the forces on the side of the British and Americans. It had been originally intended to serve as a civilian airliner, but by the end of the war it was being very usefully employed on air-sea rescue duties.

For the Royal Air Force and Fleet Air Arm there was one air-sea rescue type which held pride of place. The Supermarine Walrus with its biplane wings and fragile appearance did not look tough, but as a spotter and (later) rescue aircraft it operated in mine-infested waters close to enemy coastlines and as a shipborne spotter took the war to targets beyond the range of naval gunfire when it bombed Italian positions in East Africa in 1940. It was described as a 'ladylike' aircraft to fly, but in its military career the old lady had been used as a dive-bomber and was even looped by one enthusiastic pilot.

It is not generally known if the Germans had a nickname for the Walrus, but they certainly had a name for the big Short Sunderland. They called it the *Stachelschwein* – the Porcupine. It earned its name from the prickly defence it would put up when attacked by Luftwaffe fighters. Like any flyingboat the Sunderland was more vulnerable to attack from below, but if the pilot could get his aircraft down to sea level he was in a very good position to survive a fighter attack. The navigator became the co-ordinator of the defence plan because he would stand in what was known as the 'astrodome', a transparent bubble atop the fuselage, which gave him a complete view above the aircraft. From this vantage point he could warn the pilot when to take evasive action and also tell the gunners in their power turrets when an enemy fighter would be within range.

Running Battle

The firepower of the Sunderland was increased still further when the German U-boats began to fight it out on the surface when attacked by flyingboats. The pilot was therefore given his own battery of fixed machine-guns mounted in the nose, and as his aircraft began its depth-charging attack he could put

First flown in XP3Y-1 form in 1935, the Catalina saw service in every theatre of the Second World War.

down suppressive fire on the U-boat. The effectiveness of this defensive armament was demonstrated in 1940 when a Sunderland was attacked by six Luftwaffe Ju88s. In a running battle it downed one, damaged another (which was forced to crash-land) and drove off the remaining four.

Press Photos

The Sunderland had many enemies and was even attacked by 'fellow' seaplanes when German Dornier flyingboats attacked on one occasion and Arado floatplanes on another. The Arado Ar 196 was used against RAF anti-submarine patrols but had been designed as a shipboard reconnaissance and patrol aircraft. It first came to the public notice when press photographs showed a damaged example aboard the famous *Graf Spee* battleship in December 1939. The German battleship *Bismarck* launched similar aircraft in an attempt to drive off shadowing RAF Catalina flyingboats during her one sortie into the Atlantic.

Offensive Armament

The Ar 196 had two cannon and a

Right: **A Consolidated PB2Y Coronado long-range patrol Bomber/ transport flyingboat dwarfs everything around it.**

machine-gun as offensive armament and two machine-guns in the observer's position for self-defence. It could also carry a small bombload and when operating from bases along the coastline would attack small coastal craft, submarines and also marauding RAF Coastal Command Whitleys which patrolled the routes taken by U-boats entering or leaving their pens on the French coast.

A rather more peaceful Luftwaffe aircraft during the war years was the Heinkel He 59. Painted white with red crosses emblazoned across its fuselage sides, it was mainly used for air-sea rescue duties. But it was not long before RAF intelligence officers established that the He 59 was also being used for transmitting jamming signals to confuse Allied aircraft by means of the beams put out by its powerful radio. It had been designed as a torpedo bomber and during the Spanish Civil War (1936–9) was part of the Condor Legion, a force which operated on the side of General Franco.

Condor Legion

The Condor Legion was composed of German aircraft and crews operating in Spanish markings. The pilots soon discovered that the He 59 was an ideal night-bomber and by cutting their engines some distance from their targets they could glide in unheard by the enemy anti-aircraft gunners, hit shipping lying defenceless in the harbours, and be on their way back to base before the ground defences had time to react.

Unusual Duty

During the Second World War, the He 59 was used for mining operations and 'shadowing' convoys as well as for air-sea rescue work. In the latter role it carried more powerful radios and six rubber dinghies and had a hatch cut in the aircraft's underbelly to allow the crew to pick up downed airmen. However, the most unusual duty performed by the He 59 was as an assault troop transport. In 1940 ten He 59s landed on the lower Rhine at Rotterdam to capture the city's main bridge. Each aircraft contained six paratroops who stormed ashore to seize both ends of the bridge and so speed the Nazi drive into Holland.

If the He 59 was a wolf in sheep's clothing when it doubled up as an air-sea rescue aircraft and bomber director, the sleek He 115 was a turncoat of an aeroplane. Though German designed and built, it was used by the Norwegians and later the RAF for secret operations against the *Reich*. The Norwegians operated their own aircraft and during the German invasion of their country captured two more when they landed by accident in a Norwegian-held fjord. These two unexpected additions to the Norwegian air force were the latest models with improved bombsights, and they were used for attacks on German positions and then flown to the United Kingdom.

Secret Agents

Though there were plans drawn up to use the Norwegian and ex-German aircraft in secret operations from RAF bases this was abandoned in case Allied fighters mistook them for German aircraft. However, one was taken to the island of Malta where it flew in both RAF and Luftwaffe markings, dropping off agents in North Africa. In Luftwaffe service the He 115 was used for mining attacks far out at sea and dropped some of the first magnetic

The Consolidated PB2Y Coronado was powered by four 1,200hp Pratt & Whitney Twin Wasp radial engines – the same type that powered the famous PBY Catalina. It first flew in December 1937 and later served with the US Navy.

Above: In the Arado Ar 196 the Luftwaffe possessed a fine floatplane. *Below*: The Vought OS2U Kingfisher appeared in wheeled and floatplane versions.

mines in 1940. These were for a time a major threat to Allied shipping.

Another notable Luftwaffe seaplane was the triple-engined Blohm und Voss BV 138 flyingboat, easily recognizable with its twin tail booms and rather odd, angular-shaped hull. The German pilots had a kindly nickname for this aircraft – they called it the 'Flying Shoe'. When it was first tested just before the war, it was found to be unsuitable in rough water conditions, so it was taken away and redesigned. The new aircraft was then found to be inadequately armed, but as the war advanced its armament was increased until it mounted 20 mm cannons in both bow and stern positions. For its offensive armament it could carry

bombs or depth charges and some were also converted to operate as mine-sweepers with a magnetic loop around the hull.

'The Flying Shoe'

After all its teething troubles, the BV 138 came into service in 1941 and proved itself a formidable aircraft. One was attacked by fighters from an escort carrier for 90 minutes, yet it survived and returned to its base to fight again another day. Others destroyed a Catalina and shot down a fast twin-engined Blenheim bomber. The 'Flying Shoe' was even given rockets for catapult launching while others could carry ten passengers when serving in a transport role. In anti-

shipping operations it was fitted with radar for locating convoys for the benefit of friendly U-boats and bombers. There is a story that one Allied convoy making its way to Russia with a BV 138 circling slowly above it out of range of its anti-aircraft guns grew tired of its shadow. When a sailor picked up a signal lamp and flashed the message in German 'Could you stop doing that, we are getting dizzy', the flyingboat obligingly began to fly a new course – anticlockwise!

Ultimate Flyingboat

Before leaving German flyingboats, the Blohm und Voss BV 222 deserves a mention as the largest seaplane to reach production status. This giant had six engines and a span of 48 m (150 ft) and was used for long-range reconnaissance over the Atlantic as well as to ferry supplies to North Africa. The ultimate flyingboat of the Second World War, however, never reached production status. This was the BV 238, another six-engined giant, but the war ended before it had gone beyond trials.

Retractable Wheels

Big boats were, of course, also under design and construction in the United States and without the restrictions suffered by factories in Europe and Britain, the Americans were able to mass-produce their aircraft in comparative ease. The Consolidated PBY Catalina was not the only flyingboat built by Consolidated, but it remains their most famous, serving with all the Allied nations, including the Soviet Union. A few were amphibians – in other words they had a hull for landing on water and retractable wheels for landing on air-strips – so they had the additional advantage of being easy to pull ashore if there was any danger of high seas. Catalinas were built in Canada, the Soviet Union and in the United States, and served with great distinction in all theatres of war.

'Blister' Turrets

During the pursuit of the *Bismarck* a succession of RAF Catalinas shadowed the German warship until surface forces could be concentrated to attack her. It could carry bombs, depth charges or torpedoes and was armed with a good selection of defensive machine-guns. Two were housed in 'blister' turrets on either side of the hull, these being very useful positions for recovering downed aircrew, since the gunners were close enough to water level to lean out and pull a man aboard. Catalinas did not retire with the end of the war for they went on to become successful transports. With alterations they could accommodate up to 22 passengers and became popular with airlines in South America where they could land on the major rivers. They were in use up to the mid-sixties with various small airlines – 30 years after the prototype made its first flight.

One of the Catalina's most obvious features was the situation of its wings, mounted on a streamlined pylon high above the fuselage. Most of the big flyingboats of the time had their wings as part of the top of the fuselage. The Coronado, for example, had its wings in this configuration for it offered strength with the added advantage of keeping the engines well away from sea spray. The PB2Y Coronado, also built by Consolidated, was a big, four-engined flyingboat frequently used for coastal patrols until shore-based Liberators were introduced. In its subsequent role as a transport and ambulance aircraft it could carry 44 passengers or 25 stretcher cases.

Scale Model

A more successful, though smaller, seaplane was the Martin PBM Mariner. This twin-engined high-winged aircraft could carry a useful mix of bombs and depth charges in bays within the engine pods. The RAF operated the type in Scotland but returned their aircraft after only six weeks' service. Mariners were then used for transport work with a converted hull interior complete with strengthened floor and tie-down rings for securing cargo. In the transport role it could carry twenty passengers. An unusual feature of the Mariner was that it first flew at a quarter of its final size. The builders made a large model of the aircraft to test its general performance and take-off and landing characteristics at sea. This meant that design faults could be rectified at a fraction of the cost

Below: **A Sea Dart in flight.**

Below: **A Convair Sea Dart takes off.**

of testing a full-sized aircraft.

At the other end of the scale, the single-engined Vought OS2U Kingfisher was the floatplane workhorse of the US Navy. It equipped numerous warships and could be catapult-launched for anti-submarine liaison and aerial spotting work. An observer/rear gunner was housed in a long 'greenhouse' position and was armed with a single machine-gun. The Kingfisher was also used by the British to equip their catapult-armed merchantmen. This method of combating the German's long-range aerial shipping raiders was an inexpensive way of giving local aircover. A merchantman was equipped with a catapult and fighter and when a raider like the Focke-Wulf Condor appeared the fighter was launched to attack in a matter of seconds.

Rescue Mission

The most important advantage of an aircraft like the Kingfisher was that it could land afterwards and be recovered by crane, whereas the Hurricane fighters normally used for this work were ditched after completing a mission and sank within seconds, while the pilot scrambled over the side to be hauled aboard the parent ship. The Kingfisher also performed valuable work in an air-sea rescue role. On one occasion an OS2U taxied across 64 km (40 miles) of rough sea after rescuing Captain Eddie Rickenbacker and his crew in the South Pacific. Kingfishers even became dive-bombers during the attack on the Japanese-held Aleutian Islands when they carried 50 percent in excess of their normal bomb-load. Like many American types it had a single float below the hull with small wingtip floats for added stability in choppy water. Some big flyingboats, such as the Catalina, could retract these wingtip floats to reduce the air resistance on the aircraft when in flight.

Familiar Shapes

Some aircraft are designed as floatplanes from the start, but others are pressed into this role because of their operators' requirements. The result is that some familiar shapes appear in a new and rather unusual guise. The Germans, British and United States all produced waterborne conversions of fighters and transport aircraft. The famous Supermarine Spitfire, for example, became the fastest floatplane of the war. The Battle of Britain stopped further developments of this interesting derivative and it was only towards the end of the war when British forces began to concentrate in the Pacific that a definite role was envisaged for it. But by then carrier-borne aircraft had become more important than floatplanes.

The Fairey Swordfish was occasion-

Above: **A Convair test pilot stands in front of 'his' Sea Dart. Note the skids.**

ally converted from a carrier borne torpedo bomber into a floatplane. In this guise it served as a spotter for *RMS Warspite* during the second battle of Narvik when it flew up the Norwegian fjord observing the effect the warship's gunfire was having on the enemy. In an after-action report, Vice-Admiral Whitworth wrote of this aircraft, 'I doubt if ever a shipborne aircraft has been used to such good purpose as it was in this operation'. The aircraft had directed fire which had sunk seven destroyers, and finished off a destroyer and a submarine (the U-64) with its own bombs.

Converting single-engined types was fairly simple, but the Germans put floats on much bigger aircraft. The trimotor Junkers Ju 52 transport had been equipped with floats when it was in service with Luft Hansa before the war, while during the Spanish Civil War it ferried Moorish troops from Spanish Morocco to Spain to fight for Franco. Float-equipped Ju 52s became vital during the German invasion of Norway when former Luft Hansa aircraft were used to ferry troops to locations captured by airborne or mountain troops. When Holland was occupied by the Nazis in 1940,

the Fokker aircraft factory was ordered to produce floats so that Ju 52s could be suitably modified should the military situation require operations from water. Floatplane Ju 52s subsequently saw action during the occupation of Greece and Crete and the drive through Yugoslavia.

Jet-propelled

Meanwhile, on the other side of the world, the war in the Pacific ended with the dropping of the two atomic bombs, and so many of the plans for the invasion of Japan were never developed beyond the prototype stage. One of these was the elegant, single-seater Saunders-Roe SR/A1, the world's first jet-propelled seaplane. The idea behind its design was that the fighter could provide air superiority over the beaches without the need for an aircraft-carrier, but with a performance far superior to conventional seaplanes. Work continued after the war and one prototype set a world seaplane record when it reached speeds above 800 km/hr (500 mph), but accidents with

Seen here from an unusual angle is a Soviet Beriev Be-12 *Mail*. Its two streamlined turboprop engines and distinctive gull wings are clearly visible, as are the twin tailfins and MAD 'sting'.

two of the prototypes and the ending of the war led to the cancellation of this most promising project. A similar type of aircraft developed in the fifties was the Convair Sea Dart. This sleek, delta-winged fighter had two underbelly skids not unlike a waterskier's skis and used these for landing and take-offs. Though prototypes were built and tested, it was not adopted for general service.

Records

The Martin Seamaster was probably the most spectacular development of the jet seaplane concept. This four-engined bomber was developed to fulfil a requirement for a seaplane bomber which could operate independently of carriers or air-fields. Seamasters would be refuelled from submarines and could therefore be located anywhere offering a sheltered harbour. The general concept is no longer in vogue since atomic submarines can offer the same mobility with less of the maintenance problems and anyway, the Seamaster development programme was dogged with technical problems. But it did produce some records for seaplanes when prototypes flew at speeds in excess of 900 km/hr (600 mph). With its swept-back wings and bomb-bay fitted with waterproof rotary doors to carry an

Above: **The Martin Seamaster was a spectacular four-engined jet flying-boat of the 1950s.** *Below*: **The Fairchild Ceebee appeared in sharp contrast.**

assortment of bombs, mines or cameras, the Seamaster had a 'sting in its tail', for the tail section featured a remotely-controlled gun position. One squadron was formed in 1959 to operate this radical new aircraft, but it was disbanded after only six months.

Few nations operate flyingboats as part of their armed forces in the 1980s. Long-range land-based aircraft, and the ready availability of coastal airfields make it easier to concentrate on types like the Nimrod for maritime patrol. However, Japan is enthusiastically committed to the flyingboat idea. With limited space on land, she has a vast area of sea to the east. The Japanese Air Self Defence Force operated American-built Grumman UF-1 Albatross amphibians, rugged machines used by the US Navy and Coast Guard for patrol and reconnaissance work in the sixties. The Shin Meiwa company developed their own aircraft in the early seventies, and designated the PS-1, it entered service with the Japanese defence forces. It is a four-engined amphibian with excellent short take-off and landing (STOL) performance. In an anti-submarine role it carries equipment to search for and locate the submarine and depth bombs as well as smoke bombs to mark its position. A retractable magnetic anomaly detector (MAD) 'sting' is mounted in the tail section to detect submarines lurking beneath the surface. The air-sea rescue version carries five medical attendants and up to 36 stretcher cases.

Seagull

The Soviet Union is the only other nation to operate a military flyingboat. Their Beriev Be-12 is a modern aircraft like the Shin Meiwa and it fulfils a similar purpose. It has submarine-tracking equipment and can carry a variety of anti-submarine weapons. Known as the Tchaika (Seagull) by the Russians, it has the NATO reporting name of *Mail*. The Be-12 can carry an impressive weapon load beneath the wings and also in a bomb-bay in the hull. Its turboprop engines give a maximum speed of 610 km/hr (380 mph).

Seaplanes and flyingboats are still in service throughout the world, some like the *Mail* and Shin Meiwa are new aircraft. Others, like the Catalina, are coming to the end of a full and varied career. The water-bombers and air-sea rescue aircraft give a vital service – though the advent of bigger helicopters has made many of these roles redundant. Small numbers of flyingboats and float-planes will doubtless remain in service for many years to come in the more remote parts of Russia, Canada and the United States, but this is but a mere shadow of the majestic 'boats of old that plied the airways of the world.

Small seaplanes like this Lake Buccaneer are especially popular in the USA.

HELICOPTERS
and other Rotorcraft

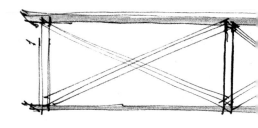

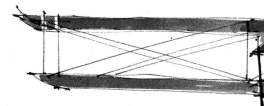

Back in the early days of aviation, long before the Wright brothers first took to the air in 1903, many experimenters were researching into rotorcraft. Simple wind-up propeller toys had long shown that rotary wings could enable a machine to climb straight up into the air, and it seemed logical to early inventors that flying machines ought to have moving wings – after all, birds appeared to fly in that way. In the fifteenth century, Leonardo da Vinci designed flying machines and among the sketches found after his death there was more than one set of drawings for a flapping-wing aeroplane.

The first person-carrying helicopter to fly was a most unlikely-looking French contraption called the Breguet-Richet No 1. This had four big biplane rotors attached to a complex framework of spindly struts and outriggers. The rotors were driven by belts and wheels from a small 40 hp motor mounted on an elevated platform, beneath which sat the pilot. He hung on to his controls as the Breguet-Richet struggled into the air on 19 September 1907, held firmly by four men on the ground for safety. The weird-looking device rose only 0.6 m (2 ft) into the air and hovered for just over 60 seconds outside the aircraft workshops at Douai, but everyone present knew that history had been made that day.

Autogyros

Two months later another step forward was made in France, at Lisieux, when Paul Cornu proved that a helicopter could fly untethered in comparative safety. He flew a fragile tandem-rotor machine of his own design on a 'flight' lasting less than 30 seconds – and promptly crashed! Cornu's helicopter was reduced to scrap but its intrepid designer lived to fly another day. By giving his machine two rotors, and making them rotate in opposite directions, Cornu had found a clever way to overcome one of the greatest initial problems associated with helicopters – namely, torque reaction. This is the tendency of the helicopter's fuselage to rotate in the opposite direction to that of the rotor itself, effectively spinning itself around the axis of the rotor shaft.

The outbreak of the First World War in 1914 called an abrupt halt to rotorcraft experiments, but progress was rapid when hostilities ceased in November 1918. It was at this period in history that the autogyro came into its own as a cheap and simple form of flying machine. The auto-gyro has a freely-rotating, unpowered rotor for lift and a conventional propeller for forward thrust. As the propeller pulls the craft forward along the ground the rotor starts freewheeling in the passing current of air and provides the lift necessary to sustain flight. Because they rely on forward movement for their lift, auto-gyros cannot take-off vertically or hover motionless like a helicopter. In the event of an engine failure, however, an auto-gyro possesses the helicopter's ability to simply descend gently to a safe landing as the rotor freewheels in the upflowing current of air.

Refined Rotors

The person responsible for the early development of autogyros was a Spaniard called Juan de la Cierva. In 1920 he began to experiment with a set of freely-turning rotor blades mounted on top of a wingless Deperdussin monoplane. Cierva's first few models twisted over and crunched into the ground on take-off, so he sat down and mathematically worked out the aerodynamics of the problem he faced. He realized that his rotor blades, which were really just large horizontal propellers, produced too much lift as they moved forward and not enough as they retreated. Cierva made two crucial breakthroughs to overcome this problem – breakthroughs that have remained at the heart of helicopter design ever since.

The first was to start thinking of a rotor as something aerodynamically quite different from a propeller. As a result, Cierva calculated that his auto-gyro would benefit from having rotors that created very little air resistance. So, instead of the steep angle of pitch he had been using on previous propeller-like rotors, he decided to build a set of gently-

Below: **This Cierva C.8L made history on 18 September 1928 when its designer, Juan de la Cierva, made the first rotorcraft crossing of the Channel.**

The extraordinary Pescara No. 3 of 1924 had two sets of biplane rotors that spun in opposing directions.

Igor Sikorsky (*below*) takes his VS-300 for its first flight. Note the short tethering wires firmly anchored to the ground for safety.

angled rotor blades. By trial and error he discovered that with the blades set at a certain low angle of pitch, a rotor mounted on an autogyro would keep turning at a constant speed sufficient to keep a light load airborne. Nowadays, this is known as 'auto-rotation'.

Controlled Flight

Secondly, to overcome the difference in lift generated between forward- and backward-moving rotor blades (a difference brought about by the additional forward speed of the helicopter itself), Cierva added a 'flapping hinge'. This series of joints works by allowing each blade in turn rise up on its mountings and absorb some of its excess lift as it moves forward. Then, as it retreats, the blade is able to sink down firmly into its original position.

By combining these two ingenious features, Cierva was able to build a balanced, autorotating rotor. He mounted it on another modified Deperdussin monoplane and on 9 January 1923 made his first successful flight in a craft he called Autogiro C.4. In the tradition of many great pioneers, Cierva continued to develop his invention to the point of commercial viability and was immensely proud when one of his later models made the first rotorcraft crossing of the English Channel. A further development, the C.40 of 1938, had a self-starting, high-revving rotor which could 'jump' the autogyro vertically into the air and keep it there long enough for the propeller to establish forward flight. But with war once again looming on the horizon, those with an interest in the future development of rotorcraft knew that even a jump-starting autogyro was not what the military planners would want. For their purposes a rotorcraft would have to be able to hover motionless for sustained periods, so the helicopter rather than the autogyro looked like being the way ahead.

By the mid-1930s helicopters had become a much more feasible proposition,

Above: **The unusual Piasecki Rescuer certainly earned its nickname of 'flying banana'.**

Below: **Hanna Reitsch at the controls of the superb Focke-Wulf Fw 61 in 1938.**

thanks to the discoveries made by Cierva and other inventors in the previous decade. The Marquis de Pescara, a Spaniard working in Barcelona, pioneered a method of tilting the rotor disc as a whole in any direction, thus allowing the pilot to 'steer' his helicopter forwards, backwards and from side to side. This came to be known as 'cyclic-pitch' control. Later that decade a 'collective-pitch' lever was added to the pilot's controls. Using this, the pitch of the rotor blades could be altered in flight, allowing them to take either a greater or lesser 'bite' at the air and thus cause the helicopter to climb or descend. Although these elementary devices have since been greatly refined, both cyclic- and collective-pitch control remain the principal method of manoeuvring almost all modern helicopters. By operating both these controls in combination, and with slight adjustments to the throttle setting, a pilot is able to exercise complete command over his helicopter.

Enter Sikorsky

The first successful helicopter with both cyclic- and collective-pitch control was France's Breguet-Dorand *Gyroplane Laboratoire*, first flown in June 1935. Powered by a 350 hp Hispano radial engine, this established numerous world rotorcraft records, including speed – 98 km/hr (61 mph), altitude – 158 m (518 ft), and endurance – 1 hr 2 mins.

By the time war clouds started gathering once again over Europe and the world, helicopter development was proceeding at a cracking pace. In February 1938, a test pilot called Hanna Reitsch, who was to be the only woman awarded the Iron Cross during the Second World War, demonstrated a new German helicopter to the Nazi hordes assembled in Berlin's vast *Deutschlandhalle* stadium. The graceful Focke-Wulf Fw 61 featured twin side-by-side contrarotating rotors to overcome the problem of torque reaction, and the successes it achieved in the world record stakes were nothing short of staggering; speed – 123 km/hr (76 mph), altitude – 3,427 m (11,243 ft), endurance – 1 hr 20 min.

In the following year, a breakthrough in the USA finally paved the way for helicopter design as we now know it. Igor Sikorsky, a Russian exile living in America who had already made a great name for himself building large fixed-wing aircraft in his homeland, realized that the practice of mounting the rotors in contrarotating pairs to overcome torque reaction was holding back the helicopter's military and commercial potential. Gradually perfecting an idea tried by a Dutch inventor back in the late 1920s, Sikorsky's experiments led him to mount a small vertical rotor at the extreme rear of the fuselage. Powered by the same engine that drove the main horizontal rotor, this would provide just enough sideways thrust to counteract the torque reaction on the helicopter's fuselage. Like most good ideas, Sikorsky's was very simple – but highly effective.

The machine he used to test these latest developments was the VS-300. It made its maiden flight tethered close to the ground on 14 September 1939, with Igor Sikorsky himself at the controls, and featured full cyclic- and collective-pitch control of the main rotor. By pulling another lever, the pitch of the new vertical tail rotor could be altered for steering purposes. In 1940, the VS-300 set a new endurance record for helicopters and ever since then, Sikorsky's main and tail rotor (MTR) layout has been featured in the vast majority of the

when saving lives.

A typical example of this, the helicopter's greatest ability came when a major explosion ripped through a US Navy destroyer cruising off the New Jersey coastline. A plea for immediate assistance reached the Coast Guard's newly-formed air division, whose Sikorsky R-4s saved the day by lifting injured men off the deck of the stricken destroyer and by relaying vital medical supplies from shore to ship. With these accomplishments, helicopters ceased to be regarded as the impractical product of eccentric inventors and took their rightful place in the structure of aviation development.

The Korean War

Although Sikorsky stole the limelight among helicopter manufacturers post-war – spurred on no doubt by the success of their products in wartime – it was the Bell company of Buffalo, New York, that received the first US commercial certificate of airworthiness for one of its designs in peacetime. The model in question was the Bell 47 of 1945 which, through various updatings, remained in production in either the USA, Italy (by Agusta), Britain (Westland) or Japan (Kawasaki) until as recently as 1976. The US Army and USAF soon snapped up the type, giving it the name of H-13 Sioux. More than 5,000 of them were built and many were exported to the armed forces of over 30 nations, while others continue to prove profitable as air taxis and crop-sprayers or are engaged in traffic-spotting work with the police. Bell 47s are easily identified by plane spotters because they have distinctive 'goldfish bowl' cockpit canopies and open lattice-work tail booms.

In the early fifties, a serious conflict broke out in southeast Asia when the Communists of North Korea invaded South Korea in a surprise attack. This brought the world's superpowers into direct confrontation when the United Nations assembled a combined force of 'western' nations to launch a counter-offensive, spearheaded by the vast American war machine. On the other side, communist China sent in troops and Russia supplied equipment – including jet fighters – to support the North Koreans. The Korean War (1950-3) was the first time that helicopters were called on to take part in combat on a large scale, and their performance exceeded even the wildest dreams of the military commanders. On the United Nations side the principal types used were Bell H-13s, Piasecki HRP-1 Rescuers, and Sikorsky S-51s and S-55s.

The Piasecki type had first flown in August 1947 and was intended to meet the heavy-lift requirements of the US armed forces. Popularly known as the 'flying banana' because of its unusual curved shape, the Rescuer was the first tandem-rotor design ever to enter military service. With this configuration a helicopter has one rotor atop the forward fuselage and another at the extreme rear, cleverly avoiding the need for a single giant main rotor and tail rotor. They rotate in opposite directions to counteract torque reaction and are synchronized to prevent the two sets of blades from touching as they overlap. This configu-

Below: **The military planners start to take an interest in rotorcraft. This is an RAF Cierva autogyro. Note the propeller at the front.**

world's helicopter designs.

With the experience they gained from the VS-300, Sikorsky's team next turned their attention to producing a two-seater version. The VS-316, as it was initially called, had an 11.6 m (38 ft)-diameter rotor and a 185 hp engine. It made its maiden flight in January 1942 and was immediately snapped up for trials by the US Army Air Force and US Navy. By 1943, as the Sikorsky R-4, it had become the first helicopter outside Germany to go into mass production. One hundred or so were built for observation and rescue as well as for training pilots to fly these new-fangled things called helicopters. In Britain, where a few found their way to the RAF in 1945, the type was used for training and was known as the Hoverfly I. But it was whilst serving with such organizations as the US Coast Guard that the helicopter first demonstrated its full potential, particularly ration was subsequently used in a number of medium- and heavy-lift helicopter designs, notably the Vertol 44 family and the more recent Boeing Vertol Chinook, veteran of air operations in Vietnam during the sixties. By this time, though, the 'banana look' had long since ceased to be fashionable.

While Rescuers certainly served in appreciable numbers, the helicopter most widely used in Korea was the Sikorsky S-51, known to the military as R-5. About 200 examples served with the US Navy and USAF, performing numerous duties throughout the conflict. Sikorsky's other major contribution to the war in Korea was the larger, radial-engined S-55. In 1949 this had become the first single-rotor helicopter in the world to lift a weight of over one tonne (.98 ton) and it was in Korea that it began a very long and successful career as a multipurpose utility type. Its deep, stocky fuselage, with the engine mounted in the nose, left enough space in the main cabin for ten troops, six stretchers, or assorted cargo. In Korea this space was quickly put to use when the S-55 became the UN's forces' principal rescue helicopter in that bitter conflict. It had the ability to fly up to 300 km (180 miles) from its home base to reach stranded soldiers or downed flyers, pick them up – often under heavy enemy fire – and then

be off again before the surprised aggressors had time to close in for the kill.

While the S-55 proved ideal for this type of operation, it must also be said that the pilots who flew them frequently displayed exceptional bravery when making these rescue flights in unarmed helicopters. After all, their only protection was to fly close to the ground, taking advantage of the cover provided by small hills and groups of trees. Using these

tactics, it has been estimated that helicopter crews saved over 22,000 wounded allies during the Korean War alone.

By the mid-fifties several countries had the engineering skills and specialized materials necessary to build the complex machines helicopters had become. At about this time the shaft-turbine engine, known as the turboprop when used in fixed-wing aircraft, appeared on the scene. Turbines use more fuel than piston

Above: **A Bell 47, specially modified for crop-spraying operations, flies low over the fields.**

Below: **An Alouette III in service with the French police force, equipped with ski landing gear.**

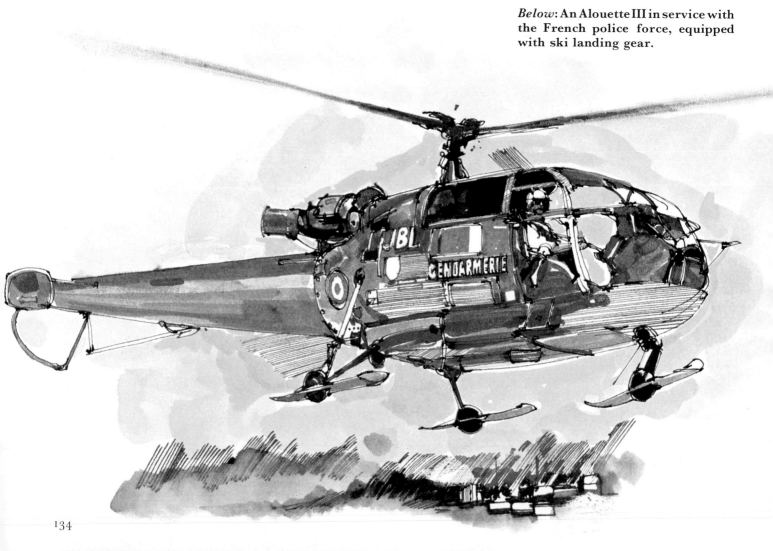

A beautiful picture of a three-seater Hughes 300 in civil use. This attractive little American helicopter also serves as a trainer with the US Army.

engines, but they are far more powerful and for helicopters they have several important advantages. Chief amongst these is their ability to put out a great deal of power over a prolonged period, whereas a piston engine might tend to overheat if it had to keep a heavy helicopter hovering for a long time. And since turbines are lighter than piston engines of equivalent output, helicopter designers can simply install more tanks to quench their thirst for fuel. As a result, helicopters became much bigger and faster during the fifties.

Cancelled

Although rotorcraft were by now well established, not every promising project got the opportunity to show its full potential. Typical of the shortsightedness that killed off more than one potential worldbeater was the sad episode of Britain's revolutionary Fairey Roto-dyne, which first flew in 1957. This 70-seater passenger aircraft employed a unique configuration that exploited the best features of both the helicopter and the conventional airliner. Just like any normal helicopter it took-off vertically, by means of a 27 m (90 ft)-diameter main rotor. The big difference with the Roto-dyne was that once airborne it was propelled forward in true airliner fashion by two Napier turboprops mounted on short wings, whilst power to the main rotor was switched off. The rotor then went into autorotation to sustain lift, as happens with an autogyro. But even more ingenious was the system Fairey devised to drive the rotor. Hot gases from the two wing-mounted turboprops were

diverted via a compressor along pipes to the tip of each rotor blade, thus dispensing with the need to carry a separate engine just for vertical take-off and landing.

With its ability to fly in and out of city centres and speed to destinations at 300 km/hr (185 mph), the Rotodyne looked set for a great future. BEA and New York Airways expressed an intention to buy up to twenty aircraft each, and the British Army took a serious interest. But in the end, the Rotodyne was probably just too far ahead of its time, for none of the interested parties had sufficient vision to finance the project's continued development.

In contrast, two other British companies – Bristol and Westland – stuck to

more conventional designs and achieved some success with them. The Bristol Belvedere of 1958 was a general-purpose transport helicopter with a tandem-rotor configuration; one rotor atop the forward fuselage and another at the extreme rear. With its long, cylindrical shape and tiny undercarriage, the Belvedere was nothing if not distinctive. Although only built in relatively small numbers, it made a good account of itself in RAF service, particularly whilst operating in the jungles of Malaya, Borneo and Singapore. Belvederes were finally phased out of operational service in March 1969.

Sub-Killer

Westland, meanwhile, had been busy tapping a very lucrative corner of the helicopter market with their multirôle Scout, first flown in 1960 and destined to enjoy orders for over 100 examples from Britain's Army Air Corps, plus smaller quantities for numerous other nations. They found a whole host of uses for these nimble little five-seaters, including liaison, armed observation and latterly (by fitting rocket pods or guided missiles) low-level attack.

Westland also built a naval version of the Scout, called the Wasp, with which the Royal Navy equipped many of its destroyers and frigates. They operated them on search and rescue missions and fitted them with torpedoes for anti-submarine warfare. The Wasp is easily distinguished from the Scout by the four fully-castoring wheels it carries as standard equipment to facilitate easier landings on the rolling, pitching decks of naval vessels. This is in sharp contrast to the Scout's more basic skid undercarriage, ideal for crunching down onto rough or muddy terrain during army manoeuvres.

During this time, the French had not

The ill-fated Fairey Rotodyne speeds across London after taking-off vertically right in the heart of the city centre. Sadly, it never saw public service.

allowed themselves to slip from the position of prominence they established with the early accomplishments of Breguet-Richet and Paul Cornu. One of their foremost aircraft constructors, the SNCA du Sud-Ouest merged with the SNCA du Sud-Est to become collectively known as Sud Aviation. One of this company's most successful ventures began with the first flight of the turbo-powered Alouette II prototype in 1955. This machine went into production in 1957 and had room for four passengers plus the pilot, who sat behind the clear plastic bubble of the cockpit windscreen which gave him an excellent view in all directions. The French military quickly put the Alouette II into action on air transport and 'flying ambulance' missions and paved the way for substantial export orders right across the globe. In fact for many years no less than 37 different armed forces were equipped with the type. A few of the 1,500 or so built have been fitted out for close-support of ground forces, but the vast majority were kept occupied with training and observation duties. Others found commercial applications as air taxis and crop-sprayers.

In the late-fifties, more powerful light-weight turbines appeared on the scene and as a result the Alouette II evolved into the Alouette III. This was a slightly larger model with an improved performance and room for six passengers. By 1970, Sud Aviation had been absorbed into the gigantic Aérospatiale organisation, but this did nothing to deter the stream of buyers for new Alouettes. Production was still underway in 1979, by which time almost 3,000 Alouettes of all versions had been built, these having been sold in over 60 countries. Many operators fitted them with missiles and guns for army support or equipped them to 'hunt and kill' submarines or surface vessels. In fact, the Alouette family of IIs and IIIs now has a battle record that includes various Arab-Israeli wars, the Indo-Pakistan war of 1971 and more recent fighting in southeast Asia.

Soviet 'Copters

Possibly due to the genius of Igor Sikorsky being 'exported' to America, the Soviet Union was slightly slower getting their own helicopter industry underway. While the UN effort in Korea was supported by an assortment of American rotary-wing types, on the other side of the 'bamboo curtain' the Communist forces had not a single operational helicopter. For although the first mass-produced 'communist' rotorcraft entered service in 1951, none found their way to Korea. The model in question was the Russian-built Mi-1, designed by Mikhail Mil and given the NATO reporting name of *Hare*. With accomodation for the pilot and three others, and a top speed of 150 km/hr (95 mph) on its 575 hp radial engine, the *Hare* has been a remarkably successful and versatile general-purpose helicopter. They were built in vast numbers in both civil and military versions in Russia and Poland until the mid-sixties and are still to be seen in many parts of the world where Communist influence predominates.

The Mil bureau continued their domination of the Russian helicopter scene when, in early 1953, the Soviet authorities introduced a much larger transport and general-purpose helicopter to their civil and military fleets in the shape of Mil's Mi-4 *Hound*. Bearing a remarkable resemblance to the Sikorsky S-55, *Hounds* have since become the most widely-used Soviet rotorcraft, and have been built in their thousands by both Russia and China. In their basic military form they have a crew of two and can carry sixteen troops or up to 1,600 kg (3,500 lb) of cargo, which may take the form of a jeep-like vehicle or a 76 mm anti-tank gun and its crew. Civilian *Hounds* first appeared in 1954, when the ten-passenger Mi-4P model entered Aeroflot service. An agricultural variant soon followed, with internal storage space for up to a tonne (.98 ton) of chemicals or 1,600 litres (350 gal) of liquid spray. This is the Mi-4S, or 'rural economy' *Hound*.

The Soviet Union was also quick to appreciate its need for a heavy transport/assault helicopter, particularly in the military field but also as a means of

This illustration shows the weird-looking Convair XFY-1 'Pogo' taking-off. It was an experimental fighter aircraft designed to combine high speed with vertical take-off and landing (VTOL).

The Boeing-Vertol Sea Knight first flew in prototype form in April 1958. It is a classic twin-rotor transport helicopter and served with both the US Navy and US Marine Corps in the conflict in Vietnam.

delivering large civilian loads to otherwise inaccessible parts of that vast country. As a result, an astounding new Soviet type, the Mil Mi-6 *Hook*, entered service in 1959. This was the Soviet Union's first turboshaft helicopter, packing two massive 5,500 hp engines in streamlined fairings above the fuselage. With its long, slender fuselage capable of accomodating a five-person crew and up to 65 troops, *Hook* retained its distinction of being the world's largest helicopter until well into the sixties. Loads totalling 15,000 kg (33,000 lb) can be wheeled up folding ramps through the big 'clam-shell' rear doors, or slung externally on a central cargo hoist beneath the fuselage. While stub wings take some of the lifting strain off its massive six-bladed rotor, *Hook* can then cruise fully-laden at 300 km/hr (185 mph) for almost three hours before stopping to refuel. The Soviet authorities have found a multitude of uses for the Mi-6 during its service life. These range from the delivery of nuclear ballistic missiles to their remote silos in frozen Siberia to water-bombing forest

fires in the heat of summer. At least 500 *Hooks* are known to have been built, most of which are still in service.

Flying Crane

Always quick to exploit a successful design to maximum effect, the Soviets built a 'flying crane' version of the *Hook* in 1960. This derivative – the Mi-10 *Harke* – has a shallower flat-bottomed fuselage and stalky undercarriage legs, between which can be slung very bulky loads of up to 8,000 kg (17,600 lb), while at the same time leaving room inside for up to 28 passengers. When carrying out 'flying crane' operations, *Harke's* crew are able to monitor the scene below the fuselage by means of a remote-controlled TV system that transmits the view to a screen on the pilot's instrument panel. Perhaps the most interesting loads so far hoisted by the Mi-10 were the complete wing assemblies for Russia's Tu-144 supersonic airliner. These were transported from Voronezh, where they are built, to the Tupolev assembly works near Moscow. Even bigger loads – up to

15,000 kg (33,000 lb) – can be carried if the *Harke's* special hydraulically-gripped lifting platform is attached to its stalky undercarriage legs.

The next Russian helicopter to appear was even more exciting, but in line with the usual Soviet policy of standardizing components for easier manufacture and

A Westland Whirlwind, the RAF's licence-built Sikorsky S-55.

maintenance, it used the same twin-turboshaft engine unit as the *Hook/Harke* family. This newcomer, the Mi-12 *Homer*, was so colossal that it required *two* of these mighty power packs – slightly uprated to generate a staggering 26,000 hp. First flown in 1968, *Homer* is still easily the largest rotorcraft the world has ever seen. It can cruise at 240 km/hr at a maximum all-up weight of around 105,000 kg (231,500 lb) – almost as heavy as a fully-laden Boeing 707! One of the three prototypes originally built is known to have been destroyed in a crash, and another is now on display in a Moscow museum. The sole-surviving *Homer's* principal task in wartime would be to convey to the battlefront such loads

as tanks, missiles and prefabricated bridges. In civilian use, of course, the duties it performs are many and varied, but they probably include supporting Russia's many remote oil and natural gas fields.

Sharp Edge

Finally, in 1971 came the first flight of what was destined to become the sharp edge of the Soviet sword. This is an armed assault helicopter known as the Mi-24 *Hind*. Applying all the lessons learned by the Americans in Vietnam, the Mil bureau surpassed itself in the design of this deadly battlefield attacker. *Hind* is a modern *blitzkrieg* weapon, intended to deliver ten combat-ready troops into the heat of battle and blast its way through any opposition it may encounter on the way – particularly enemy tanks. It has a maximum speed of 275 km/hr (170 mph) and is armed with a four-barrel rapid-fire machinegun in the extreme nose, with stub wings to carry six rocket pods or a formidable variety of guns and air-to-surface missiles. The Mi-24 has been designed with 'battlefield survivability' very much in mind. Its two-person crew, armour-protected troop compartment and twin

1,500 hp Isotov turboshaft engines are all clustered together within the classic narrow fuselage of a gunship – the most difficult target to hit during a head-on attack. Literally hundreds of *Hinds* are now in Soviet service, most of them stationed close to the 'Iron Curtain'.

The Mil bureau is undoubtedly the USSR's main source of helicopter designs but other bureaux do exist, chief amongst these being Kamov. Their leading current model is the twin-turbine Ka-25 *Hormone*, which entered service in 1967. In its civilian configuration it has room for twelve passengers and has the ability to work as a 'flying crane' with underslung loads, but it is most important in the anti-submarine rôle. For this purpose it carries a large radar scanner within a prominent bulge beneath the nose and is armed with homing torpedoes, nuclear depth charges and air-to-surface missiles. In addition, some highly-secret *Hormones* are fitted out for electronic warfare. Kamov's other major product is the Ka-26 *Hoodlum*, easily recognizable with its distinctive quadricycle undercarriage, bulbous engine pods and twin tail booms. Both *Hormone* and *Hoodlum* employ a most unusual

Left: **A *Hormone* closes in for the kill. Note the prominent radar bulge under its nose.**

The Kaman Huskie is ideal for fighting fires. It has an underslung extinguisher to douse the flames.

rotor configuration, with two separate sets of blades spinning around the same axis, one above the other.. This type of arrangement requires a rather complicated rotor shaft system, but is a novel way of avoiding the torque reaction problem, for the two sets of blades rotate in opposing directions.

A decade earlier, the small American helicopter manufacturer, Kaman, had displayed an equally interesting variation on the 'one up, one down' theme. The rotors on their neat little H-43 Huskie spun in opposing directions, too, but unlike those on the Soviet Kamovs they were mounted on separate shafts placed close together, with a synchronizing mechanism between them to ensure that the blades intermeshed without contact. This arrangement must have worked well, for the Huskie performed admirably in the 'air ambulance' and airfield fire-fighting rôles.

America's Weightlifter

There is no disputing the fact that the Soviet Union has built itself a most formidable armoury, but the USA has managed to maintain its position as leader of the 'western' powers by continuously improving their military capabilities, adding new weaponry whenever necessary. For example, with helicopters becoming more and more specialized, it was perhaps inevitable that the American armed forces would request one of its major suppliers to design a 'flying crane' like the Soviet Union's mighty *Harke*. The Sikorsky company met this

challenge by producing a smaller, though more manoeuvrable machine called the S-64 Skycrane. Over 100 of these odd-looking helicopters have seen service with the US Army since 1964, a handful more having been bought by commercial operators. Skycranes are designed to operate with special containers that can be carried under their spindly spines. These serve as field hospitals, command posts or 'universal military pods' (capable of transporting up to 87 combat-ready troops into the battle-zone). Skycrane's three-person crew

includes a rear-facing 'pilot' for the central hoisting winch, used to lift loads too bulky to clamp into the pod recess between the spiderlike undercarriage legs. In Vietnam, the S-64 proved itself to be an efficient weightlifter, carrying loads of up to 9,000 kg (20,000 lb). The Skycranes used in that conflict are estimated to have saved in the region of $210 million worth of shot-down aircraft by picking them up from otherwise inaccessible places.

Sikorsky introduced what was to become yet another American success

A Sea King prepares to lift *Apollo* astronauts out of their ditched module.

story in the helicopter field when the boat-hulled shape of the S-61 entered widespread service in the early sixties. This basic twin-turbine design has since been developed into a whole host of sub-variants, both civil and military, with various models being produced in the UK, Japan and Italy as well as in the USA. The portly lines of the amphibious S-61N model are now a familiar sight on and around the landing pads of offshore oil rigs right across the globe, while many a shipwreck victim has had cause to praise the Sea King version's splendid reliability record in the vital air-sea search and rescue rôle. Sea Kings are the navalized S-61 derivatives and are usually equipped to engage in anti-submarine warfare, carrying a sophisticated collection of sonar detection gear and an all-weather navigation system. They serve with the naval forces of many nations, notably Brazil, Canada, Denmark, Great Britain, West Germany and, of course, the USA.

Astronauts

A favourite tactic of Sea King crews is to hover at low level over the waves and lower the helicopter's special sonar 'dipper' into the water. This sends out radar impulses and picks up return signals as they bounce back off submarines lurking below the surface. In a wartime situation, the Sea King would then swing into action with its deadly armament of torpedoes and depth charges. Although they are advanced submarine 'hunter-killers', perhaps their most glamorous duty was performed whilst in US Navy service, retrieving splashed-down American astronauts after the famous *Apollo* moon missions.

While operations at sea gained the most publicity, it is also notable that a land-based troop transport variant known as the HH-3 *Jolly Green Giant* achieved the distinction of becoming the first helicopter to fly the Atlantic non-stop. By using its long, retractable refuel-

A Westland/Aerospatiale Lynx of the British Army performs a hair-raising 360 degree roll!

ling probe, the HH-3 was able to top up with fuel from a USAF Hercules tanker-plane whilst *en route*. In Vietnam, the *Jolly Green Giant's* principal duty was to fly deep into enemy-held territory to pick up downed aircrew. To help it accomplish this risky task it had special fuel tanks that automatically sealed when hit by gunfire, plenty of armour plating, and bristled with up to four 7.62 mm Miniguns.

Although the Piasecki company had by this time undergone a change of name to become Boeing-Vertol, their ability to design and build the distinctive tandem-rotor helicopters that had become their trademark was far from lost. Boeing-Vertol's most notable product thus far has been the CH-47 Chinook. With their watertight hulls, all-weather performance and ability to cruise for up to eight hours at 260 km/hr (160 mph), Chinooks have proved themselves to be worthy successors to the illustrious 'flying banana' family. Both turboshaft engines are mounted atop the rear fuselage on short pylons, leaving the interior completely unobstructed for the speedy loading and unloading of troops, small vehicles and cargo via the folding rear ramps. In Vietnam, where it began

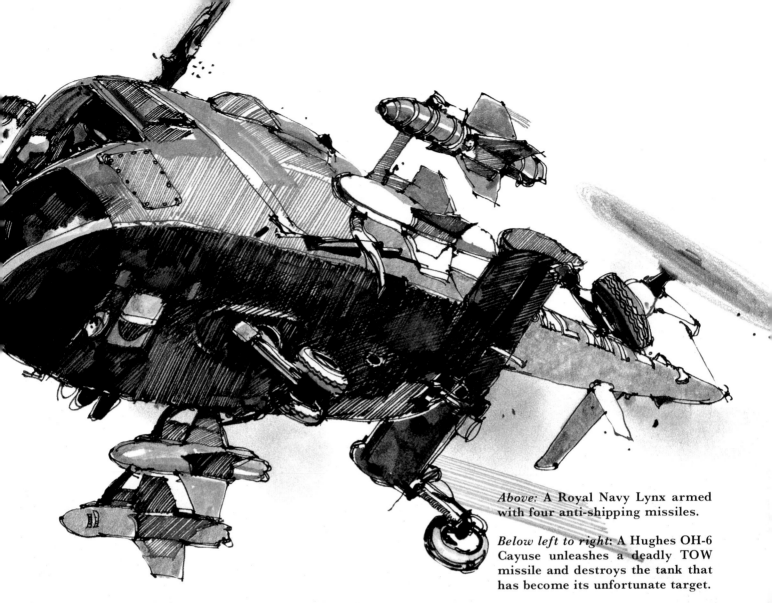

Above: **A Royal Navy Lynx armed with four anti-shipping missiles.**

Below left to right: **A Hughes OH-6 Cayuse unleashes a deadly TOW missile and destroys the tank that has become its unfortunate target.**

active service in 1962, the CH-47 quickly established itself as the US Army's principal troop transport helicopter, and went on to achieve staggering success recovering crashed aircraft for salvage or repair. In fact, it has been estimated that Chinooks in Vietnam recovered over 11,500 downed aircraft – worth at least $3 billion to the American taxpayer. Although it is 'officially' capable of carrying 44 fully-equipped troops, on one occasion a Chinook carried no less than 147 refugees and their belongings to safety during an emergency airlift.

The US Army's 'go anywhere, do anything' helicopter since the early sixties has been the Bell Iroquois, a multi-rôle utility machine with room for up to twelve fully-equipped troops. Powered by a single Lycoming T53 turbine engine of 1,100 hp, the Iroquois gained a reputation for toughness and reliability whilst serving in the dreadful southeast Asian conflict. They were most frequently used to carry squads of soldiers into jungle clearings close to the front line, allowing the military commanders to switch their forces from one battlezone to another at very short notice. Others did valuable 'air ambulance' work, swooping into clearings hurriedly prepared by infantrymen with chain-saws and explosives to pick up wounded soldiers and rush them to nearby medical posts. Enemy gunfire was not the only danger on such mercy missions, for sharp obstacles like tree stumps littered the landing zones and could easily pierce the helicopter's vulnerable undersurfaces.

In a fascinating demonstration of design ingenuity, the Iroquois formed the basis of an exciting new combat model in 1965. When Communist missiles and gunfire started taking a high toll of Chinook transport helicopters in southeast Asia, the US Army issued an urgent request for a fast, well-armed escort to provide fire-support. As time was short, Bell hit on the idea of mating the engine, transmission and rotor system of the Iroquois with an entirely new fuselage, only 0.97 m (38 in) wide at its widest point. This produced the AH-1 Huey-Cobra, a slender 'gunship' helicopter with fighter-like manoeuvrability and a top speed of 320 km/hr (200 mph). The HueyCobra's two-person crew are seated in tandem, the pilot above and behind the navigator/gunner for improved visibility, with the crew seats and cockpit sides being armour-plated for protection

the gunner's helmet, and are guided to the target by a long, thin wire attached at one end to the 'parent' helicopter and at the other to the missile itself. After HueyCobra, the rôle of the helicopter in warfare took on a whole new dimension.

Super Styling

Although helicopters had enjoyed steady improvement over the years, both in visual appearance and 'under the bonnet', the late-fifties demonstrated that one of the barriers to civilian sales was simply that they still looked rather ugly. As a result, business executives who cared more about prestige than the technical or economic sides stayed with the sleeker fixed-wing alternatives. Bell was the first manufacturer to cotton onto this problem and thus in 1962 was born the highly-successful JetRanger family, configured specifically for the civilian market, where attractive lines, high-gloss paintwork and luxury seating rapidly took sales well over the 5,000 mark. Here

Egg-Shaped!

A new trend had undoubtably been set, for another helicopter with attractive looks followed on soon after, and then found its way into the tough world of the US Army. This was the Hughes OH-6 Cayuse, a highly-manoeuvrable military observation helicopter whose fuselage had egg-like contours that conferred exceptional strength on the passenger cabin without spoiling the superb streamlining. Over a period of seven years, the US Army took delivery of almost 1,500 OH-6s, many of them serving with distinction throughout the Vietnamese conflict. This initial success encouraged Hughes to develop civil variants and eventually a new military model, the armed Defender, currently in production as an anti-submarine version for export to Taiwan and as an anti-tank weapon for South Korea and Kenya.

Meanwhile, in Europe, the British and French helicopter builders had decided

A battlefield attacker of supreme efficiency, the Hughes AH-64 here demonstrates its awesome firepower.

against enemy gunfire. The HueyCobra packs a big punch. In the extreme nose is a rotating 7.62 mm multi-barrel Minigun and a remote-controlled 40 mm grenade launcher. Attachment points under its stubby wings carry a deadly assortment of up to 76 small rockets, more Minigun pods or TOW (Tube-launched, Optically-sighted, Wire-guided) missiles. As the name suggests, these fearful projectiles leave their underwing missile tubes at very high speed, are guided automatically through a sight fitted to

was a helicopter with car-like styling and charisma – something the business executive could readily appreciate and something that other manufacturers, such as Enstrom with their Shark, were not slow to copy. That is not to say that the JetRanger failed to introduce technical refinement, for the use of a turbine engine lowered cabin vibration levels and increased speed and carrying ability considerably when compared with products of the previous generation. The helicopter had a new image.

to combine resources in a cooperative programme to re-equip their military forces during the seventies. Both countries needed a mixture of helicopters of various sizes for training, communications, cargo carrying and naval duties, and both countries had some glaring gaps in available designs. The first Anglo-French helicopter was the Puma, designed by Aérospatiale as a twin-turbine transport machine able to carry sixteen fully-armed troops at speeds approaching 270 km/hr (170 mph). The prototype actually flew two years before the cooperation agreement was implemented in 1967, but Pumas subsequently went into mass production on both sides of the English Channel, with Westland and Aérospatiale sharing the construction of major components. In 1971 the Puma entered service with the French army and the RAF, and since then over 500 have been delivered to a variety of military and commercial operators. Technical improvements such as plastic rotor blades have helped keep Puma abreast of the times and Aérospatiale are now testing a new Super Puma, with a larger cabin and more powerful engines, for production in the eighties.

Gazelle was the second Anglo-French helicopter, designed by Aérospatiale to replace the highly-successful Alouette II in French military service, and the Sioux and Hiller HT2s still serving with the British. The Gazelle introduced a new word to the helicopter dictionary – 'fenestron'. This can be best described as a multi-bladed fan set into a circular cutout in the helicopter's tailplane. It was designed to replace the conventional open tail rotor with a far less dangerous alternative, with the additional benefits of greater manoeuvrability and better streamlining without needing more power. Pilots soon found that in the Gazelle they had quite a tiger, for its top speed of 310 km/hr (190 mph) and superb aerodynamics made it very swift indeed. In fact, pilots had to learn to 'start braking' a lot sooner than in contemporary helicopters if they wanted to avoid overshooting their intended landing point!

The third in the line of Anglo-French helicopters is the Lynx, this time a British design built in two distinct versions for that country's army and Royal Navy, plus the French *Aéronavale*. First flown in 1972, the army variant – distinguished by its skid undercarriage – carries up to ten armed troops and can also be used in an anti-tank rôle when fitted with a variety of weapons, including up to eight TOW missiles. The naval version employs a fully-castoring wheeled undercarriage and a retractable 'harpoon' to hold it firmly down on the deck of a heaving frigate. It is now in service with several navies worldwide, including those of Brazil and Argentina. The Lynx was one of the first helicopters to successfully employ a 'rigid' rotor, a system which excludes the complex linkages found at the head of a conventional rotor, greatly simplifying maintenance.

A JetRanger of the New York City Police keeps an eye on traffic jams.

A Bell 222 prepares to whisk a group of top executives from a city-centre heliport to a business engagement.

It also bestows exceptional agility – even to the extent of allowing such manoeuvres as loops and 360 degree rolls!

And what of the 1980s? On the civil front the first Bell 222s and Sikorsky Spirits are now entering service, taking the executive look still further and using new materials, such as carbon fibre, to increase performance and cut vibration to previously unheard-of levels. These new machines are also quieter than anything that has gone before, despite the fact that they use two engines for enhanced safety. Companies like Bell and Sikorsky are now making great efforts to gain widespread public acceptance of helicopters using city centres, where they may one day compete with the more conventional forms of transportation. New materials and new technology are also to be found in the next generation of military rotorcraft, exemplified by the Sikorsky UH-60 Black Hawk troop transport and Hughes' AH-64 armed attack helicopter. Over 1,000 Black Hawks are expected to replace the war-weary Iroquois of the Army over the next decade, and in battle these would be protected by some 500 AH-64s – armed with up to sixteen anti-tank missiles, or 76 unguided rockets backed up by a 30 mm chain-gun in a ventral turret. Formidable opposition by anyone's standards!

Bell's extraordinary XV-15 looks like a sure pointer to the future. A conventional helicopter's biggest shortcoming is its restricted top speed, because of the strain on its rotors caused by the oncoming torrent of air. To overcome this, the XV-15's two engines are mounted on pivots. By setting them vertically for VTOL performance, and tilting them forward in flight to attain high forward speeds, it enjoys the best of both worlds! The experimental XV-15 is exploring this unusual method of flight.

LIGHT AND GENERAL

Light Aircraft and General Aviation

In the very early days of aviation, before the First World War, most flying was 'private'. The first small-scale attempts at running commercial airlines did not begin until around 1912–13 and were almost immediately stifled by the outbreak of war. Most experts agree that the first really practical aeroplane was the 1905 version of the Wright brothers' *Flyer*, and as nothing that could be called a reliable aircraft emerged in Europe until 1908–9, the real pioneer days did not last for long. At first, of course, everybody had his own ideas as to what an aeroplane should look like, how it should fly and indeed why it flew at all. Very few of them actually had the right answers to any of these questions, but by the time of the first international air meeting, in France in 1909, two different types of design accounted for all the successful models.

Framework

The prototypes of these designs were all French. France was the leader of the European aviation movement, just as she had led the world in motor car design a few years earlier. The first and most common type was the 'boxkite', which was a big, light but strong framework of biplane wings, with many struts, supporting wires and control surfaces carried on long wooden outriggers fore and aft. The pilot sat on a crude seat on the lower wing (with no safety belt) and behind him was the engine, driving a big and rather slow-moving propeller.

This was crude and cumbersome, but it was comparatively easy to build and to repair and was usually easy to fly. The Voisin brothers and Henry Farman in France pioneered this type of design and when it was successfully built under licence in England by the Bristol company, many early army pilots learned to fly on it. Other manufacturers in Italy and Germany also built them in some quantity. Putting the engine up front meant the designer could concentrate on a clean, strong fuselage and attach the stabilizing and control surfaces directly onto it at the rear. Breguet in France and A V Roe in England both turned out highly successful biplanes of this kind.

The second basic type was the monoplane, a single wing version of the 'puller' biplane, and eventually this was to become almost the only type of aeroplane built. It was certainly the faster and stronger of the two types, with the least amount of struts and wires, although at this early period not enough was known about aircraft design and materials to build strong monoplanes without a lot of bracing wires and pylons. In fact, follow-

ing a couple of accidents when monoplanes broke up in mid-air, the British War Office put an official ban on monoplanes as being too dangerous. Once again the French seemed to excell in this field. Louis Blériot, one of the most famous of early designers, turned out a whole series of highly-successful monoplanes. After he had made history by making the first flight across the Channel to England on 25 July 1909 in one of his

Above: Early light aircraft were often promoted and sold at motor car shows. The layout of this early Cessna model is somewhat typical of those produced by this famous company right through to the present day – a single engine at the front with a high-mounted monoplane wing. *Below*: The Piper Cub remains one of the most popular aircraft ever built.

own monoplanes, they became the best-selling machines on the market.

In those early days, flying was a very expensive sport, but by 1914 there were several hundred licensed pilots in each of the major European countries. Flying schools were flourishing and the number of pilots grew larger. The old 'boxkites' had almost vanished and strong front-engined monoplanes and biplanes with more or less reliable engines of 60–100 hp

were flying at speeds up to 110 km/hr (70 mph). Curiously enough, in the United States, where powered flight had started, progress was very much slower. The Wrights had been terribly secretive about their work and the close exchange of ideas that characterized aviation in the various European countries was lacking. Only Glenn Curtiss was really building aircraft, founding a long and line of mostly military planes.

Right: The Stinson company of America produced many hundreds of these single-engined Voyagers, but they were never able to compete with the might of Cessna, Beech and Piper.

After the First World War, civilian flying got underway again quite quickly. The public were now much more accustomed to the idea of men taking to the air, and in France, Britain and America there were large numbers of unemployed ex-military pilots to keep flying in the public eye. And this they did, with the travelling aerial circuses giving joyrides and the fantastic aerial stunt flying of the American 'barnstormers'. Slowly, an increasing number of private pilots and private owners of aircraft came on the scene.

The sudden cutback of wartime orders made most aviation firms bankrupt and few new designs were produced in any numbers for about five years. Joyriding,

Below: The Cessna 195 was introduced in 1947 and was a very straightforward design, powered by a single six-cylinder Continental air-cooled engine. Some are still flying today. *Below right*: Most Beech Bonanzas are easily recognizable with their distinctive vee-shaped tail surfaces.

Beech are one of America's largest light aircraft producers. They produced the first of many twin-engined Beech 18s in 1937 and could surely never have guessed that some would still be in service in the 1980s. Beech 18s are used as small airliners by some operators.

barnstorming and private flying were all done in ex-military trainers that could be picked up for a little money at war surplus depots. The Avro 504 in Britain, with its ancient rotary engine throwing burnt castor oil all over everything, and the Curtiss JN-4 'Jenny', the equivalent American type, were almost the only civil aeroplanes any of the public ever saw. The 'Jenny' had a big, solid engine (also designed by Curtiss) called the OX-5. So many thousands of these engines were built that for the next seven or eight years at least half the aircraft in America had one. There even grew up an OX-5 Club, the only fan club in the world to be organised around an aeroengine!

While all this was going on, a curious series of designs emerged around 1922–3, mostly in Britain and France but spreading to America for a short while. These were to embody the idea that aeroplanes should be as economical and small as possible (what we would now call ultralight aircraft) and in Britain an official competition was staged to encourage their design. Some very interesting results were obtained, the winner of the economy contest, for example, claiming 121 km (76 miles) flying on a single gallon of petrol.

But there was one man watching these trials who very soon saw that the whole thing was absurd, and that none of these pretty little aircraft were practical. What was wanted was a bigger aircraft, with enough power to fly in strong winds, carry two people and their luggage in some comfort and be strong enough to stand the rough usage of training flying and landings on bumpy airfields. This man was Captain Geoffrey de Havilland, a distinguished wartime designer, and within three years he had flown a light aeroplane that was to start a revolution

Above: Britain's de Havilland (later Hawker Siddeley) Heron has been used for a variety of tasks since the prototype made its first flight in May 1950. These duties include those of aerial ambulance, small airliner and executive transport. *Below*: Canada's de Havilland DHC-6 Twin Otter is a more modern aircraft but it performs similar duties with great success.

Above: **This picture gives a good impression of modern general aviation at work. Crates of merchandise, spare parts, perishable foodstuffs and busy executives are the most frequent loads.**

in private flying – the Moth.

This was an open-cockpit, two-seat biplane that flew a reasonable distance at about 135 km/hr (85 mph). It was light enough to manhandle on the ground and had folding wings to allow easy storage in a motor car's garage. It was safe, simple, strong and easy to fly and many people bought them for private use. Its Gipsy engine was based on half a wartime unit, of which there were many thousands easily available. It was the first practical light aircraft in the world and it was sold, built under licence and copied all over the world. The British government even started a scheme to subsidise flying clubs that operated Moths, a distinction that proved, sad to say, unique.

De Havilland produced many versions of the Moth and later many more sophisticated designs. It made all Europe air-minded and factories, flying clubs and aerodromes flourished everywhere.

Avro produced a similar aircraft called the Avian, and other manufacturers followed suit.

Biplanes like the Moth continued to be popular until about 1930, but by then de Havilland and other contemporary designers realized that however convenient open cockpit aeroplanes were for training, being easy to get in to and get out of, the private owner wanted something more comfortable. Before long, the small monoplane with an enclosed cabin and the luxury of a heater, began to become popular. Now men and women – for women had taken to the air as readily as men – could fly in their ordinary clothes, without having to dress up like Arctic explorers. This was the next major step forward in 'selling' private flying. The monoplane with a cabin was much more streamlined, and therefore fast, and engines were improving apace, now giving up to 200 hp. By 1939 some of the best light aircraft available, like the Percival Gull series, were capable of speeds up to 240 km/hr (150 mph). There were also several designs with retractable undercarriages, reducing air resistance and increasing speed still further.

A very similar pattern was followed in

Above: **Although it would win no prizes for beauty, the Short Skyvan is certainly a winner when it comes to moving large and unwieldy loads from one place to another. Basically a rectangular container with wings, it has become very popular.**

France, where private flying developed in much the same way. In Germany, and to a lesser extent Italy, the postwar revival of flying was coloured very much by political considerations. Germany had been virtually forbidden by international law to develop an aviation industry of her own after the First World War and had to content herself initially with constructing gliders. When the Germans began to design and build light aircraft in the early 1930s, not only did they have a lot of ground to make up, but it was necessary that they attract the maximum publicity to the successes of their new government. As a result, new German aeroplanes such as the Messerschmitt Bf 108 were very advanced, designed mainly to win competitions and prestige, and to double up military trainers. The Messerschmitt was eventually developed, despite Allied restrictions on Germany's military activities, into the famous Bf 109 fighter of the Second World War.

Cheap Petrol

In the USA the picture developed rather differently. The same enthusiasm for flying arose and soon became even more intense than in Europe. Petrol was much cheaper in America than in Europe and so operating expenses did not prevent the development of aero-engines much more powerful than those

in Europe. Together with the prevalent American desire for speed and size, it was not surprising that some of their private aircraft were being fitted with engines of 250–600 hp from about 1926 onwards. At first, private flying developed more slowly than in Europe, but the popularity and performance of the big Travel Air and Waco biplanes and scores of other designs had begun to lay the foundations of a whole new industry. Charles Lindbergh's first solo crossing of the Atlantic in his Ryan NYP (meaning 'New York–Paris) started such a great national wave of interest in flying that even the Wall Street stock market crash two years later could not extinguish it.

Designers

Many of the smaller aircraft companies did not survive the Depression and owing to a particular feature of the American aircraft industry, many familiar names disappeared. The reason was that in the United States the actual designer was seldom the man who founded or ran the company, while in England and the rest of Europe the man who marketed a successful design series did so under his own name. In consequence, American designers moved around the industry a good deal, working sometimes with others, sometimes in competition with them.

Only quite gradually did the familiar

names of today's general aircraft industry first emerge. Walter Beech, for example, began as a designer for Travel Air and only started under his own name in 1931 with a beautiful and very fast biplane called the Beech 17 'Staggerwing'. Surviving 'Staggerwings' are vintage collector's pieces today.

Bill Piper, whose name now covers a huge range of aircraft, as does Beech and Cessna, began by working for a man called Taylor. In fact it was the Taylor Cub of 1932 that provided America with its first really popular, low-cost sport aircraft. When Piper set up on his own it was with his version of the Cub that one of American aviation's greatest success stories began. Oddly enough, Clyde Cessna (who had started designing aircraft in 1912) stopped running the firm bearing his name in 1934, handing over control to his nephew Duane Wallace; yet this company went on to become the world's greatest single supplier of light aircraft with a new team of designers drawing up the plans. Clyde Cessna himself did however maintain his link

One of the latest trends in light aircraft design is the incorporation of T-shaped tails. This configuration is said to increase the efficiency of the rudder and elevators by positioning them out of the turbulence caused by the aeroplane's fuselage and propeller.

with the company in the capacity of a senior consultant.

The Americans pioneered many advances in private flying, such as instrument flying, all-metal aircraft and tricycle undercarriages (ie, nosewheel rather than tailwheel). The Luscombe, for example, was not only the first production all-metal light aircraft in the world to enter production, it was also the most popular aircraft type in the United States before the Second World War, some 6,000 examples being built in all. With the advent of the Second World

War all passenger and private flying in Europe ceased, but America's industrial potential and her sheer size meant that the development of these activities could continue without interrupting her war effort. This was to prove a great advantage to the Americans after the war, when they were also fortunate enough to have a continuing demand for light aircraft, a booming economy and an industry geared to the resumption of private flying.

The British light aircraft industry was based largely on small and long-established family firms and with little real industrial interest it withered away

completely. In France, where the government was making strenuous efforts to revive their aircraft industry, the private owner and flying club movement was seen as a part of this national drive, and accordingly their light aircraft industry flourished, as indeed it still does. It was in France that a very special kind of light aviation grew up after the war, in parallel with a similar, but larger movement in the United States – do-it-yourself aircraft building.

Encouraged by the subsidies granted by their government, hundreds of Frenchmen in every walk of life began, from 1946 onwards, to design and build their own aircraft. If they built an aircraft entirely from French materials and allowed it to be used for some of the time for flying club instruction, they got back quite a large proportion of the original cost price. These aircraft were all either single- or two-seaters and were powered in the first few years by 55 or 65 hp engines. As the demand for more per-

Above: Possessing excellent STOL characteristics, the Pilatus Britten-Norman Islander is a tough, economical mini-airliner and general-purpose transport. *Below*: This dazzling Swiss-built Helio Courier has a ski undercarriage.

formance (and the added margin of safety that goes with it) grew, so engine power went up to 90–95 hp.

Currently, the majority of homebuilts are fitted either with one of the numerous varieties of the modified Volkswagen car engine or with the excellent Continentals and Lycomings, rated at about 100 hp The Volkswagen engine was the foundation of a whole generation of ultralight single-seaters, to the considerable embarrassment of this famous car company at first, for they were still under the post-Second World War embargo on aviation activities imposed on Germany.

René Fournier of France has produced a series of very attractive looking aerobatic aircraft, both single- and two-seaters. These have gained a reputation for being extremely pleasant to fly and are powered by variants of the basic Volkswagen engine.

The home-building craze spread to Britain, where there had been a number of promising ultralight designs flying before the Second World War, and it was helped by the increasing practice of designers selling plans for the more popular types for others to build. There are flourishing and more or less self-governing national bodies in both Britain and France who are charged with the technical and training aspects of amateur aircraft construction. Every year sees numerous additions to the ranks of homebuilts and ultralights as each individual builder tries to outdo his comrades.

It is in America, however, that the home-building movement has really taken off. The widespread technical ability and constructional skills of many Americans, especially among the ranks of employees of the aircraft-building and airline industries, has led to a vast national movement which turns out with several thousand homebuilts at their annual convention held each year at Oshkosh, Wisconsin.

The interest generated by such conventions has resulted in the building and flying of aircraft with extremely advanced aerodynamic ideas, for many of these little aircraft are sophisticated all-metal designs with retractable undercarriages and include such features as delta-shaped wings, tail-first configurations, and suchlike. There are even some solar-powered ultralights now flying in the

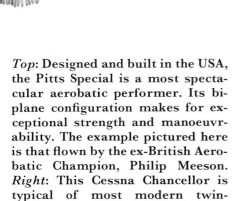

United States, perhaps serving notice that these keen amateurs intend pointing the way ahead, rather than waiting for the 'real' aircraft manufacturers to do so.

The light aircraft industry in Britain never recovered from the effects of the Second World War, for by 1960 there was little left of it. The splendid single- and twin-engined designs of the Miles brothers had come to an end. The old Auster, a kind of throwback to the prewar American Taylor Cub, soldiered on (it had been an artillery spotter during the war) and it says a good deal for the soundness of the original design that many hundreds were sold all over the world and still fly in some numbers.

In a last desperate attempt to revive the once supreme position held by Britain's light aircraft industry, Miles and Auster joined forces and eventually emerged as a new company called Beagle. Headed by Peter Masefield, an aviator of vast experience, the company produced some promising new designs, among them the single-engined Pup and

Top: Designed and built in the USA, the Pitts Special is a most spectacular aerobatic performer. Its biplane configuration makes for exceptional strength and manoeuvrability. The example pictured here is that flown by the ex-British Aerobatic Champion, Philip Meeson. *Right*: This Cessna Chancellor is typical of most modern twin-engined executive aircraft.

Pilatus, the Swiss-based aircraft constructors, have long specialized in the construction of aeroplanes capable of STOL performance. Here, a PC-6 Turbo Porter model demonstrates this useful capability in a most spectacular manner.

the twin-engined 206 Bassett, both admirable aircraft and a joy to fly. But it was too late to break back into the market outside Britain and the company even failed to build up a strong home-sales position. There was not even a new British aeroengine available by this stage, for while the old Gipsy Major continued, and still continues, to give sterling service, insufficient funds were there to provide a successor. And so it was that the Americans moved in.

Until 1960–1 customers couldn't even buy an American aircraft in Britain if they wanted to, and the ageing Tiger

The Embraer company of Brazil is making sizeable inroads into the fiercely-competitive world general aviation market with the sleek Bandeirante.

Moths, Percival Proctors, Miles Magisters and de Havilland Rapides, released from their military service, were the mainstay of flying clubs and the majority of private owners. A strict ban on imports reflected the Treasury's view of the relative positions of the pound and dollar, and Britain's shortage of the latter. After 1960 however, under a government concession, the dollar imports were allowed when their comparable British product was not available and the floodgates were opened. The Pipers, the Cessnas and the Beechcraft were soon swarming over British airfields. They brought with them a number of attractive innovations. Cabin comfort was usually better than on contemporary European types, for they had better-designed and equipped instrument panels. Many of them also had tricycle undercarriages.

A Brazilian-built Embraer Ipanema engaged in crop-spraying work.

There was another great change coming up, initially no bigger than the smallest cloud upon the private pilot's horizon. Where the average American private pilot of this period was growing up with the earliest examples of radio navigational aids, his British counterpart trained on non-radio aircraft, often featuring open cockpits, and was taught to navigate entirely by map, watch and compass. He bitterly resented the invasion of these new devices, and considered them unnecessary, expensive and somewhat bewildering. Above all, their greatest 'crime' was to introduce ground control into private flying, thus destroying the feeling of freedom that drew many people towards flying.

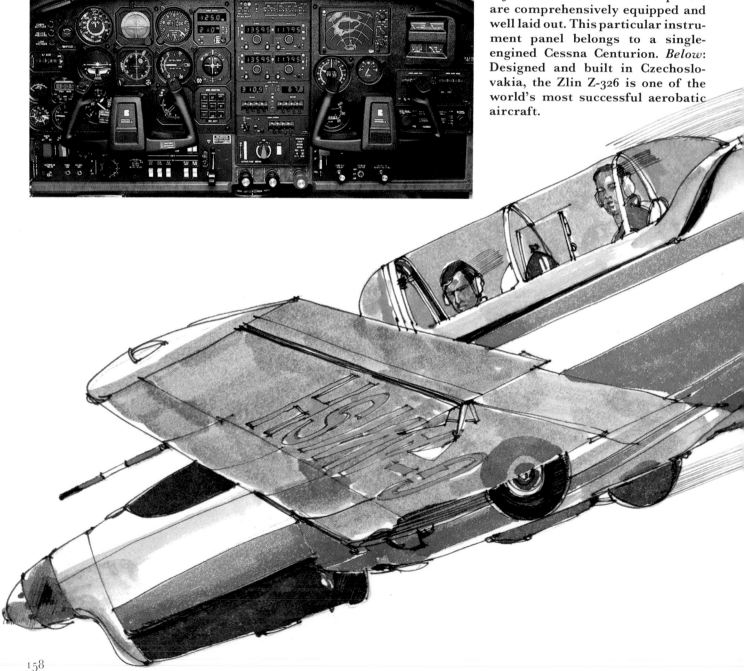

Left: Modern GA instrument panels are comprehensively equipped and well laid out. This particular instrument panel belongs to a single-engined Cessna Centurion. *Below*: Designed and built in Czechoslovakia, the Zlin Z-326 is one of the world's most successful aerobatic aircraft.

Left: Carrying stretcher patients to hospital in doublequick time is one of the most important aspects of general aviation. Here a French-built Dassault-Breguet Falcon, powered by two rear-mounted jets, acts as an air ambulance.

It is difficult now, looking back on that period of transition to realize how serious the situation seemed to many pilots. The modern flyer, travelling around in even the smallest two-seater, is at home with a radio that will tune in to 380 different channels (the new ones can be tuned to no less than 700), a radio compass and a very high frequency (VHF) Omni receiver, the latter two for obtaining directional bearings. In 1960, if a European light aircraft had a radio at all it would have been an ex-RAF one capable of operating on either four or nine frequen-

cies at the most, and these could only be altered by changing the crystals inside the set. This could and often was done in the air but it was not uncommon to hear a pilot confess that he could not fly to a particularly airfield because he didn't have the frequency.

What was happening meantime in the United States? As we have said, the production and development of light aircraft continued throughout the Second World War. There was, however, a strong break in continuity in that few of the big prewar makers survived with peace. Luscombe, the all-metal favourites of the late-1930s faded away, as did Waco, Aeronca and many others. Beech (who had only started on his own in 1931) survived, and continued the tradition towards greater luxury, power and performance that was started with his famous 'Staggerwing'. Cessna had been something of a 'one-design' company before 1945 with their big radial-engined Airmaster, but postwar they began the series of light two-, four- and later six-seater single-engined types that

today fill the skies. Meanwhile, Bill Piper built on his success with the little single-engined Cub (which is still in production) and began to branch out into larger and more powerful types of aircraft.

The American light aircraft industry is backed by a strong economy, and a population that has taken to the air in large numbers to cover the great distances of their land. The need to sell larger and larger numbers of aircraft to keep ahead in a market as buoyant as this, not to mention the intense rivalry between the big companies, has resulted in the domination of the world light aircraft scene by American products. And the aeroengine market, too, has been pretty well tied up by the major American manufacturers.

Executives

The smallest aircraft for training and flying club use and for use by the economically-minded tend to have two seats and engines that generate around 100–150 hp. These use about four gallons of fuel per hour and cruise at a little over 60 km/hr (100 mph). After the two-seaters come a whole wide range of four-seaters, with engines rated at up to 300 hp and capable of speeds approaching 320 km/hr (200 mph). There are, in addition, a few six-seater singles, these being almost entirely intended for commercial and charter work; taking business executives to meetings in distant cities in double-quick time, or serving as airborne ambulances.

The twin-engined aircraft first came about because there were no engines of sufficient power to give the required higher performance alone, and this is still largely true today. The extra power gives different advantages; more seats, higher speed, better flying and take-off performance – and, of course, greater safety standards. Twin-engined aircraft are certainly more expensive, but their speed and ability to carry comprehensive 'avionics' (aviation electronics) for communications with the outside world and navigation assistance make them popular for long-distance commercial flying. A more recent development in the aero-engine field has produced a whole new realm of business aeroplanes – namely, the jets. Aircraft fitted with this type of engine are a long way from the true private aircraft of the old days and approach the small airliner in terms of size and performance.

Aerobatics

Unfortunately, the standardization imposed by very large production runs of the more popular types has taken a lot of the individuality of light aircraft away and the requirements of modern training means that they are all safe and fairly easy to fly, though a little dull in external appearance. But if the majority of modern light aircraft find themselves looking the same as their competitors, it is pleasing that there have arisen a number of specialist types in other fields that are still exciting and highly individualistic. The requirements of such

These three Dassault-Breguet twin-jets sum up the future of general aviation – sleeker shapes are the way ahead.

activities as aerial photographic surveying, agricultural work such as crop-spraying and the growing need for short take-off and landing (STOL) characteristics have produced a rather more eccentric series of aircraft.

Probably the ultimate in this line are aircraft specifically designed for the purpose of performing aerobatics. The sport of aerobatics is almost as old as air racing and the increasing complexity of manoeuvres demanded by the judges at national and international competitions the world over has resulted in a range of specialized aircraft as carefully designed and refined as any wartime fighter. Apart from the purpose-built air racers and the vintage types carefully preserved and brought out only for flying displays, aerobatic single- and two-seaters are really the last demanding and truly individual light aircraft to be built. For the ordinary private pilot, the skills of the challenge now consists of learning the new techniques of flying with instruments and mastering the complexities of following the restrictive – but highly necessary – airways that now criss-cross the continents.

What of the future? It seems fairly certain that new design trends will be in the direction of increased economy, reduced engine noise and even higher standards of safety, and that the fastest growing sector will probably be that of business and charter operations. The use of small aircraft in business is spreading down to the light single-engined types, and in the United States, general aviation is now the largest single sector of all, having outstripped even the airlines in terms of take-offs and landings.

PATROL AND RECONNAISSANCE
Search, Spy and Special-Mission

In any kind of conflict, it has always been an advantage to have some idea of what your opponent is about to do. Even during some of the earliest battles in history, scouts were sent out from the main force to see if they could gather any information on the size and movement of the enemy. It was obvious that the best place to view something was from the top of a hill and, of course, the higher the hill the more the scouts could see. This realization, coupled with man's lust to fly, did much to bring about the first recorded use of military aviation. It was on 26 June 1794 that Captain Coutelle of the French army floated above the Battle of Fleurus beneath a tethered balloon filled with hydrogen gas and spent the whole day signalling every move made by the enemy forces. As a result, a great deal of credit for the subsequent victory must go to him.

Once one side has an advantage over the other it does not take very long before the other side makes efforts to equalize the odds, so balloons began to play quite a large part in battle strategy and continued to hold their position of prominence until well into the twentieth century, reaching the peak of their popularity during the First World War. Under heavy combat conditions however, the weaknesses of the balloon as a means of reconnaissance had long since been shown up. They had to be attached to the ground by means of a line to stop them drifting away from the scene of the battle or, even worse, drifting towards the enemy lines, and so the height to which they could climb was severely restricted. This, together with the fact that the balloons had to float reasonably near to the enemy lines in order for their crews to see anything, made them sitting ducks for enemy guns. They were ideal targets – being both large *and* stationary!

The fragile aeroplanes of the early 1900s would have proved the ideal answer to these problems, but in those

early days of aviation the army wanted nothing to do with them. These strange devices seemed to struggle just to get up into the air, let alone stay there for sustained periods. So it was not until 22 October, 1911 – almost eight years after the Wright brothers first flew, – that an aeroplane was used in a military role. Then Captain Piazza of the Italian army, sketch pad in hand, flew a reconnaissance mission over Turkish positions in a frail-looking Blériot monoplane. Piazza also became the first man ever to fly a photo-reconnaissance mission when he took a large and clumsy box camera up with him on one of these risky excursions.

Scribbled Notes

Aircraft were by this time slightly more reliable, so it was perhaps inevitable that the world's first air force should come into being – namely the Royal Flying Corps, formed in April 1912. The main aircraft to be flown by this enthusiastic but inexperienced body of men was the BE.2. It was built primarily for

The observer in this Henschel Hs 126 photographs enemy shipping.

use as a reconnaissance aircraft, with an emphasis on stability to allow the pilots to concentrate on operating the cumbersome cameras of the day and on taking down scribbled notes about what they spotted below. When war broke out in 1914 the RFC found out just how much they had to learn about aerial reconnaissance. The pilots frequently mistook shadows cast by trees onto roads for columns of enemy troops, and they quite often lost their way and were forced to land to ask someone where they were –

Royal Flying Corps groundcrew surround a BE.2c

Moments before embarking on a night mission, the crew of an RFC RE.8 show signs of tension. The RE.8's 'flexible' and fixed side machine-guns are clearly visible.

on many an occasion to find out that they had strayed far behind enemy lines!

By 1915 however, the RFC pilots had learned how to recognise certain signs and reconnaissance aircraft were supplying ground troops with detailed photographs of enemy positions, as well as directing ground artillery fire. This was done by imagining the target as the centre of a clock face and directing the gunners by quoting a time and a distance; for example '3 o'clock, 100 yards' meant that the next shell must land 100 yards further to the right, and so on until the target was hit.

The Germans soon realized that the only way of preventing RFC reconnaissance aircraft reporting what they had seen was to shoot them out of the sky as quickly as possible. This is exactly

A Focke-Wulf Fw 189 Uhu, *das Fliegende Auge*, **bombs enemy tanks while on a reconnaissance mission.**

Japan's twin-engined Mitsubishi Ki-46 Dinah.

what happened on numerous occasions to the BE.2s. They were such stable aircraft for their time that their manoeuvrability suffered as a result. Their inability to escape from enemy fighters, especially the latest Fokker Eindeckers, gained them the unfortunate nickname of 'Fokker fodder'.

Because so many BE.2s were being lost, the Royal Aircraft Factory came up with a new design to replace it. The new plane was known as the RE.8. Although more than 4,000 of these aircraft were built their service record was far from impressive. They had fragile wings, went into a spin at the drop of a hat and because the fuel tanks were placed right behind the engine, they frequently burst into flames if forced to crash-land. The RE.8 was nicknamed 'Harry Tate' and was noted more for the large quantities in which it was built than for any qualities it had in the air.

Better Cameras

Between the two world wars great progress was made not only in the reliability and speed of aircraft but also in the quality of cameras, film and photographic equipment available. When cameras were first used for aerial reconnaissance purposes the one type of film available was only capable of recording colours at the blue end of the spectrum. Anything that was a reddish colour, therefore, very often did not show up in early photographs. With new scientific discoveries however, cameras were soon being made that not only recorded everything regardless of colour but also worked almost completely automatically. At first this was achieved by using cameras powered by tiny 'windmills' sticking out from the fuselage into the passing airflow, but it was not long before these gave way to cameras operated by small electric motors. This innovation, and the use of a whole bank of cameras rather than just a single one, made it possible to record entire strips of land with a series of overlapping photographs. With one camera mounted in the fuselage pointing straight down, and one one either side of the fuselage pointing down at an angle, it was possible for the strip of land covered to be as much as sixteen kilometres (ten miles) wide, provided the reconnaissance aircraft flew high enough.

With the advent of the Second World War, the development of military aircraft was stepped up. Reconnaissance was even more vital than it had been in earlier conflicts, and before any major bombing operation pilots carefully studied detailed photographs of the target area. It also became important for air force intelligence officers to know how much damage had been done by

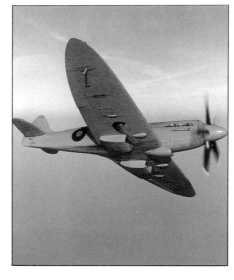

Above: **A photo-recce Spitfire in standard colours.**

Below: **The array of radar antennae on a Bf 110.**

their bombing raids, so photographs of the target area taken just after an attack were brought into use to help ascertain the effects.

By this time, the RAF's Coastal Command had a large number of patrol and photographic reconnaissance (PR) squadrons, which were gradually equipped with aircraft more suited to their high-specialized needs. These aircraft were either 'pure' patrol aircraft such as the portly Short Sunderland flyingboat, or – for PR – special variants of the fastest and most manoeuvrable contemporary combat types available. Probably the best known of these were the Spitfire PR variants. They were renowned for their spectacular performance, particularly their long range, and regularly flew dangerous photographic missions over occupied Europe. It was on one of these routine sorties that it was discovered that the Nazis were using defensive radar in western France. This came as a surprise to the Allies as they thought that they had a monopoly on equipment of this

kind. On another occasion a top-secret V-I 'flyingbomb' installation was spotted quite by chance on a photograph taken by a Spitfire flying at high altitude over Peenemunde on the Baltic coast of Germany. Another famous British aircraft adapted for reconnaissance duties was the de Havilland Mosquito. As they were made almost entirely out of wood, parts for Mosquitos were built in such unromantic places as furniture factories and the workshops of piano-makers. Photo-recce 'Wooden Wonders' were externally similar to standard aircraft, but carried neither armament nor any other pieces of 'unnecessary' equipment. This improved performance by reducing weight, and also saved space for vital photographic gear. Being unarmed, their only defence lay in their ability to fly very fast, often climbing to high altitude to avoid enemy interception. In fact they were so difficult to intercept that towards the end of the war they had reduced their loss rate to only one aircraft in every 2,000 missions.

'Painted Cloud'

The use of reconnaissance aircraft during the Second World War was certainly not restricted only to the Allies. The Japanese possessed what was undoubtebly one of the finest photo-recce aircraft of the war in the beautifully streamlined Mitsubishi Ki-46 *Dinah*. Powered by two 1,050 hp piston engines, the *Dinah* was so fast that in 1942, the first year of Japan's participation in the war, they were almost free to take pictures of anything they wanted because nothing the Allies had could catch them. Another Japanese aircraft which excelled in reconnaissance work as a result of its high speed was the Nakajima C6N Saiun, which frequently left the American Corsair and Hellcat fighter pilots aghast with astonishment. Saiun was a

The jet-engined Avado Av 234 was very advanced for its time.

Lockheed's PV-2 Harpoon, USA's principal postwar patrol aircraft.

beautiful Japanese aircraft whose name meant 'painted cloud' but the Allies who referred to all enemy aircraft by special code names, called the C6N *Myrt*.

The Germans enjoyed a greater degree of success than Japan, for the Luftwaffe's

reconnaissance effort was geared to high-altitude operations beyond the reach of enemy fighters. The Junkers Ju 86P and R variants were converted bombers developed for high-level photo-recce. To be successful at photo-recce and to survive,

The RAF's sturdy Westland Lysander excelled at aerial spotting work.

an aircraft must either fly very fast or be capable of climbing to extremely high altitudes to avoid enemy interceptors. Thanks to its pressurized cockpit, the Ju 86 could certainly fly high enough to escape marauding fighters, and this thwarted British interception.

The Luftwaffe also operated one aircraft successfully in the tactical reconnaissance role against the Soviet Union with their twin-engined Focke-Wulf Fw 189 Uhu (Owl). Often called *das Fliegende Auge*, 'the flying eye', it was notable for its excellent handling qualities and performed well under difficult combat conditions. With an uncanny ability to withstand heavy battle damage, the Fw 189 was always flitting across the front line looking for chinks in the enemy's armour. While the Uhu was serving with distinction against the Russians, another Focke-Wulf product, the big four-engined Fw 200 Condor, maintained the Luftwaffe's relentless patrol over the Atlantic Ocean. Operating in cooperation with packs of German U-boats, the Condor became the scourge of Allied shipping, with many a convoy falling prey to its deadly bombardment.

It was not only with very large aircraft like the Condor that the Germans asserted their expertise, for at the other end of the scale was the tiny Fieseler Storch spotter plane, designed for take-off and

A Storch lands on a desert strip.

landing in extremely restricted spaces. Characterized by its spindly undercarriage legs and a deceptively frail general appearance, the Storch was used extensively for staff transport, but achieved far greater fame operating in close cooperation with ground forces. They would

The LV-2 was one of the US Navy's many maritime patrol and reconnaisance versions of the famous Constellation airliner. The electronic reconnaisance equipment situated on top of the fuselage and mars the Constellation's lines.

frequently fly up to take a closer look at the enemy's activities and land again to pass on vital information to the commanders who sat planning their next move. During the desert campaign in North Africa the Storch proved particularly suitable for this type of activity.

In 1944 the Luftwaffe brought into action the world's first jet-propelled reconnaissance aircraft, the Arado Ar 234 Blitz. This aircraft was fitted with two Jumo turbojet engines, one mounted under each tapered wing, and succeeded brilliantly on high-level photographic missions throughout mainland Europe and even over Britain, thus becoming the first German reconnaissance aircraft to do so in comparative safety since the early days of the war. As if its jet engines were not enough in the way of technical innovation, the Blitz featured a pressurized cockpit, an ejector seat, a rear-firing, periscope-sighted cannon and an autopilot. Developments in the field of jet propulsion in the latter stages of the Second World War were of great benefit to the designers of reconnaissance aircraft. The speed bestowed by these radical new engines promised a significant increase in a pilot's chances of survival when overflying enemy territory to secure photographs.

Lumbering Giant

Sleek little jets certainly looked like being the way ahead, but this did not mean that the day of the lumbering giants was entirely over – least of all in the USA, where there was a strong tradition of modifying operational bomber aircraft for photo-recce duties. This was partly because only very large

aircraft were capable of carrying the enormous loads of fuel required to keep airborne on flights over very long distances, not to mention the masses of cameras and electronic equipment

A Tupolev Tu-16 *Badger* banks over the gigantic waves of the North Sea at low level. This aircraft has performed with distinction in Soviet naval service. *Above right*: Tupolev Tu-126 *Bear* seen from an unusual angle.

needed to maintain adequate surveillance.

The giant RB-36, for example, was derived from the B-36 bomber and served with the USAF during the fifties. It was

One of Britains fleet of Vickers Armstrongs Valiants is loaded with cameras before a reconnaissance flight in the late 1950s.

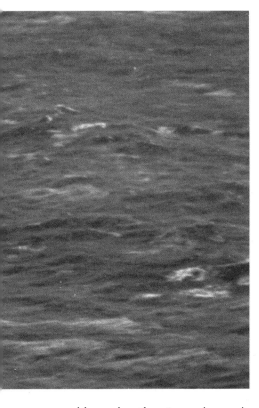

powered by no less than *ten* engines – six 'pusher' radials and four turbojets – and introduced new standards of sophistication to the field of airborne reconnaissance equipment. A crew of 22 was needed just to fly it and tend to the fourteen cameras it carried in its gigantic fuselage. Unrefuelled flights of up to 24 hours were regularly flown, and if the underbelly bomb-bays were used to house extra fuel then the flight duration could be extended to 30 hours or more. A standing joke between RB-36 crews was that a calendar featured prominently amongst the aircraft's instruments!

Britain followed the tried and tested American policy when they introduced PR versions of the Vickers-Armstrongs Valiant and English Electric Canberra jet bombers in the mid-fifties. Just as converted bombers were ideal recce aircraft for times when a lot of photographic and electronic equipment needed to be carried over very long distances, so converted fighters are perfect for times when a fast reconnaissance sweep is called for.

Recce Pods

This is particularly true when heavy anti-aircraft fire is anticipated in the vicinity of the target. In these conditions the pilot must try to get in under the radar cover, climb over the target to get his pictures and head for home at top speed with fingers crossed.

In the fifties the USAF operated a special photo-recce version of the McDonnell Voodoo fighter, designated RF-101. It was later used by the nationalist Chinese of Taiwan. Cameras were mounted in a modified nosecone fitted with toughened glass panels, and more were angled to take photographs from positions in the fuselage.

Another McDonnell product, the ubiquitous F-4 Phantom, has been turned out in sixteen different variants, among these being three reconnaissance versions now in service with the US Marine Corps and USAF, and such countries as Japan, Iran and West Germany. Phantoms serving with the RAF in the photo-recce role have pods slung either under the fuselage or on special pylons beneath the wings which can be opened up to reveal cameras and a multitude of intricate sensors. When a Phantom lands after a mission, ground crew race out to collect the cameras and will remove the rolls of film – already developed automatically

Below: **A Vigilante maintains a close watch over ships of the US Navy.**

against it! Its maximum level speed is 3,384 km/h (2,115 mph) and it can reach 25,000 metres (82,000 ft) in 2 min 34 sec. The PR version has camera windows in its nose and some have been seen with sideways-looking radar. The *Foxbat* is built largely of steel with titanium wing-edges to allow it to withstand the very high temperatures which result when travelling at high speeds. The Japanese and Americans had a chance to look at a *Foxbat* in detail when a Soviet pilot defected to Japan with his fighter in September 1976. Experts took his plane apart and after they had examined it, crated it up and sent it back to the USSR – without the pilot.

Soviet Union

The idea of using bombers as a basis for reconnaissance versions seems to have appealed to the Soviet Union too. Soviet long-range reconnaissance aircraft make a frequent practice of trying to infiltrate western airspace to test NATO early warning systems and fighter reaction. Among the types used on these missions is the veteran Tupolev Tu-95 (known to NATO as *Bear*). This vast silver aircraft has a long thin fuselage and graceful swept-back wings. The *Bear* made its maiden flight in 1954 and was designed primarily as an intercontinental strategic bomber. It was an obvious choice for adaptation to reconnaissance duties, as it had plenty of internal space to cram with banks of complex electronics and the very latest in sophisticated camera equipment.

A Lockheed P-3C Orion sweeps over a vast, sparkling expanse of sea. It has been the mainstay of the US Navy's maritime patrol for many years.

whilst in flight. By using two separate cameras, photo-recce aircraft can produce stereoscopic pictures that give a clear idea of the terrain and whether it is going to be hard work for foot soldiers.

Another exciting photo-recce jet is the North American Rockwell RA-5C Vigilante. Capable of reaching 2,230 km/hr (1,385 mph), this hefty carrierborne aircraft has a considerable advantage when overflying enemy territory, as it can outfly most enemy interceptors. The Vigilante took over from the Vought RF-8 Crusader, a single-seat fighter and reconnaissance aircraft first flown back in 1955. One advantages of types such as Crusaders was that they were less recognizable to the enemy as PR aircraft, since

they were outwardly very similar to the fighter and strike versions they were derived from. They can be mixed in with an attack on ground positions, though the smoke and explosions from the battle make good photography very difficult. It is normally better to have them fly with armed escorts on their own reconnaissance missions.

One aircraft that does not need an escort and can safely rely on sheer speed is the Soviet MiG-25, known to NATO as *Foxbat*. This sleek single-seater appeared over Israeli airspace at the height of a major conflict against the Arabs, but the four Phantoms 'scrambled' to intercept it could not shoot it down, for it was even faster than the missiles they fired

A Grumman E-2 Hawkeye shows off its huge flying saucer-shaped radar.

Contrarotating propellers are a notable feature of the Avro Shackleton.

The Soviets did not follow the trend towards jet engines with this and similar large aircraft, preferring the better fuel economy of four massive 15,000 hp Kuznetsov turboprops. When RAF fighters 'scramble' to escort *Bears* away from North Sea rigs and the eastern coastline of the UK, they slide into close formation with the intruding aircraft until it finally turns for home. A very similar machine to the *Bear* is the *Moss*, the Tupolev Tu-126. It has the same engines as the *Bear*, and a similar general appearance, but mounted above the fuselage is a sinister-looking radar disc. The *Moss* carries a crew of twelve, allow-ing for more than one watch to be maintained.

The *Bison* is a much older type with four jet engines, the reconnaissance version having a long refuelling probe in the nose which allows it to top up with fuel whilst in flight. The Tupolev Tu-16, or *Badger*, is about the same age as the *Bison*. It has two jet engines, and has a radar fairing in the nosecone which contains a special vantage point for the bomb-aimer. *Badger* has been used by com-munist China, Egypt and Iraq as well as the naval and air arms of the USSR. It is one of the types used to shadow NATO naval exercises in the Atlantic. Another shadower of naval activities is the Ilyu-shin Il-38. This prop-driven patrol air-craft has a MAD(Magnetic Anomoly Detector) tail sting and is used to collect ELINT (Electronic Intelligence), the technical jargon for radio conversations between ships and aircraft. If ELINT is tape-recorded and analysed it gives a good idea of drills and reaction times on ships and aircraft of a rival nation, but this is only a fraction of the data that can be gathered.

Homing Torpedoes

At first glance there is a close similarity between the Il-38 and Canada's primary maritime reconnaissance aircraft, the Canadair Argus. Both have MAD tail stings, four engines and a single rudder. The Argus however, is a converted Brit-annia airliner with somewhat larger overall dimensions. It carries homing torpedoes in its massive bomb-bay with additional weaponry slung under the wings. The Canadians are heavily in-volved in peace-keeping work for the United Nations along with Sweden who have also maintained a strong army, navy and air force. Among the fighter and reconnaissance types which the Swedes use to cover the Baltic and the Gulf of Finland is the Saab Viggen.

Infrared

The Viggen is easy to spot because it has its 'tail' surfaces at the front and delta wings close behind. The two photo-recce versions carry the usual range of cameras and infra-red sensors, the latter being capable of detecting the heat differences of objects on the ground, so as to show where men and vehicles are working. Infra-red photography will even show which aircraft on an airfield have been fuelled up ready for take-off, by 'seeing' through their outer skin and into their fuel tanks! The PR version of the Viggen is armed with two air-to-air missiles for self defence, while the maritime version carries a comprehensive radar system and ECM (Electronic Counter-Meas-ures) pods. Though neutral, the Swedes

maintain a thorough patrol of their coastline borders.

A rather more specialized application for aircraft than photo-reconnaissance is that of airborne ground command. The most spectacular examples are the Boeing E-4 AABNCP, highly-modified Boeing 747 airliners that have been specially equipped for the President of the United States. These unbelievably expensive aircraft are fitted with elaborate communications equipment and one would take the President out of Washington in the event of a nuclear war

but would keep him in close communication with his forces wherever they happened to find themselves in action. A simpler version of this idea is the Boeing EC-135, which is a flying command post and radio tracking station. The Israelis used a 707 in this role when they raided Entebbe in June 1976 to rescue one of their airliners which had been hijacked and forced to land in Uganda. The 707 remained airborne over the airport and monitored short-range transmissions from stations below. These were then passed on to Israel so that the cabinet

was able to listen to the entire operation as it was happening. More recently, the Rhodesians employed this method on their raids into Zambia.

Indo-China

The idea of a control ship is not new. The French were the first to employ one in Indo-China in the 1950s, when the commander of a paratroop raid deep into enemy-held territory worked from a Dakota. This aerial command plane could carry much more powerful radio equipment and had no hills to block its transmissions to friendly territory. Moreover, the commander was not entangled

A Lockheed Viking is catapulted off the deck of a US Navy carrier.

Counter-Measures) equipment. Even the bulbous pod on top of the tailfin is packed to capacity. The odd-looking probe on the nose is used for receiving fuel during mid-air link-ups with tanker planes.

An OV-10A Bronco in aggressive mood.

in the ground fighting and could get a clearer view of the overall situation. This is perhaps the biggest advantage of aerial reconnaissance.

In Britain the classic patrol aircraft of the postwar years has been the Avro Shackleton, first flown in 1949 and directly descended from the Lancaster bomber of the Second World War. During its long career into the seventies its engines and equipment have been continuously updated and improved. The Shackleton is due to end its service in the RAF sometime in the early eighties, but South African aircraft still patrol from the Cape of Good Hope to cover the South Atlantic and the Indian Ocean. In its final role with the RAF the Shackleton became a AEW (Airborne Early Warning) aircraft with a flight crew of three 'up front' and an additional eight

Gannet

electronics operators situated in a special compartment deep in the fuselage.

Prior to the installation of early warning radar in the Shackleton, this task had been performed by the Fairey Gannet, an aircraft designed at the end of the last war to make use of the then new turbo-prop engine. In the aircraft-carrierborne anti-submarine warfare role it carried weapons in an internal bomb-bay, later crammed with sophisticated radar equipment. The two radar operators worked huddled within the fuselage, while the pilot sat in a little bubble-shaped cockpit canopy overlooking the Gannet's unusual contrarotating propellers. With this type of arrangement, the pilot could save fuel by turning off one propeller while cruising, but could immediately switch to full power (both propellers) if an attack was imminent. Contrarotating

propellers both turn around the same axis, but spin in opposing directions.

The United States has a vast coastline, so somewhat predictably it, too, has taken care to develop several very effective maritime patrol aircraft over the years. The Lockheed P-3 Orion is a good example. Not only is it being used by the US Navy, but substantial numbers have seen service with Norway, Australia, New Zealand and Spain. The P-3 Orion is a four-engined turboprop aircraft, that can patrol an area far out at sea for up to three hours at a time. The Orion made its first flight in 1958, which makes it a fairly old aircraft by the standards of the eighties, yet it is still in production.

Flying Saucer-Shaped

Although the Lockheed Orion is serving in large numbers, it is the Grumman company that must be regarded as the principal supplier of patrol and surveillance aircraft to the United States armed forces, for they have been building them

since the 1950s. Their E-2 Hawkeye is a turboprop-powered, carrierborne AEW aircraft with a characteristic flying saucer-shaped radar dish mounted high above the fuselage on reinforced pylons. It has a computer on board which in the latest versions can detect targets even against a background of 'clutter' – interference on the radar scanner caused by features rising up out of the ground, particularly undulating terrain.

Older American carrierborne types in the patrol and anti-submarine team were the Grumman Tracker and Grumman Tracer. The Tracker, as its name suggests, was a submarine hunter and was readily recognizable with its stocky fuselage and long, retractable MAD sting. Among the weapons carried by the Tracker were echo-sounding depth charges for blasting enemy submarines lurking below the waves, and up to six torpedoes slung beneath the wings. The Tracer was even more eyecatching however, for although both aircraft were piston-engined with a crew of four highly-skilled airmen, only the Tracer carried a huge oval radar scanner high above its fuselage, Hawkeye-fashion.

Despite the fact that this configuration has been common to certain AEW aircraft for a number of years now, the technical jargon for the latest equipment being carried is AWACS, (airborne warning and control system). The advantage of AWACS is that it can detect and track enemy aircraft over both land and water and is particularly effective in detecting aircraft flying at very low levels. Normal land-based radar stations pick up lots of 'clutter', so by hugging the terrain an intruding strike aircraft can fly under its beams and avoid detection. The AWACS system looks *down* at the scene rather than up at it, and so allows radar coverage to start well beyond the coastline. By plotting incoming flights it

can work out an interception route for friendly fighters and pass this back to bases ashore.

Grumman also produce the EA-6B Prowler, which operates as an ECM (Electronic Counter-Measures) aircraft. ECM is the technique of jamming radar and radio by locating an enemy frequency and broadcasting 'noises' over it or simply blanking it out with a stronger transmission. This means that the enemy's missiles cannot receive radar guidance and their fighter pilots are prevented from receiving outside information. The Prowler carries five self-contained ECM pods with a total of ten jamming transmitters. It can scan the radio bands, pick up an enemy station, jam it, and still be looking for other enemy wavebands at the same time. Prowlers were an essential part of the US Navy's operations over Vietnam in the

late sixties and early seventies, where they caused havoc with Communist air and ground forces alike.

The Grumman Intruder looks like the Prowler, and also has a wide cockpit since it has a side-by-side seating arrangement for its two-person crew. It performs aircraft carrierborne strike, electronic reconnaissance and tanker aircraft duties, so different versions of the basic model are used to ensure that these very different tasks are carried out to maximum effect. The electronic warfare version has no less than 30 different antennae protruding from its fuselage and wings to detect, locate and classify, record and jam enemy transmissions. It can also attack ground positions with bombs, rockets and special missiles that follow the enemy's radar beams to destroy their transmission stations.

Powerful Flares

The latest addition to the US Navy's impressive fleet of aircraft carrierborne submarine killers is the Lockheed S-3A Viking. This very advanced warplane, powered by two small turbofan engines, made its first flight in 1972 and carries a

Left: **A crewman prepares to photograph a Soviet battleship.**
Below: **A *Star Wars* shape come true! The Lockheed SR-71 'Blackbird' is the fastest aircraft ever to see operational service.**

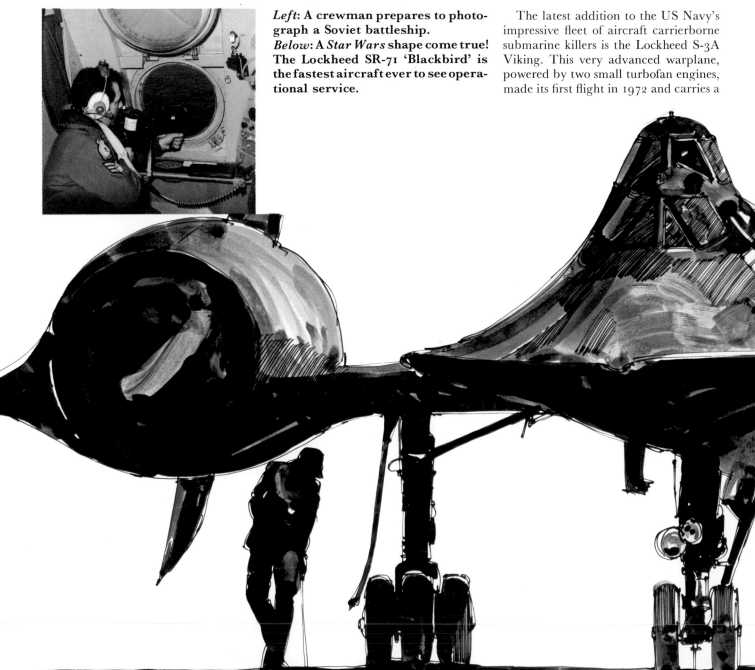

aircraft and the Rockwell OV-10 Bronco has one which was developed during the war in Vietnam for the use of forward air controllers and as a COIN (COunter INsurgency) aircraft.

In its forward air controller role it would mark targets with smoke rockets prior to a major assault by strike aircraft, but as a COIN aircraft it was armed with a variety of underwing weapons, bombs, rockets and four M-60 machine-guns. The new NOGS (night observation gunship) version has a 20 mm gun turret under its fuselage and a forward-looking infrared sensor in its lengthened snout, complete with laser sight. In its COIN configuration the Bronco was designed to operate from short and hurriedly prepared landing strips, but it could double-up as a military passenger aircraft or stretcher-carrier.

A Nimrod shadows the Soviet battleship *Mosova* to take photographs.

crew of four. It replaces both the Tracker and the Tracer in US Navy service. The Viking is normally armed with a mixture of flares, mines, rockets and depth charges. It can locate submarines that have been foolish enough to surface and then light up the entire area with its powerful flares so that it can deliver a ferocious attack with those deadly underwing rockets even at night.

Not all the Grumman types operate from aircraft carriers. The OV-1

Mohawk, for example, is a two-seater observation aircraft. One of its variants has SLAR equipment – sideways looking airborne radar – allowing the aircraft to fly across country and scan to considerable distances either side. In some versions it can also build up a radar map of the area which can be very useful in remote and inaccessible places. There is also a version equipped with an infrared mapping sensor and cameras. An eye in the sky is essential for controlling strike

The sinister Lockheed U-2.

Probably the most famous reconnaissance aircraft ever built was the Lockheed U-2. A joint venture undertaken by the CIA (Central Intelligence Agency) and the USAF, this sinister-looking spy plane was hand-built under a veil of strict secrecy in 1955. With its very long wingspan and extremely lightweight construction, the U-2 is virtually a big glider crammed full of complex electronic devices that just happens to be propelled by a jet engine. The USAF set up a squadron of U-2s under the innocent title of 1st Weather Reconnaissance Squadron at Lakenheath, England, but even this soon aroused suspicions and when awkward questions were asked about the unit's true purpose, the squadron was quickly moved to Western Germany. Other bases in Japan, Turkey, Pakistan and Alaska played host to U-2 detachments, forming a global 'web' across which the CIA could perform their most important reconnaissance function, namely overflying Communist territories to monitor missile sites, satellite launches and military activities in general.

The U-2 Incident

In May 1969, though, the plan came terribly unstuck, when a U-2 piloted by a CIA agent called Gary Powers was shot down over Sverdlovsk in the USSR by eagle-eyed Soviet missile crews. Powers was held by the Russians on a spying charge for some time, but was eventually exchanged for a Soviet agent who had been serving a similar sentence in the United States. The U-2 was back in the news again in 1962 when one of them took a series of photographs from high altitude revealing that the Russians were building missile bases on the Communist-governed island of Cuba, dangerously near to the United States mainland. After a nerve-racking few days when John F. Kennedy, the US President, demanded that the bases be dismantled, and sent the US Navy steaming towards the island, the Soviets backed down and dismantled the bases, much to the relief of the rest of the world.

But the Cuban missile crisis had proved beyond any shadow of doubt just how important reconnaissance aircraft had become, even in the tension-filled world of international politics. In 1980 the U-2 production line was opened up again for a brand new version, the TR-1 (the initials stand for Tactical Reconnaissance). This is intended mainly for use over Europe and will have the added advantage of an all-weather sideways-looking radar system, allowing it to maintain surveillance over enemy territory without endangering itself by actually overflying it.

Into the 1980s

The Lockheed U-2 may have stolen the publicity limelight, but across the Atlantic in the United Kingdom is an aircraft that steadily and undramatically fulfills its duty of patrolling the UK's sovereign waters and vital offshore oil interests. The aircraft in question is the BAe Nimrod submarine hunter-killer, undoubtedly the most advanced machine of its kind anywhere in the world. Although the Nimrod has completely superceded the elderly Shackleton in the anti-submarine role, it is itself directly descended from one of yesterday's classics – the Comet airliner. Appropriately enough, the new aircraft is named after the biblical 'mighty hunter' and has an aggressive shark-like shape that is instantly recognisable. In the extreme tail section is its MAD sting, which registers the presence of submerged submarines.

The ultimate in reconnaissance aircraft today is Lockheed's incredible SR-71 'Blackbird' – a *Star Wars* creation come true in the glamorous world of aerial espionage. 'Blackbird' can travel for sustained periods at speeds in excess of 3,200 km/hr (2,000 mph) and carries vastly expensive camera equipment that can photograph golf balls on a green from an altitude of 24,400 m (80,000 ft). Before each mission, the SR-71's two-person crew undergoes a rigorous series of physical fitness tests and take nearly three hours to get into their elaborate space suits – essential in the event of an emergency escape at high altitude.

TRAINERS
Purpose-built for Learners

The earliest training of pilots was very elementary and often informal, for early aircraft builders were more concerned with proving that their machines could actually fly rather than with training the flyers themselves. As a result, many early pilots learned through trial and error or were taught by friends. This inevitably led to high casualties. By 1914, with the onset of the First World War, military flying training had accelerated in Europe and the United States, but the aircraft used tended to be combat or general-purpose types rather than machines specifically designed for learners. The use of such aircraft meant that the pupil was often cramped into a tiny cockpit, learning by watching the instructor using the one set of flying controls available. The poor pupil had to learn solely from memory, rather than through direct experience and continuous practice, and it soon became obvious that a purpose-built training aircraft was badly needed.

Safety

Undoubtedly the most important early trainer used by Britain's Royal Flying Corps (RFC) was the Farman Longhorn, a large and comparatively heavy French biplane with a 'pusher' propeller, and its useful 1914 development, the Shorthorn. Both types were used by the other Allied air forces in the First World War. Another notable aircraft to fulfil the RFC's urgent need for trainers in the autumn of 1916 was the Airco DH.6. This was a two-seat biplane which lacked the usual style of its designer, Geoffrey de Havilland, but was practical and easy to build and maintain, with a good safety record. Interestingly, its four rectangular wing panels were interchangeable for ease of maintenance following crashes, as were the tailplane panels. The DH.6s began to be phased out of service in late 1917 and at the end of the war the RFC (now part of the RAF) still possessed over 1,000 examples of the type, as a result of the large orders they had placed during wartime.

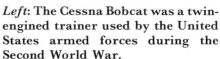

Left: The Cessna Bobcat was a twin-engined trainer used by the United States armed forces during the Second World War.

Two Avro 540s resplendent in the all-yellow colour scheme that has typified training aircraft for many years. The strong undercarriage units were essential if heavy-handed landings by new pupils were to be withstood.

Despite the significant contribution made by aircraft of this type, pilot training during the war was patchy and hurried, and often undertaken by instructors who had been wounded or were being rested from combat duties and were therefore downhearted. There was at this time still no definite syllabus or technique, until Robert Smith-Barry drew up the first detailed scheme of pilot training and in doing so formed the basis of all methods used to the present day. Smith-Barry wanted specially-designed trainer aircraft, instead of just anything that was available at the time. This meant aircraft with proper dual controls for instructor and pupil and handling qualities that permitted the pupil to fly precisely and safely. He also required that the instructors be specially selected and trained for the job. The now world-famous RAF Central Flying School was the result of the effort Smith-Barry put in. Reliability, simplicity and versatility were henceforth to be vital for future trainer aircraft specifications.

The method of training pilots has not changed much since the days of Smith-Barry. Before then, possibly half the pupil's early flight-time was taken up with monotonously circling the airfield and in trying to perfect his landings, aiming at all times for consistency and safety. Pupils were not allowed to fly solo until they had completed about eight to ten hours of instruction and they qualified for their 'wings' after a minimum of 80 hours.

British involvement in the First World War meant large orders for virtually any aircraft which could be manufactured quickly, and so the Avro 504, which was first flown in 1913, soon replaced the Farmans and DH.6s as the foremost standard trainer. 504s were also used as

Above: **As shown in this illustration the rear (instructor's) seat of the Miles Master could be elevated slightly, and the cockpit top tilted up to form a windscreen, so that the instructor could keep an eye on his pupil's progress.**

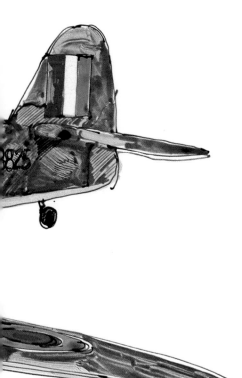

Above left: **The Vultee BT-13 first flew in 1937 and provided single-engined flying training for USAAF pilots during the Second World War.** *Above*: **Affectionately known as the 'Annie', the Avro Anson performed many useful training tasks during the Second World War, including air gunnery and navigation.**

bombers and single-seat fighters during the war. The major trainer development in wartime was the 504J, which was the first purpose-designed military trainer to be mass-produced, and it was this aircraft which laid the foundations for all subsequent flying training machines throughout the world. It was made in larger numbers than any other aircraft prior to the Second World War, some 8,340 examples being built in all.

The 504 had a simple wooden structure with fabric covering, and the instructor sat in a separate cockpit behind the pupil. After the war the new 504K version was designed to be powered by any available engine. This model was in turn replaced by the 504N or Lynx-Avro (so named because of its Lynx radial engine), which continued in production as the RAF's primary trainer until 1933. Interestingly, a substantial number of 504s were built under licence in the Soviet Union, where the type became known as the U-1.

'Jenny'

During the First World War, the Americans, too, produced a number of notable trainers. Among them was the E-1, made by the Standard Company which had been shrewdly formed to anticipate the United States' entry into the war. It was designed originally as a fighter, but this small and sleek machine was soon found to be underpowered, and lacked the speed and agility needed for frontline service. As a result it was re-assigned to the advanced training role.

The Curtiss JN-4. or 'Jenny', was

another significant American trainer to emerge during the war. The 'Jenny' took to the air for its maiden flight in 1916 and although it was not an exceptional aircraft in terms of sheer performance, its distinctive character earned it a great reputation. In the basic training role it was used in military flying schools all over the United States, Great Britain and France throughout the First World War. Early trainers usually offered their pilots poor visibility from their cockpits, but the 'Jenny' was well-known for its splendid all-round view.

'Barnstorming'

Curtiss was the main supplier of aircraft to the air arm of the US Army at this point in time but at the end of the war, contracts for some 4,450 JN-4s were cancelled. As a result, a multitude of them found their way onto the civilian market. Not surprisingly they proved ideal for flying school use and saw sterling service all over the United States until new safety regulations which were framed to fit more modern designs compelled their retirement. The JN-4's final fling came in the form of 'barnstorming' flights in the hands of high-spirited display pilots. They thrilled the crowds at countless air displays, being used to give daring demonstrations of wing-walking and other such antics.

In early 1917, B.D. Thomas, one of the designers responsible for the 'Jenny', branched out on his own to design the Thomas-Morse S.4. This was acquired by the US Army for the advanced training of future fighter pilots and had a

Below: **The big Convair T-29 served with the USAF in the 1950s and provided comprehensive training facilities for up to fourteen student navigators. Each student had his own map table complete with a radio compass panel, an altimeter and various other instruments for long-distance navigation.**

superior performance to the 'Jenny'. It was yet another military trainer that proved popular on the civilian market after the war. The S.4, also known as the 'Tommy', enjoyed an unexpected spell of fame in the postwar years, when it was modified to 'play' British, French and German aircraft with convincing realism and appeared in numerous famous feature films.

initially to observe enemy movements on the ground, and to undertake dangerous photographic missions high over territory earmarked for attack. As designs became more sophisticated, bombing and fighting duties played a larger and larger part in the aircrafts' role. Airmen had to be trained to perform these tasks with confidence, so aircraft like the 'Jenny' became the first to be modified for such purposes.

Useful Tasks

As the First World War progressed, the role of the aircraft became increasingly important. Aircraft were employed

Despite the great surplus of trainers at the end of the 1914–18 war, new designs continued to be accepted for mass production. One particular company,

Below: **The DHC-1 Chipmunk had no unpleasant handling characteristics and was very popular.**

Stampe in Belgium, was established in 1922 to specialize solely in building trainer aircraft. By far their greatest success was the Stampe SV.4 series of two-seat biplane trainers, first built in 1933 and famed for their excellent manoeuvrability and immense strength. Production finally petered out during the Second World War when the Antwerp factory where they were built was destroyed by fire, but a few Stampe SV.4s live on to this day and continue to impress pilots with their agility and reliability when performing demanding aerobatic manoeuvres.

By the 1930s, the sharp increase in the variety of duties aircraft were called upon to perform had given birth to two distinctly different types of trainer. On the one hand was the primary trainer, so called because a student pilot would be given his initial background experience of flying in it. On the other hand was the advanced trainer, the final stepping stone before a trainee pilot joined his first squadron.

Open Cockpit

A primary trainer was of simple construction and was relatively easy to fly,

thus providing an ideal means for pilots to learn the basic principles of control, particularly at the critical points of take-off and landing. One of the classic primary trainers of the interwar period was the Boeing PT-13 Kaydet biplane, noted for its substantial size and strength and powered by a variety of radial engines. The Kaydet represented the pinnacle of open-cockpit biplane design and featured a massive single-strut under-carriage unit to withstand the heavy and frequent landings of trainee pilots.

Due in part to its dependability on landing, the Kaydet became the first

Below: **The propeller blades of the North American T-6 Harvard produced a fiercesome noise.**

183

aircraft ever to fulfil the often conflicting needs of both the US Navy and US Army. Painted in a striking all-yellow colour scheme, these trainers soon earned the nickname of 'Yellow Perils' when their antics in the hands of keen but inexperienced young flyers frequently took them far beyond the bounds of safety! Production of Kaydets ended in February 1945, and many surplus ex-military examples went onto the civilian market at very cheap prices. The majority of them were snapped up to form the backbone of the new aerial enterprises that were springing up all over postwar America, such as the well-established crop-spraying industry.

While aircraft like the rugged Kaydet certainly occupied a place of considerable importance in the basic training role, many would agree that the most famous aeroplane ever to perform this vital duty was a bird of a very different feather – the neat little de Havilland Tiger Moth. This was a completely British aircraft and was the culmination of a series of light aircraft designs which had begun in 1925 with the DH.60.

Built mainly of wood and covered almost entirely in tough fabric, this elegant aeroplane first flew on 26 October 1931. In the years before the Second World War it was used by most civilian flying schools in Great Britain and was the standard trainer during the early war years for military flying throughout the Commonwealth. The secret of its success lay mostly in its simple, resilient construction, its low cost, and the reliability of its Gipsy Major engine. The war obviously stimulated production, which was handed over to the car manufacturers Morris Motors Ltd and other de Havilland factories worldwide. This made it possible for de Havilland to concentrate on combat aircraft development, especially the twin-engined wooden Mosquito.

Radio-Controlled

During the war the Tiger Moth found itself performing an unusual yet necessary duty when certain examples were modified to become radio-controlled targets for anti-aircraft artillery training! After the war, the RAF declared their Tiger Moths obsolete, but most of them finished up on the civilian market. Flying clubs competed to buy them because the world's planemakers were not immediately able to satisfy the peacetime demand for light trainers. The demand for a military replacement was later met by the de Havilland Canada company with their famous Chipmunk in 1946.

In 1936, the British air ministry and RAF considered it essential to introduce a monoplane trainer alongside the Tiger Moth to help cope with its expansion programme, which demanded crew for large numbers of monoplane fighters and bombers. One result was the two-seat Miles Magister, which was constructed entirely of wood. A total of nearly 1,300 were built between 1936–41 and they served widely in both Britain and her Commonwealth. The Magister and the Tiger Moth had distinctive features in the fabric hood that could be pulled over their rear cockpits for 'blind-flying' training. Deprived of any view of the outside world, the student pilot was forced to navigate solely by his instruments.

Deafening

The blind-flying instrument panel, introduced into the RAF in the 1930s, carried five basic flight instruments – altimeter, airspeed indicator, turn and slip indicator, gyro compass and artificial horizon. This panel was made common to all aircraft in RAF service, including the trainers, and the instruments were grouped in the same positions on each panel, thus providing familiarity of use for pilots whatever aircraft they were flying. This clever innovation considerably improved the standard of instrument training and gave trainee pilots in particular an extra source of confidence in the aircraft they flew.

After trainee pilots had received their initial grounding in the art of controlling an aeroplane, courtesy of the primary trainer, their next step was to clamber into the cockpit of something far more substantial. It was at this point in their careers that they progressed to the more demanding advanced trainer; an aircraft that could give them experience of a much more powerful engine and a higher performance. A prime example of this type of trainer was the North American AT-6 Texan. Known to the Commonwealth air forces as the Harvard, this stocky yet nimble all-metal monoplane provided virtually every Allied pilot with his advanced training during the Second World War. One of this aircraft's most distinctive features was the piercing whine caused by the tips of its propeller

These Potez-Air Fouga C.M.170 Magister jet trainers serve with *La Patrouille de France*, the formation display team of the French air force. *Top*: A Lockheed T-33 of the USAF.

blades under certain conditions, as they sliced through the air at a speed faster than that of sound itself.

As American involvement in the war became increasingly likely, a second assembly line was established at a new aircraft plant in Dallas to cope with the immense demand anticipated. The AT-6C model was an interesting variation, because for fear of shortages of certain materials during the war it was decided to build its fuselage with as little aluminium as possible, with plywood replacing metal. This version therefore represented a fascinating step back into the past.

After the war, to tide the United States armed forces over until a new trainer aircraft arrived, the 2,000 remaining Texans were rebuilt and modernized in 1949. With improved cockpit layout, modified landing gear, increased fuel tankage and new instruments, the Texan trained American pupils in the use of modern combat aircraft until March 1955. Meanwhile, other types of trainer, some of them twin-engined, had been used to teach aircrew such specialized techniques as air gunnery, aerial photographic reconnaissance, communications and bombsighting.

Typical of the twin-engined aircraft

that saw service in the advanced training role during the Second World War were the Avro Anson and the Airspeed Oxford, both British designs. The Anson earned the affectionate nickname of 'Annie' from its crews and was a solid, dependable performer, while the Oxford, which entered service in late 1937, was known to those who flew her as the 'Ox-box'. A military development of a successful civilian aircraft, the Airspeed Envoy, the Oxford was used for all aspects of aircrew training, and like a number of Ansons, some it featured a revolving gun turret atop the fuselage to help train air gunners under 'genuine'

conditions. Oxfords and Ansons were also employed as air ambulances and communications aircraft during the war, some being called upon to transport high-ranking officers from one place to another in comparative speed and comfort.

Great Britain and her Allies were not, of course, the only ones to employ advanced training aircraft during the Second World War. The Luftwaffe, for example, had the Arado Ar 96B, an elegant two-seater monoplane to fulfil such a purpose. This extremely attractive machine had a tandem seating configuration, with the instructor situated just behind his pupil under a long, streamlined cockpit canopy.

Adaptability

First ordered in 1940, Ar 96Bs were built in great numbers during the war and became the standard equipment of most Luftwaffe fighter trainer squadrons. Most of them had a machine-gun fixed just above the engine on the right-hand side and possessed a full range of night-flying instruments, though some served as dive-bombing trainers. To fulfil this difficult role these Ar 96Bs carried underwing bomb racks and were fitted with a manually-aimed machine-gun in the rear cockpit. This is a good example of the way in which a trainer aircraft can if necessary be adapted to provide a speedy backup for weakened air forces. It is a practice that has continued right through to the jet-propelled trainer aircraft of today, though the Ar 96B itself has never actually been called upon to serve in combat conditions.

The Japanese, too, relied heavily on

Top: Folland (later Hawker Siddeley) Gnats of the RAF's *Red Arrows* aerobatic team. *Above*: The Hawker Siddeley Dominie is powered by two rear-mounted Rolls-Royce Viper jet engines and performs navigational training duties for the RAF.

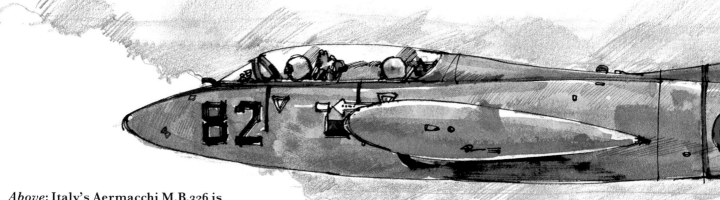

Above: Italy's Aermacchi M.B.326 is also powered by a Rolls-Royce Viper engine. This nimble aircraft has provided many hundreds of Italian air force pupils with their first taste of jet flying. There is also an attack version.

The interior of a Vickers Varsity navigational training aircraft during a typical mission. The Varsity served with the RAF in this role throughout the 1960s and was then replaced by the Dominie (see page 188). The young students are plotting their position on special charts with the aid of the Varsity's built-in instrument panels. Varsities were also used as bomb-aimer trainers.

purpose-built trainer aircraft to keep their operational squadrons well-stocked with highly-skilled young pilots. Their standard trainer for future crews of multi-engined aircraft during the Second World War was the Tachikawa Ki-54. Japanese pilots, navigators, bomb-aimers, radio operators and air gunners alike trained on this twin-engined monoplane. The curious Allied system of codenames for enemy aircraft listed the Ki-54 as the *Hickory*.

Because of Japanese involvement in the Pacific war against the United States there was an overriding need for a good naval trainer aircraft. For a time the Yokosuka K5Y fulfilled this need. Codenamed *Willow* by the Allies, this small

biplane was designed in the early 1930s and had a performance similar to several more modern types of trainer. It became very popular in the air arm of the Japanese navy, and served right through the war on various aircraft-carriers. Most Japanese aircraft possessed sleek looks and had simple structures, but a notable exception was the lumbering Kyushu K11W Shiragiku.

First flown in the summer of 1943, the Shiragiku was for some unknown reason never allocated an Allied codename, despite the fact that it was one of Japan's most common aircraft. Codenamed or not it would always have been easily recognizable to Allied fighter pilots and anti-aircraft gunners, as it featured such

a pot-bellied fuselage structure. Powered by a single 515hp Hitachi nine-cylinder radial engine, the Shiragiku had an unusual way of accommodating its crew, for trainee pilot and radio operator (or gunner) were seated in a cockpit situated atop the high-sided fuselage, while the student navigator and bomb-aimer were housed with the instructor in another cockpit below wing level.

The Shiragiku was a very hefty aeroplane to say the least, and would probably have achieved greater success had it been fitted with two engines rather than one. Nevertheless, it proved itself a workmanlike if somewhat cumbersome performer, though many were needlessly wasted – along with their precious pilots – in the infamous *Kamikaze* suicide raids on the US Navy's battleships and aircraft carriers stationed out in the Pacific.

Chipmunk

The Second World War ended in 1945, but it was not long before another major conflict began. The Korean War (1950–3) saw the introduction of the United States armed forces' first operational jet fighter, the Lockheed F-80 Shooting Star. A trainer version, the T-33 was soon flown, and went on to serve in the air arms of over 30 nations. Not all trainers in the early 1950s were high performance jets however, for 1946 saw the maiden flight of the de Havilland of Canada DHC-1 Chipmunk.

Built in Toronto, the single-engined Chipmunk proved to be a reliable workhorse, with no unpleasant handling characteristics to upset the confidence of young trainee pilots. Complete with blind-flying panel and radio, it provided many military airmen with their first experience of flying, and continues to do so to this day in the hands of civilian owners, its service career long finished.

In RAF operation the Chipmunk has been replaced by the faster and slightly more agile Bulldog, another single-engined type with impeccable handling characteristics. The Bulldog has another slight advantage over the Chipmunk in that it seats pupil and instructor side-by-side rather than in tandem, thus providing both crew members with the opportunity to study the other's operation of the flying controls.

MM 54282
AERMACCHI No 326

Left: A large proportion of a pupil pilot's time is spent in the class-room learning the theory of flight and the use of the aircraft's instruments. But the real test of his skill comes when he straps into the cockpit of his aircraft (in this case a BAe Hawk).

The development of flying training in the Communist bloc countries after the Second World War has centred largely on four major aircraft, one Soviet, one Polish, and two Czech. In 1946 the first prototype of the Yak-18 primary trainer took to the air for its maiden flight. The original version, which had metal covering the engine area, but was fabric-covered behind, stayed in production until 1955. It was superceded by the more powerful Yak-18A. This version was given the NATO codename *Max*, and saw service in many different versions. These have been widely used as the standard primary trainer in Eastern Europe in the 1950s and 1960s. These versions include the Yak-18P, an aerobatic trainer and competition aircraft, and the Yak-18PM.

Poland's Iskra TS-11 (with a turbojet engine) on the other hand first flew in 1960, and by the end of 1965 it was in service with most Polish training units. Its low-level attack derivative, the Iskra 100, was introduced in 1972. Meanwhile, the Czechs have not allowed themselves to lag behind the other countries of the Communist bloc. Their Aero L-29 Delfin became one of the first to demonstrate that nations other than the Soviet Union could win competitive evaluation for major East European equipment contacts. It is clear to Western observers, however, that there is a deliberate Soviet policy of giving secondary construction tasks to its Warsaw Pact neighbours by assigning all manufacture of modern trainer aircraft to Poland and Czechoslovakia. Competing against the Soviet Yak-30 and the Polish TS-11, the L-29 prototype had made its first flight in April 1959 and was selected as the standard jet pilot trainer by all the Warsaw Pact countries except Poland.

A Hawker Siddeley (now BAe) Hawk being flown on a weapons training mission by a young pilot. This is surely the most exhilarating part of the pupil's training syllabus.

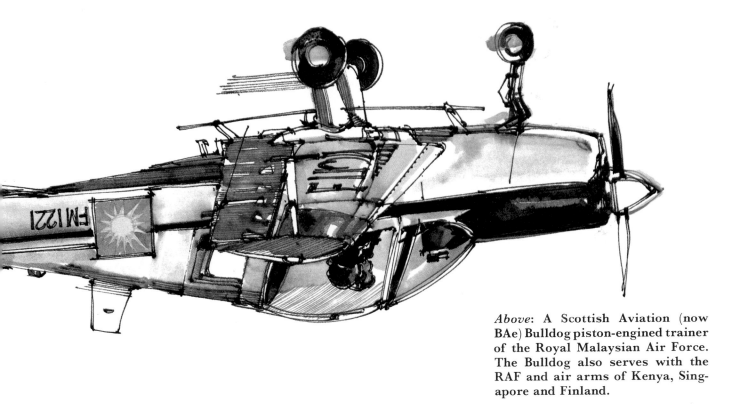

Above: A Scottish Aviation (now BAe) Bulldog piston-engined trainer of the Royal Malaysian Air Force. The Bulldog also serves with the RAF and air arms of Kenya, Singapore and Finland.

The trainer aircraft of today are nimble little machines with a bewildering variety of secondary capabilities. This trend towards compactness was started by such aircraft as the famous Hawker Siddeley Gnat, famous all over the world for its long spell with the *Red Arrows* aerobatic demonstration team. Typical of the new breed is France and Germany's twin-engined creation, the Dassault-Breguet/Dornier Alpha Jet. Built as a cooperative venture by the two nations, the Alpha Jet is in reality almost two different types of aircraft. The French version now performs a fairly straightforward training role, while the Luftwaffe's machine will double-up as a multirole attack aircraft offering close support to friendly forces on the battlefield.

The Alpha Jet's cockpit is fully pressurized and seats its two-person crew in tandem. In the French version, the occupant of the rear seat is, of course, a straightforward instructor, but the Luftwaffe's battlefield attack Alpha Jets will seat a combat observer in the rear, to keep an eye on enemy troop movements on the ground and take charge of his aircraft's sophisticated array of navigation and missile guidance systems. The

A pupil strapped into the trainer version of the Harrier jump jet.

RAF have a somewhat similar-looking advanced trainer/attack aircraft in their new Hawk T.1. This impressive swept-wing machine is sure to achieve world-wide fame even if its routine training missions do go largely unnoticed, for the type has now replaced the Gnat in RAF service and so gains the honour of equipping the *Red Arrows*.

Versatility

So the present-day sleek and smooth monoplane trainers are far removed from the ponderous all-wood biplane aircraft which trained the pioneer pilots of the First World War all those years ago. It is true that in principle the syllabus and techniques of pilot training have hardly changed since the days of Smith-Barry, for the courses followed today still include demonstrations of the effect of the controls, all the normal modes of flight, recovery from accidental spinning and incidents, aerobatics, night flying and so on. But today's trainers are, of course, far more powerful and, above all, faster and safer. They are also far better designed and are now required to undertake more sophisticated tasks. In short they have kept pace with modern air defence requirements. But as the cost of aircraft manufacture and operation escalates, it is the versatility of the trainer that will remain the key to its future use.

TRANSPORT AIRCRAFT
Workhorses of the Skies

MILITARY AIRLIFT COMMAND

When air travel first became a reality, the possibility of carrying cargo quickly and over long distances was soon realized. As so often happens with aircraft however, it was the military requirements that encouraged the first developments in transport aircraft.

During the First World War, aircraft were only used for military transport duties in special emergencies. It is true that troops isolated in their trenches were occasionally supplied from the air, but the methods used were both hasty and improvised. Ammunition, food, water and medical supplies were usually wrapped in blankets or canvas and dropped at low-level from fighters or bombers. This method usually meant that the supplies missed their targets; sometimes falling into enemy hands or landing in no-man's land, or being destroyed on impact.

Just as there was no organized system of air supply, there was hardly any movement of troops by air. There were isolated incidents of men being flown in large bombers, such as Russia's massive Sikorsky *Ilya Mourometz*, but there is no record of aircraft being specially equipped to carry troops by either side. In a conflict as 'static' as the First World War, where troops were bogged down in trenches across fronts hundreds of kilometres long, where any movement was on foot across difficult terrain, or in trucks or trains which were open to attack, the crucial importance of air transport was easy to see. If troops could be moved quickly by air, even in small numbers, any future war could be easily won, it was argued, simply by taking key points on the battlefield.

Moreover, the potential of military transport aircraft would be especially

Above: **British troops, dressed in standard desert uniforms of the period, about to board a Vickers Vernon biplane to fly on a peace-keeping mission in the Middle East. This was one of the primary tasks of early transport aircraft.**

significant to countries such as Britain and France which had large colonial empires. The problem these countries faced was that they had to control huge areas of land which were often thousands of kilometres away from the ruling country. If a rebellion was planned or had arisen, the ruling power had to be able to send a well-armed force quickly to the point of disturbance and keep that force well supplied until the rebellion was quashed. To keep large forces permanently stationed throughout the colonies was becoming increasingly expensive, both in terms of men and materials. The alternative of ferrying troops by sea and land, as had happened in the nineteenth century, was difficult and time-consuming. By contrast, air transport offered a means of shuttling adequate forces from one place to another in a matter of hours. Colonial powers soon saw the advantages of this, so military air transport was quick to develop.

Policing Duties

Initially, military transport aircraft were similar to everyday commercial airliners. Both types had small side doors that could admit nothing larger than troops, stretcher casualties, drums of fuel and so on. Military transports were also

Above: **Vickers Valencia troop transporters were mainly used in desert regions such as Messopotamia, Iraq and India.** *Left*: **A few aircraft were fitted with defensive guns to keep feuding tribesmen at bay when they attempted to take pot-shots at British aircraft. Large transport aircraft were, of course, particularly vulnerable to this type of attack.**

similar in appearance to early bombers, except that the former had bigger fuselages which accommodated more bulky loads.

Britain's first purpose-designed military transport aircraft was the Vickers Vernon which was based on the Vimy Commercial airliner. The Vernon entered service with the RAF in 1922 and could carry twelve troops at a time. Vernons were used extensively in the Middle East, especially in Iraq. Apart from their 'policing' duties, they were tasked with helping to establish reliable air routes, firstly from Cairo in Egypt to Baghdad, capital of Iraq, and eventually to places as far afield as India.

Because the Vernon's range was only about 512 km (320 miles), well-guarded landing strips had to be prepared at various intervals along the route, where the plane could take on petrol, oil and water. In late 1922 British troops in a remote area of northern Iraq were struck down by disease. Vernons were sent in and all the soldiers were successfully removed to a Baghdad hospital within hours of the outbreak. The following year a possible war between the Kurds and the Arabs in Kurdistan was quickly halted by the timely intervention of British troops – airlifted in by a squadron of Vickers Vernons. This was the first operation of its kind anywhere in the world and proved once and for all how useful transport aircraft could be.

Throughout Britain's Middle and Near Eastern empire, policing grew in efficiency as new techniques were introduced. On several occasions, Vernons (and their replacements, Vickers Victorias) were used to drop leaflets warning troublemakers that if they did not stop fighting amongst themselves, their villages would be bombed into submission. This was much cheaper than airlifting troops and more often than not these warnings proved sufficient!

Riots

There was one striking exception however, involving the Vickers Victoria troop transport which took over from the Vernon in 1927. The Victoria closely resembled the Virginia bomber, in much the same way that the Vernon was similar to the Vimy Commercial. One interesting feature of the Victoria was that stretcher cases could be loaded in through a special hatch in the nosecone of the aircraft; a taste of things to come. Victorias served mainly in Iraq and Egypt, and proved their worth during the Kabul riots in Afghanistan. Between 12 December 1928 and 25 February 1929, eight Victorias assisted other aircraft from India to evacuate 586 civilians and their luggage to a place of safety. They also flew out the King, his family and numerous high-ranking government officials. This operation, completed with great efficiency, was the first largescale airlift in history.

The Victoria was the RAF's most important transport aircraft of the interwar period and was much more reliable than any of its predecessors. In 1935 the RAF replaced the Victoria with a developed version – the Vickers Valentia – as the mainstay of its Middle East transport force. The Valentia was characterized by a tailwheel, rather than a tailskid. The wheel made it more controllable on rough landing strips and the Valentia did such splendid work in difficult desert conditions that some were still flying as late as 1941, when they took part in the evacuation of Habbaniya during the Iraqi rebellion of that year.

In the 1930s the Italians were trying to build up an empire in Africa and de-

Two Junkers Ju 52/3ms drop paratroopers on to an enemy airfield. This triple-engined workhouse was affectionately known as 'Auntie Ju'.

veloped a range of 'colonial' aircraft. One of these aircraft was the Caproni Ca 101, a sturdily-built machine with three engines. It was developed also as a bomber and was used for both attack and supply duties during the Italian invasion of Ethiopia in 1935-6 and by the Nationalist forces during the Spanish Civil War (1936-9). Some Ca 101s were still in service during the Second World War, employed as transports during the conflict with Russia until 1943. It is worth noting that these early military transports could carry only a fraction of the weight that a modern transport can cope with. For example, the Vickers Vernon could only carry 2,086 kg (4,600 lb), while the Ca 101 – because it was grossly underpowered – could only lift an astonishingly low 500 kg (1,100 lb). By comparison, the modern

American C-5A Galaxy can carry loads exceeding 200,000 kg (440,000 lb)! Obviously, the carrying capacity of transport aircraft developed with the increase in available engine power and in the sheer size permitted by the materials from which their airframes were built.

One event which accelerated this development – and the variety and quantity of transport aircraft – was the Second World War. It was obvious even in the 1930s that the looming war was going to be far more mobile than the first, and would be fought on a truly global scale. It was also realized that aircraft would play a major part in moving troops and supplies to the battlefronts. Moreover, men could now be carried hundreds of kilometres and actually parachuted from the air in large numbers. Heavy guns and tanks could also be safely ferried by air to

strategic points anywhere across a wide front line. The Russians certainly believed this to be the way ahead.

'Auntie Ju'

In the early 1930s the Junkers company had built a three-engined workhorse of a transport aircraft called the Ju 52/3m. Before the war they were used extensively as commercial transports by Luft Hansa and various foreign airlines. However, with the Nazi involvement in the Spanish Civil War, they were used initially to carry troops and military supplies to the Nationalist forces. Later, they were used on bombing missions. In this latter capacity they were soon replaced, however, and in 1937 the Ju 52/3m reverted to its original role as a transport aircraft. It was affectionately nicknamed '*Tante Ju*' ('Auntie Ju')

A Messerschmitt Me 323 Gigant (meaning Giant) being loaded with horses during the conflict on the Eastern Front.

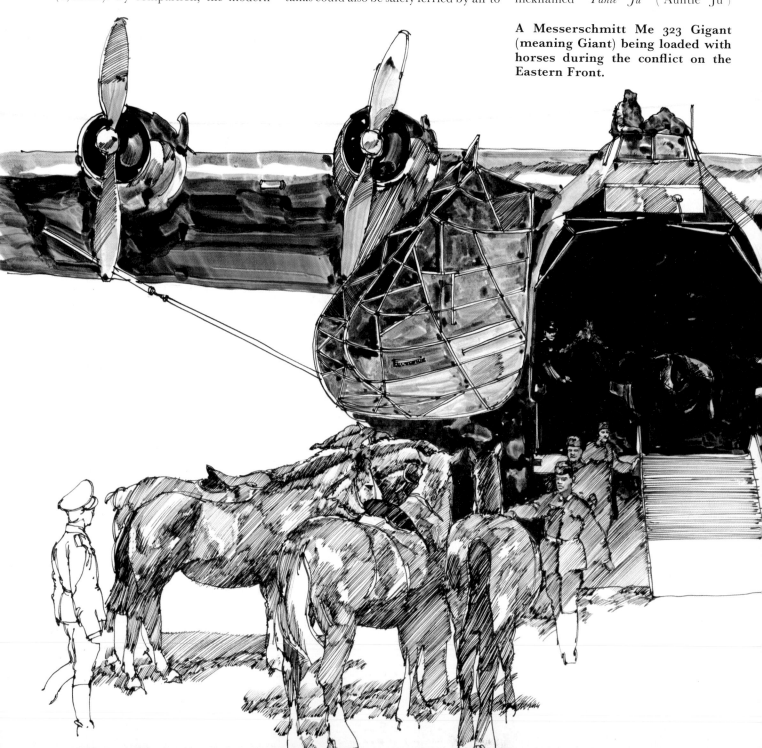

during the Spanish War, and 'Iron Annie' during the Second World War, when it became the Luftwaffe's principal troop transporter.

The 'Iron Annies' had armour plating around their cockpit areas to protect their crews, and a machine-gun armament to ward off any attackers. They were used extensively in the invasions of Norway and Denmark in April 1940, when about 600 saw operational service. A larger number figured in the battles for France and the Netherlands. Tough, reliable, slow but very versatile, these transports were used to carry seventeen troops at a time, and served as ambulance aircraft, being able to accommodate up to twelve stretcher cases. They were also used as supply transports and glider tugs – pulling gliders full of parachutists to capture key military positions. As if this were not enough, they could also be easily adapted to accept ski or float landing gear.

Secret Tests

Sufficient new Ju 52/3ms were built to ensure that the type continued to service in the Balkans, North Africa, Crete and on the Eastern Front during the conflict with Russia. In Crete over 270 were lost, while in Russia the loss rate was even higher. Despite this they were among the last aircraft flown into and out of the besieged German 6th Army garrison at Stalingrad in 1942–3. The Germans had intended to replace their ageing machines with the newer Ju 252s and Ju 352s, but these were not produced in sufficient numbers to be of any real use. Ju 52/3ms therefore continued to serve throughout the war and for many years

Above: **Gotha Go 242s were usually towed aloft by Junkers Ju 52/3ms and had rear clamshell doors for loading guns and troops.**

afterwards as both a military and civilian transport. In fact, three still fly regularly in Swiss air force service!

Although the success of the Ju 52/3m was virtually a foregone conclusion, even before the Second World War began, the Germans started developing a totally new concept in aerial warfare – the assault glider. In late 1937 flight tests were made in great secrecy on a glider called the DFS 230, but it was not until May 1940 that this aircraft was first used in the attack on the fortress of Eban Emael.

Assault Gliders

The idea was to tow parachute troops to a battle target – in this case the DFS 230s were pulled aloft by Ju 52/3ms – and drop them into a position where they could capture that target and then hold out until the arrival of ground troops. So successful was this operational initiation of the assault glider that the Germans used them again in the invasion of Holland and Belgium, in Crete and in Russia. Almost inevitably, the British and Americans followed Germany's lead and designed troop- and freight-carrying gliders of their own.

The Germans, however, were still not satisfied. The DFS 230s could carry only nine fully-equipped troops and loading could only be done through a small door for the troops and a detachable panel under the wing for freight. An easy answer had to be to build a glider with a

Above: **A Thor ballistic missile being pushed into the capacious hold of a Douglas C-124 Globemaster II.**

much larger fuselage, preferably with a level cargo floor close to the ground with front or rear doors giving access to the entire fuselage. The Gotha Go 242 provided part of the answer. It was built largely of wood with a hinged tail, allowing the desired easy access to the interior. This aircraft was accepted by the Luftwaffe in August 1941 as an airborne freighter, while a version fitted with additional doors saw service in the assault role, packed with battle-ready troops. These models were involved in the battles on the terrible Eastern Front.

Clamshell Doors

The glider to beat all gliders, however, was the massive Messerschmitt Me 321 Gigant. Access to its enormous interior was by the left- and right- hinged panels that constituted the aircraft's nose section. The popular term for these panels is 'clamshell' doors. This made the Gigant the first aircraft in history to feature such a configuration. Through these doors an 88 mm field gun, a light tank, most German wheeled vehicles or halftracks, or up to 150 troops could be loaded. At long last bulky equipment could be loaded into an aircraft with ease, thanks to these massive hinged doors. The Gigant was intended to carry tanks and other such heavy equipment on the planned invasion of Britain, which of course never materialized. Having the cargo doors situated in the extreme nose had the one disadvantage that loads could not be dropped whilst the glider was actually airborne. Against this drawback

This DHC-2 Beaver only just fits through the doors of a Bristol Freighter.

however, were ranged a whole host of big advantages.

Needless to say, pulling such a gigantic glider into the air required a tremendous amount of pulling power. In the early days of the Gigant's career this power was provided by the *troika-schlepp* (triple-tow) – groups of three twin-engined Messerschmitt Bf 110s, assisted in their hair-raising task by auxiliary take-off

rockets fitted to the glider. Later came an even more ingenious solution when the Heinkel company hit on the idea of joining together two of their He 111 medium bombers and fitting an extra engine into the centre-section where the two wings were bolted together. The result was an extraordinary five-engined hybrid called the Heinkel He 111Z. Only twelve of them saw active service. The

Above: The RAF's Blackburn Beverley of the 1950s could easily carry bulk loads like this Whirlwind helicopter.

The massive fixed undercarriage and twin tailfin configuration of the Blackburn Beverley are well shown in this picture.

need for such incredible aircraft was removed when the Luftwaffe ordered the construction of a powered version of the Gigant. All that weight needed no fewer than six 990 hp radial engines to heave it up into the air. Both the Me 321 glider and the powered version (the Me 323) had two long rows of wheels along the bottom of the fuselage, fitted with low-pressure tyres for landing on rough airstrips close to the front line. Because the Me 323 version had the benefit of engines to keep it aloft, the extra weight imposed by an improved armament was considered permissible. As a result, four machine-guns were fitted to the Me 323, as compared with the Me 321 glider's modest two-gun armament.

Both models of the Gigant performed with distinction, but not all German assault gliders proved so successful. The Junkers Ju 322 Mammut, for example, was built entirely out of wood for lightness and was designed to carry a *Panzerkampfwagen IV* tank or over 100 fully-equipped troops. But on initial landing tests the tanks just crashed through the Mammut's wooden floor, so the whole project had to be abandoned in 1941!

Many of the RAF's large aircraft in the 1930s were known as bomber-transports, such as the Handley Page Harrow. Bomber-transports were dual purpose planes but did not bomb as efficiently as a single-purpose bomber or transport as efficiently as a single-purpose transporter. Until well into the Second World War the British had hardly any really useful military transports because the loading capacity of the aircraft then in service was so much like that of civil airliners. The RAF was quick to learn from the Germans however, especially in using gliders, and although the Germans were the pioneers, it is interesting that the Allies used gliders in far greater numbers during the Second World War. Three examples were Britain's GAL Hamilcar and Airspeed Horsa, and America's Waco CG-4A.

The Hamilcar was originally intended

Above: **A Boeing C-135 Stratolifter of the USAF.**

Below: **A Canadian-built DHC-4 Caribou of the Royal Malaysian Air Force. Its radar unit is enclosed in its bulbous nose.**

to carry a light tank or bren-gun carriers, but it was later adapted to carry a great variety of loads. It had a hinged nose to enable it to load the tanks, and was towed into the air by aircraft such as the Halifax, Lancaster or Stirling bombers. The sleek-looking Airspeed Horsa had two large sliding doors set into the fuselage sides to facilitate the easy loading and unloading of troops and freight. It normally served as a personnel transporter, carrying up to 25 fully-armed troops, but a wide variety of military equipment could be stored in the long cylindrical fuselage.

On a combat mission, the Horsa's undercarriage unit was dropped away as the glider was pulled off the ground, later landing on its belly to disgorge its load. After coming to rest the entire rear fuselage could be detached to allow the troops and cargo to be offloaded in a matter of seconds. An improved version, the Horsa II, was introduced towards the end of the war in 1944 and featured an upward-hinging front fuselage section to permit field guns and jeeps to be carried.

In RAF service Horsas were used in the Sicilian operations of July 1943, having been towed there non-stop from bases in Britain. On D-Day (6 June 1944), 250 Horsas arrived at Normandy for the all-important landings. One batch of Horsas had been fitted with parachutes to help them make very short landings. Horsas were again employed at Arnhem and at the famous crossing of the Rhine, when 440 machines carried the British 6th Airborne Division into action. The Horsa was the leading Allied assault glider during the war and was towed behind a wide variety of aircraft, including Dakotas, Albermarles, and Stirling and Halifax heavy bombers.

The American Waco CG-4A, known as the Hadrian to the RAF, could carry either freight or fifteen fully-armed troops, including the pilot and his co-pilot. It too had a hinged nose for the direct loading and unloading of equip-

The Soviet Union employs transport aircraft in massive quantities.

ment, but the normal troop entrance was set into the side of the fuselage. One Waco was modified so that it could be fitted with two detachable cells, each of which contained an engine, fuel tank and engine instruments, enabling the glider to become a conventional powered aircraft when necessary. These cells were known as 'power eggs'.

In its Hadrian guise, the Waco was originally delivered to the North African theatre in 1943, where it went into operation, rather disastrously, in the Allied invasion of Sicily in July of that year. Greater success was achieved in March 1944 in the Far East during the second 'Chindit' operation in Burma, which involved landing in a jungle clearing at night 240 km (150 miles) behind the main Japanese lines. Subsequently the CG-4As took part in many major airborne operations, especially the D-Day landings in France in June 1944, the action at Arnhem and the Rhine crossing. They were the only gliders used in any great numbers by the USAAF.

It is plain that gliders played a very important part in assault, transport and supply throughout the war, but the bulk of the work was, of course, carried out by conventional transport aircraft. Such machines were built in truly vast quantities to satisfy the great demands for fast military transport. One such aircraft was the American Curtiss C-46 Commando, one of the leading transporters of the conflict. It was designed in 1939 as a 36-seat commercial airliner, the CW-20. With an exceptionally roomy interior by the standards of the day, the CW-20 had obvious military possibilities and the USAAF ordered a large number of them in 1941. It had room for 40 troops, 33 stretchers or 4,500 kg (10,000 lb) of military cargo, and was in fact the largest and heaviest twin-engined aircraft ever to have been employed by the USAAF up to that time.

Himalayas

Because of their greater load-carrying ability and better performance at high altitudes compared with contemporary transport types, Commandos were assigned mainly to the Pacific theatre and were especially successful in the Far East, where they made round-the-clock supply and casualty evacuation flights across the Himalayas between China and India after the Japanese had captured

Throughout the 1960s the Lockheed C-141 StarLifter served with the USAF's Military Airlift Command.

Burma. Commandos were also used during the Korean War (1950-3) and the early stages of the Vietnamese conflict in the 1960s, by which time they had been progressively modified to the point where they could carry as many as 50 fully-equipped troops.

One of the Commando's main rivals in the Far East during the Second World War was Japan's Mitsubishi Ki-57 (known to the Allies as *Topsy*) which served mainly as a troop and paratroop transport. It too was developed from a commercial transport, the MC-20, but was not as big as the Commando and could only carry eleven soldiers at a time. However, it featured notably in the paratroop attack on Palembang airfield in Sumatra and the nearby oil refineries.

In 1941 the US Army decided they needed a specialized military freighter, instead of making do with types derived from commercial airliners. This was the first time a completely new aircraft had been designed in the United States specifically for use as a military transport. Fairchild undertook the project and the design centred around the idea of obtaining a large cargo hold, uninterrupted by side doors, with direct access for loading at near ground level. The result was the C-82 Packet, which had twin tail booms and clamshell doors at the rear to enable jeeps, tanks and trucks to be driven up a

ramp and straight into the aircraft.

The Packet first flew in September 1944, and there followed a number of fascinating developments. For the air-dropping of vehicles for instance, the rear fuselage doors were removed completely and a system was developed in which a parachute was released into the airstream as a means of drawing the vehicle out of the aircraft's interior, after which a main parachute opened to slow the load down on its way to the ground. Small

which fulfilled the USAF's need during the Vietnamese conflict for a large and heavily-armed 'gunship'. These were formidable weapons of warfare, packed with sophisticated night sensors and special communications and navigation systems. Known to the Americans as the 'dollar-nineteen', the Flying Boxcar is a tough and reliable transporter, still in service in some parts of the world.

By far the most numerous and popular transport aircraft both during and after

and well in every theatre of the Second World War. It was among the first types of aircraft to be delivered by the United States to Britain under their wartime aid scheme. The British called the aircraft the Dakota, and it was soon proved that it could operate from even the most primitive landing strips. In 1942 the C-47 joined the RAF's Air Transport Command, primarily to carry military equipment, and soon began to play a big part in the movement of troops.

One of the Dakota's most important wartime duties was to transport para-

Loading a Sikorsky helicopter into an On-Mark B-77PG freighter.

doors set into each side of the fuselage allowed up to 42 paratroopers to make a speedy exit, or the Packet could alternatively carry up to 34 stretcher cases.

The Packet just missed seeing action in the Second World War, and production was cancelled on VJ-Day in 1945. But in 1949 deliveries began of a revised version, the C-119, soon to be called the Flying Boxcar. This had room for 62 troops, and saw action in the Korean War with the USAF, being based in Japan. There were many variants, not least of these being the AC-119 models,

the Second World War, however, was yet another type derived from a commercial airliner – namely the Douglas C-47 Skytrain. This was a revised version of the famous DC-3, which was built in huge numbers for US domestic airlines from 1935 onwards. The redesign work included a stronger cabin floor, strengthened rear fuselage with large loading doors in the sides, and more powerful engines.

The C-47, alternatively nicknamed 'Gooney Bird' or 'old bucket seats', was in service by 1941 and served reliably

Above: Ex-military transport aircraft such as the Armstrong Whitworth Argosy now serve in increasing numbers with civilian cargo operators. *Below*: The unbelievable On Mark B-77PG is derived from the Boeing Stratocruiser airliner of the 1950s. The entire superstructure hinges open to allow unprecedently large loads to be carried. The B-77PG can carry larger items than any other transport plane.

troops and act as a glider tug. In the first largescale Allied airborne invasion of Sicily in July 1943, transport aircraft (mainly C-47s) dropped 4,381 paratroops in a single day. An airborne invasion of Burma in March 1944 saw C-47s pulling Waco gliders, while the Normandy landings saw the use of no less than 1,000 Dakotas. In the first 50 hours of this mammoth operation they carried a staggering 60,000 paratroops and their equipment into action. Little wonder that the C-47/Dakota family is regarded as the most significant transport aircraft in history. They continued in use until well after 1945, of course, and hundreds of Dakotas are still busily flying in and out of airstrips and airports right across the globe.

Looking back over that long and distinguished career, perhaps the best-remembered postwar use of transport aircraft was the Berlin Airlift, which started on 24 June 1948 and again saw the C-47 at the heart of the action. The USSR was controlling the eastern sector of Berlin and severed the west of the city (which was controlled by Britain, the USA and France) from the rest of West Germany by means of a total blockade of all land routes. The people of West Berlin were faced with starvation on one hand and Soviet occupation on the other.

The West refused to be bullied and as the Russians had not closed the air corridors, a giant airlift began with C-47s flying food, coal and other supplies into Tempelhof Airport in West Berlin. However, the C-47 on its own was not enough for such a massive operation, so the larger Douglas C-54 Skymasters were given the task of flying the relatively short distance of 240 km (150 miles) each way. The C-54s carried a full load of 10.2 tonnes (10 tons), and despite the hazards of weather, heavy air traffic and political harassments, take-offs followed a split-second schedule. Aircraft were landing and taking-off every three minutes, the average number of flights per day being 700.

Blockade

On 15 July, the 'Big Lift' transported 1,554 tonnes (1,530 tons) of supplies into Berlin in 24 hours. Landings in bad weather were made using Ground Control Approach radar, developed during the Second World War and now perfected. The Russians tried to harass air

Drums of steel cable being loaded aboard a Canadair CL-44. The entire tail unit of this aircraft hinges to one side to facilitate large loads.

traffic, but Allied fighters patrolled the air lanes to prevent them forcing transport aircraft off course. Even so, when the blockade ended on 12 May 1949, 400 aircraft and a number of men had been lost. As far as transports were concerned, however, the Berlin Airlift proved the feasibility of largescale aerial supply under any weather conditions, and served as a yardstick by which other airlifts would be compared for years to come.

203

The significance of the contribution made by military transport aircraft both to victory in the Second World War and in the Berlin Airlift forced governments and their advisers to pay more attention to the size, power, design and development of specialized military transports. The American government led the world in 1948 in establishing the Military Air Transport Service (MATS) to consolidate the long-range airlift capability of the USAF and US Navy into one huge organization. The 'brush fire' wars in Africa and Korea in the fifties and other such crises needed fast-reacting, highly mobile forces offering effective means to deter, contain and end a conflict in the shortest possible time.

War-Readiness

In 1965 MATS was renamed MAC (Military Airlift Command), charged with the duty of maintaining in a state of war-readiness the airlift capability necessary to fulfil tasks that would include global movement of combat troops and equipment, and aerial drops into battle areas. They also had to be ready to deliver thousands of tonnes of cargo anywhere in the world in a matter of days. The age of the real giants of air transportation had finally dawned.

One of the first aircraft to serve with MATS was the Boeing C-97 Stratofreighter, a variant of the B-29 Superfortress heavy bomber. The Stratofreighter made its maiden flight in 1945 and represented a great advance in transport aircraft performance. It could carry 134 fully-equipped troops, compared with a typical capacity of twenty for the C-47!

A dramatic view of a Lufthansa Boeing 747 being loaded.

Another interesting development by Boeing was the KC-97 Stratotanker, which was a Stratofreighter fitted out as a convertible tanker/transport plane. If it was not fitted with the new in-flight refuelling equipment, the full transportation capability was retained. However, if it was fitted with refuelling 'boom', it could refuel (in mid-air) bombers – such as the B-47 and other large aircraft which needed to undertake long journeys – and still have partial transport capability. The 'boom' was attached to the underside of the fuselage in the KC-97's extreme tail section, thus allowing easy access to aircraft refuelling.

Ballistic Missiles

Two other long-range heavy cargo transports which were used by MATS were the Douglas Globemaster I and II. The Globemaster I first flew in 1945 and was essentially a much-enlarged C-54 with a long cylindrical fuselage. It could carry up to 125 troops or 25,400 kg (56,000 lb) of cargo. The Globemaster II featured a redesigned fuselage which was much deeper than that of its predecessor, and had clamshell doors in the nose. These opened to allow the use of a built-in ramp to help load Thor ballistic missiles and other fearsome weapons. A versatile cargo and troop carrier, the Globemaster II could carry 200 fully-equipped troops, or military vehicles, or it was possible to convert it to an ambulance aircraft with 127 stretcher cases, plus a full complement of doctors and nurses. They operated especially in the war zones of Korea and Vietnam, as well as in peacetime in the US, Europe and the Pacific.

Cargomaster

Following the USAF decision in 1952 to adopt the more powerful turboprop engine as a replacement for piston engines on future transport aircraft, the Douglas company was tasked with producing a heavy strategic transport that filled this requirement. The C-133 Cargomaster was the result. The first prototype flew in 1957, with MATS taking over all the aircraft produced. The enormous freight-hold of the Cargomaster, with its clamshell doors at the back, allowed it to carry huge ballistic missiles such as the Atlas, Thor, Jupiter and Titan.

Rocket Units

An even more successful result of the turboprop decision was the Lockheed C-130 Hercules. It still survives as an excellent military transport, incorporating all the features learnt through hard experience with previous types. These features include a level floor and a large fold-up door at the rear for loading bulky

Above: **A Boeing 747 freighter of CP-Air, the Canadian state airline, being loaded through the side doors by a large truck fitted with hydraulic 'scissors'.**

Because of their high selling price, the cost of airfreighting motor cars (here, in a Lufthansa Boeing 747) can be swallowed up. It is not normally economical to airfreight low-cost, bulky goods.

items or for dropping cargo whilst airborne. In addition, it had full all-weather navigation equipment, rough-field landing gear, and even the facility for rocket units to assist take-off at maximum weight.

The Hercules was designed to a 1951 specification for an eightfold increase in payload and range performance over its piston-engined predecessor, the Flying Boxcar. It fulfilled that specification and amazingly is still in production today, with over 1,500 built. In fact, the Hercules has become one of most widely-used transport aircraft in history. Used operationally in the Far East, Middle East and Africa, including Zimbabwe/Rhodesia, it can operate even from short grass strips. Many variants of the Hercules undertake a whole host of duties, including maritime search, rescue and recovery. But in its standard role as a medium long-range combat transport, Hercules can take 92 troops, 74 stretcher cases, or 64 paratroops.

Massive Newcomer

In 1963 transport aircraft development took a further step forward with the first flight of the Lockheed C-141 Star-Lifter. It was designed in 1960 to provide MATS with high-speed transportation over very long ranges, and proved its capabilities by airlifting a cargo of 22,680 kg (50,000 lb) in stages over 12,000 km (7,500 miles) in only $18\frac{1}{2}$ hours. In contrast, the Hercules would have taken 30 hours and the Globemaster II nearly 42 hours! Indeed, the C-141 was the first jet aircraft designed from the start for military transport duties and as such it ushered in a new age of air transport.

The StarLifter was the USAF's standard heavy transport aircraft until the introduction of a massive newcomer – the Lockheed C-5A Galaxy. Because of her ever-increasing responsibility as 'leader' of the western powers, the United States needed an aircraft of such size that it would dwarf anything else in the sky. The resulting C-5A Galaxy is the world's largest aircraft, yet it can take-off from the same runways used by the much smaller StarLifter and inherits that aircraft's ability to land on hurriedly-prepared landing strips right in the middle of combat areas. Typical loads include two M-60 tanks, or sixteen small trucks, or one M-60 tank and two helicopters, or ten Pershing missiles complete with their towing and launching vehicles. Loading and unloading can be carried out via front or rear doors, or even both together. Like the StarLifter, the Galaxy was used extensively in Vietnam and is today used by the USAF throughout the world.

Algeria

The United States is not the only country whose transport aircraft have played an important part in the postwar scene. France, for instance, developed the Nord Noratlas, which, like the Fairchild Packet, had twin tail booms and clamshell doors at the rear. The *Armée de l'Air* employed it under actual combat conditions on more than one occasion, notably in campaigns against nationalist forces in Algeria and during the Suez invasion of 1956.

The Germans had already built the Noratlas under licence, so it was logical for them to team up with the French to produce a successor. As a result of this merger an aircraft known as the C-160 Transall was born. It has the distinction of being the first aircraft in history to be conceived from the outset as a joint international design and construction programme. Very similar in outward appearance to the C-130 Hercules, the Franco-German C-160 is nonetheless slightly smaller than its American counterpart and has a smaller lifting capacity. Typical loads include 93 fully-armed troops or 81 paratroops.

Firefighting

Italy has not allowed herself to slip behind the other European countries on the transport aircraft scene, for the Aeritalia G 222 ranks as one of the finest machines of its type. It was originally intended to become NATO's first vertical/short take-off and landing (V/STOL) transport aircraft, but gradually the design evolved and the vertical lift jets were removed, leaving a fairly conventional turboprop-powered aircraft with rear-loading doors. Aeritalia made both civilian and military G 222 derivatives, and even a firefighting version that can drop water from a large internal hold onto raging forest fires. In its military form the G 222 is a useful performer, with room for up to 44 troops, 36 stretcher casualties or 32 paratroops.

Above: A Lockheed C-130 Hercules of the RAF performs an ultra low level cargo drop. The parachute helps to pull the load from the aircraft's hold.

Below: The same type of drop being carried out at a much higher altitude.

Above: The cargomaster's job is one of the most responsible as it is up to him to ensure that each parachute drop goes smoothly.

Above: The Short Belfast, designed and built in Northern Ireland, was the largest aircraft ever to have served with the Royal Air Force. Here its cargo of armoured cars is being safely unloaded during a training exercise.

Below: In order to prevent damage during parachute drops, loads like this jeep are carefully packaged. The shock of landing is absorbed by a thick bed of corrugatred cardboard. Once on the ground, the packing frame is quickly removed.

STOL

Meanwhile, across the Atlantic, the de Havilland company of Canada has produced two notable battlefield transports, both possessing the short take-off and landing (STOL) characteristics that prove so helpful in modern warfare. The first was the DHC-4 Caribou, its maiden flight taking place in 1958. This aircraft was designed to combine the carrying capacity of the C-47/Dakota family with STOL performance. It sold in appreciable numbers to both civilian and military customers worldwide, including the US Army. They bought 160 of them and, many of them served in the southeast Asian conflict. Caribous were largely superceded by the more powerful turboprop-equipped DHC-5 Buffalo, which first flew in 1964 and could carry more troops and casualties than its forerunner. The STOL performance of this aeroplane is truly outstanding, a fact borne out when the Buffalo set several new world 'time-to-height' records in 1976.

Across the 'Iron Curtain' the progress of Soviet military air transportation has been an interesting one. Russia's leading source of postwar transport aircraft is the Antonov bureau. Their first mass-produced aircraft entered service in 1949. This was the An-2 (codenamed *Colt* by NATO), a light transport and general-purpose biplane powered by a single 1,000 hp Shvetsov piston engine. Although the *Colt* was intended mainly for civilian use, no Soviet aircraft is designed without there being at least some consideration given to its possible uses in wartime. An-2s have seen service in a great many Communist countries, including Albania, Hungary, North Korea and Rumania. They are still used to perform such varied duties as paratroop training, casualty evacuation and crop-spraying.

Smyro

At the opposite end of the scale, both in terms of time and in sheer size, are the An-24 *Coke* and its more refined development, the An-26 *Curl*. Both are used in general transport roles and also see civilian service with the Soviet 'civilian' air transport bureau, Aeroflot. *Curl* is the more interesting, as it can accommodate

The mighty Lockheed C-5 Galaxy is one of the largest aircraft ever built. It can carry two M-60 battle tanks or three CH-47 Chinook helicopters.

large vehicles but is also capable of being converted on the battlefields for paratrooping duties, the transformation taking less than 30 minutes to complete. *Curl* can land in very rough fields and is used by a number of Communist air forces, notably those of the Warsaw Pact.

Probably the most remarkable Soviet military transport aircraft is also the largest and heaviest, the massive An-22 Antei. This is a cavernous long-range aircraft which is able to carry tanks and a whole host of other military vehicles, plus earthmoving equipment. The An-22 has four enormously-powerful turboprop engines driving large eight-bladed propellors, and its existence has played a significant part in the Soviet Union's attempts to maintain its global presence. It has enabled the Soviet air force to send vast quantities of modern weapons over long routes to such places as Angola and Ethiopia in Africa – a task which would have been impossible until the early seventies.

Civil Cargo

As we have seen, military transports can be derived from commercial airliners, or they can be designed specifically for the job. Cargo has been carried by air ever since the airlines first started operating, but this task has only become a sizeable part of commercial aviation since the late 1950s. Before that time civilian airliners mainly carried passengers and mail. The design and construction of cargo aircraft for commercial use has evolved hand-in-hand with the growth of the specialized air freight business. Today commercial cargo is carried by all-cargo and regular passenger aircraft with special compartments

set aside for the carriage of goods. These include such airliners as the Boeing 747, with a modified nose to permit bulky loads to be hoisted aboard with comparative ease.

Swing Tail

The most significant of the early all-cargo civilian aircraft is the Canadair CL-44, first flown in 1960. This can carry a payload of 28,576 kg (63,000 lb) over a range of 5,600 km (3,500 miles). The CL-44's most notable feature is its rear fuselage, which swings round in its entirety to make way for oncoming freight. Most all-cargo planes have a multitude of tiny rollers across their floors to permit preloaded pallets of freight to be quickly pushed in. An interesting development has been the 'quickchange' aircraft such as the Boeing 727QC. This model carries passengers during the day but at night is converted to a cargo carrier when fewer passengers are scheduled to fly, thus giving the airlines a substantial increase in profits.

It is an indisputable fact that transport aircraft are now an integral part of our everyday lives. In conclusion, it should be mentioned that military transport aircraft undertake all kinds of civilian life-saving duties. A good example of this came in 1974, when fleets of C-5A Galaxies proved invaluable in a mercy dash to the flooded areas of Chile and Pakistan. During the Nicaraguan earthquakes too, Galaxies ferried much-needed equipment and food supplies to the hapless victims, while in 1977-8 the same aircraft carried snow-clearing equipment to several isolated areas in the United States which had been blocked off by terrible blizzards. .

The Making of a Giant
How Boeing build a 747

When we go on holiday by air, we take the aircraft we fly in increasingly for granted. After all, when an airliner packed with hundreds of passengers takes-off from one of the world's major 'gateway' airports and disappears into the gathering haze, it is difficult to imagine the time when nothing existed of that aircraft but a few pieces of metal on a factory floor.

For this reason, this chapter is devoted to a pictorial account of the massive operation that takes those few pieces of metal through various complex stages to produce, after many hundreds of thousands of hours hard work, a finished aeroplane. The vast Boeing 747 makes an ideal subject for our step-by-step picture sequence as the sheer scale of the operation, and the number of individual components that have to be shipped in from various parts of the world, is nothing short of breathtaking. Every component built by outside contractors must be constructed to an exact specification so that no problems are encountered when the time comes for the Boeing engineers to fit all the individual components into larger sub-assemblies. Sub-assemblies include such parts as the wing, nose-section, central fuselage, etc. The next phase of construction is joining these big sub-assemblies together to complete the main airframe.

Then comes the task of 'fitting-out'. Seats, windows, instruments, lighting, fuel supply pipes and many similar small but vital components must be fitted in the correct sequence and to a tight time schedule to ensure that the gigantic 747 production line is constantly moving and Boeing's airline customers kept happy. After that comes the all-important first flight, still a momentous occasion long after the maiden flight of the first prototype back in 1970.

While all this has been going on, the huge administrative task that makes an operation of this kind possible has been proceeding quietly behind the scenes, in offices far from the hustle and bustle of the production line. Supplies of raw materials and individual components must be ordered many months before they are needed, and delivery dates quoted and monitored. Deciding the quantity of each order is another difficult aspect of this constant process, for the shortage of a single component could bring the whole production line to a standstill and leave thousands of skilled technicians and engineers, not to mention vastly expensive manufacturing machinery, lying idle.

Here, stage-by-stage, is the story of a 747's construction . . .

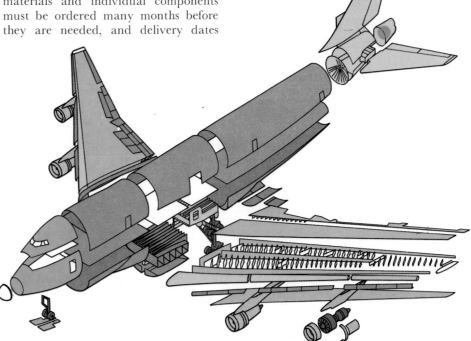

The diagram on page 209 shows the main sub-assemblies that go together to build a complete 747.

Production of 747s takes place in the Boeing Airplane Company's vast assembly plant at Everett Field, near Seattle, Washington, USA. In the background are various completed 747s awaiting flight trials before delivery to customer airlines.

Fabrication of these wing sub-assemblies takes place in one corner of the assembly plant. Over-slung power lines (A) provide electricity to rivet guns that join the pre-cut pieces of metal together.

Right: The 747's fuselage sections are assembled in another area of the factory. Special multi-level gantreys (B) provide easy access for technicians and inspectors, while the fuselage sections themselves are shaped around red-painted jigs (C) that ensure that every one is built to exactly the same specification.

The completed wing assemblies (D) are now lifted into place by a powerful overhead crane (E). They will later be joined to the main centre-section fuel tank (F) that forms the middle section of the 747's fuselage.

G

Above: The middle section of the fuselage (G) is now lowered into place and will be attached to the centre-section fuel tank.

Left: When this operation is completed the wings are finally attached.

H

J

Above: The middle section of the fuselage, complete with wings, is mounted on huge multi-wheeled trolleys that enable it to be manoeuvred around the factory floor. Here, two hefty vehicles (H) push this gigantic structure into such a position that it can be attached to the forward fuselage section. Adjustable jacks (I) are already in position to support the massive wings when the join-up has been completed.

A close-up of the delicate forward fuselage attachment operation. Note the hoist (J) that helps support the forward fuselage from above.

Next, the rear fuselage is moved in.
A huge hoist (K) lifts it into position.
The trestles under the wings are
now taking some of the strain, while
another huge trestle at the rear (L)
awaits its share of the load.

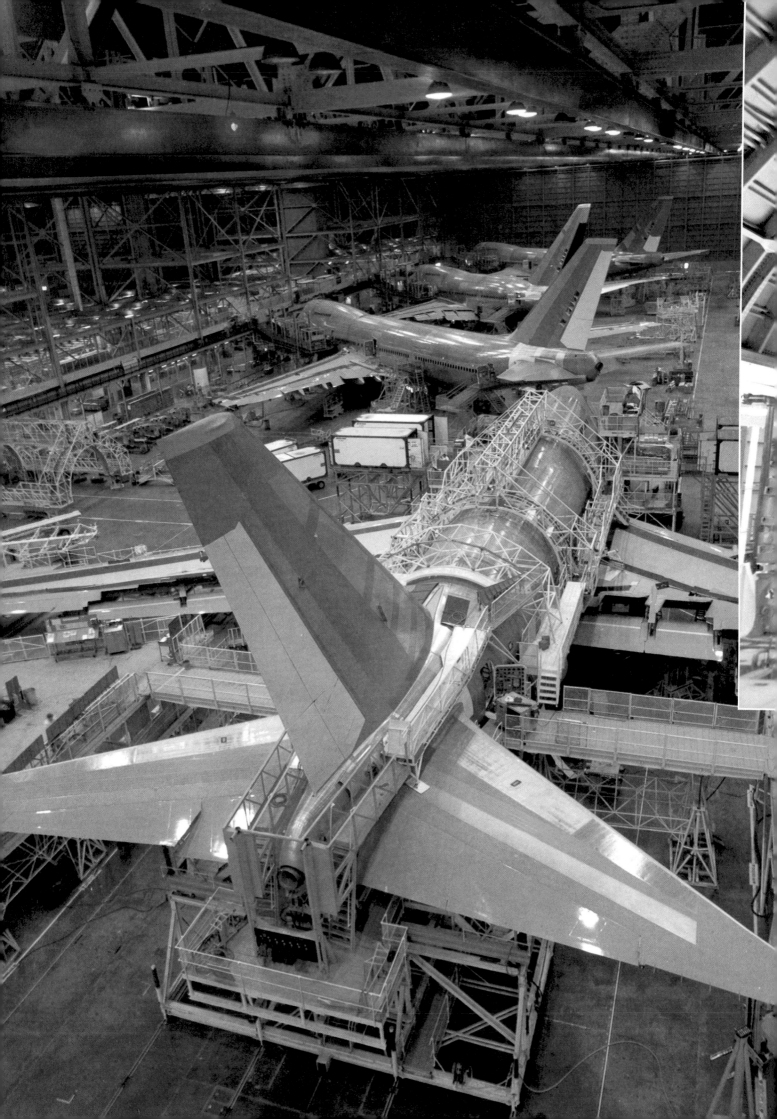

Left: This general view of the Everett plant shows the vast scale of the 747 construction programme. It also illustrates an important point; while one aircraft is undergoing a particular operation, others are receiving the next stage of treatment. This really is a production *line* – thousands of small pieces arrive at one end and are joined together into the finished product by the time they reach the other end.

Above: Highly-skilled inspectors check the 747's interior structure before 'fitting-out' with such equipment as seats, luggage racks and carpets begins.

Above: Next stage in the production of a 747 is the fitting of engines. In this picture one of the 747's four Pratt & Whitney turbojet engines (M) is lined up with the appropriate underwing pylon (N) prior to attachment. Note the daunting collection of exposed electrical cables (O) hanging from the leading edge of the 747's wing!

Right: While all this is going on, various sub-assemblies – such as these undercarriage units – are being readied for installation. The technicians (P) seen working on the undercarriage units in this picture give some impression of the size of these gigantic sub-assemblies.

Above: With the undercarriage units and most other sub-assemblies now installed, the 747 is given its first coat of paint – a special 'primer' to prevent corrosion. Polythene sheets have been taped over the 747's windscreen, windscreen wipers, passenger windows and other areas not requiring paint. The huge sheet of polythene taped around the 747's undersurfaces ensures that this area too remains unpainted. This is because most airlines prefer to have this area highly polished to a bright silver finish.

Above: After receiving further coats of primer and then the actual colour scheme of the customer airline, each 747 is rolled out of the main assembly plant, where all systems are double-checked. In this picture are 747s destined for various airlines. Some have just been rolled out of the factory, while others have already been checked over and have had their fuel tanks filled in preparation for the momentous first flight. *Left*: The 747, now resplendent in the livery of the South American airline, Avianca, makes its first flight.

So that is the story of one aeroplane's progression from just a few pieces of metal on the factory floor to a finished product ready for delivery to the customer airline and, soon after, the first passenger-carrying services.

INDEX

223

ACKNOWLEDGMENTS

As well as thanking all those organizations and individuals listed below for their kind permission to reproduce copyright illustrative material in this book, the authors and publishers also wish to extend their grateful appreciation to Elfan ap Rees, John Blake, Cal Brown, John Davies, Jeff Daniels, Mike De Luca, Will Fowler and Mike Johnstone for their individual contributions to the end product. Many thanks are also due to the dozens of people behind the scenes whose names have never been known to us but whose participation was still of great value.

Listed below are the various organizations and individuals who kindly granted permission to use copyright illustrative material in this book. Particular thanks are due to Airfix Products Ltd whose superb collection of oil paintings was placed at our disposal. These illustrations are usually to be found on the box-tops of the Airfix range of plastic construction kits, so for the benefit of modellers we have listed the code numbers in brackets alongside the page numbers. When more than one picture appears on a page, pictures are credited from top to bottom, left to right.

---

page references in italics indicate illustrations

front endpapers: Fairchild Republic; title page: Pilot Press; title spread: General Dynamics; contents spread: Starless collection (the private collection of Nigel and Nicola Macknight) 6–7: via Miss Sheila Scott; 8: via Imperial War Museum (2); 9: Imperial War Museum/MoD; 10–11: Lufthansa/Starless Collection; 14: MoD; 14–15: Starless Collection; 15: MoD; 16: United Airlines; 17: Starless Collection; 18: Lufthansa; 18–19: Lufthansa/Starless Collection; 20: Lufthansa/Sabena; 20–1: Starless Collection; 21: Sabena; 22: Airfix (00000–0)/Lufthansa (2); 23: Lufthansa(2); 24: Lufthansa (2); 24–5: Starless Collection; 25: Lockheed; 26: United Airlines/Lockheed; 26–7: Lockheed; 27: Balair; 28: Cathay Pacific/Airfix (00000–0); 29: United Airlines/Boeing; 30: Airfix (03167–5)/TAA; 31: Lufthansa/CP-Air/Boeing/British Airways; 32: British Airways/Lufthansa; 33: Starless Collection; 34: via M. J. H. Taylor (2); 35: Starless Collection; 36: Starless Collection; 36–7: Starless Collection; 38–9: Starless Collection; 39: Airfix (01013–9); 40: Frank Mormillo; 41: Frank Mormillo; 42: Frank Mormillo; 43: Frank Mormillo/via Formula Air Racing Association; 44: via Formula Air Racing Association/Starless Collection; 45: Frank Mormillo; 46: Frank Mormillo; 46–7: Frank Mormillo; 47: Frank Mormillo; 48: MoD; 49: Starless Collection; 50: Airfix (00000–0); 51: MoD/Airfix (02151–4); 52: Pilot Press/Airfix (02032–3); 53: Airfix (02014–5); 54: Airfix (04006–0)/Imperial War Museum; 55: Pilot Press/Starless Collection; 56: Airfix (02022–6)/Pilot Press; 57: Airfix (02054–3); 58: Imperial War Museum/Airfix (03027–4); 59: Fairchild Republic/Airfix (05011–5); 60: Airfix (03163–5); 60–1: Starless Collection; 61: MoD; 62: Starless Collection; 63: Fairchild Republic/MoD; 64: MoD; 65: Starless Collection; 66: Starless Collection; 66–7: Starless Collection; 67: Airfix (00000–0); 68: Imperial War Museum; 68–9: Starless Collection; 69: Pilot Press; 70: Imperial War Museum; 70–1: Starless Collection; 71: Imperial War Museum; 72: Pilot Press; 72–3: Airfix (05006–3); 73: Imperial War Museum (2); 74: Airfix (04005–7)/Pilot Press (2); 75: Starless Collection; 76: Airfix (06002–4); 77: Boeing/Pilot Press; 78: Boeing; 78–9: Starless Productions; 79: MoD (2); 80: General Dynamics; 81: Starless Collection; 82: Starless Collection/Imperial War Museum; Airfix (00000–0); 84: Airfix (01055–3); 84–5: Starless Collection; 85: Imperial War Museum; 86: Imperial War Museum/Starless Collection; 87: Airfix (02140–3); 88: Airfix (01002–9); 88–9: Airfix (03141–9); 89: Imperial War Museum; 90: Imperial War Museum; 90–1: Pilot Press; 91: Airfix (02051–4); 92: Lockheed; 92–3: Imperial War Museum; 93: Airfix (01046–9)/Pilot Press; 94: Airfix (02023–9); 94–5: Starless Collection; 95: Airfix (01030–4); 96: Airfix (01063–4); 97: Starless Collection; 98: Pilot Press; 98–9: MoD; 99: Airfix (02061–1); 100: MoD; 100–01: Starless Collection; 101: General Dynamics/MoD; 102: Lockheed; 103: MoD; 104: MoD/Pilot Press; 105: MoD/Airfix (02010–3)/Pilot Press; 106: Pilot Press; 106–7: Starless Collection; 107: Airfix (02039–4); 108–9: Starless Collection; 109: General Dynamics (4); 110: Northrop/Airfix (03036–8); 111: General Dynamics; 112: Airfix (05013–1); 113: Starless Collection; 114: Imperial War Museum; 114–5: Starless Collection; 115: Lufthansa; 116–7: Airfix (04172–6); 117: Lufthansa (2); 118–9: Starless Collection; 119: Imperial War Museum/Airfix (00000–0); 120–1: General Dynamics; 121: Imperial War Museum; 122: General Dynamics; 123: Airfix (02019–0)/Airfix (02033–6); 124: General Dynamics; 124–5: General Dynamics; 126–7: General Dynamics/Starless Collection; 127: Fairchild Republic; 128 Starless Collection; 129: Starless Collection; 130: Blandford Press; 131: Sikorsky; 132: Starless Collection; 132–3: Starless Collection; 133: Imperial War Museum; 134: Bell Textron/Starless Collection; 135: Hughes Helicopters/Airfix (00000–0); 136: General Dynamics; 137: Airfix (02065–3)/MoD; 138: Starless Collection; 139: Peter March/Airfix (03010–6); 140: MoD; 140–1: Starless Collection/Hughes Helicopter; 142: Hughes Helicopters; 143: Bell Textron/Starless Collection; 144: Bell Textron (3); 145: Starless Collection; 146: Starless Collection; 146–7: Cessna/Starless Collection; 147: via M. J. H. Taylor; 148: Cessna; 148–9: Starless Creations; 149: Beech; 150: Airfix (03001–2); 150–1: Starless Creations; 151: Piper; 152: Airfix (04018–3); 153: Beech; 154: Airfix (02041–7); 154–5: Starless Creations; 155: Marlboro/Cessna; 156: Pilatus; 157: via M. J. H. Taylor (2); 158: Cessna; 158–9: via M. J. H. Taylor Starless Collection; 160: via M. J. H. Taylor; 161: Starless Collection; 162: Airfix (03028–7); 162–3: Starless Collection; 163: Imperial War Museum; 164: Airfix (02037–8); 164–5: Airfix (00000–0); 165: MoD/Imperial War Museum; 166: Lockheed/Airfix (00000–0)/Pilot Press; 167: Airfix (01047–2)/Lockheed; 168: MoD; 168–9: MoD; 169: MoD/Airfix (04012–5); 170: Lockheed; 170–1: Starless Collection; 171: MoD; 172: Lockheed; 172–3: Starless Collection; 173: Airfix (02035–2); 174: MoD; 174–5: Starless Collection; 175: MoD; 176: Lockheed; 177: Starless Collection; 178: via M. J. H. Taylor; 178–9: Starless Collection; 180: General Dynamics; 180–1: Starless Collection; 181: Airfix (02009–3); 182: Airfix; (01054–0); 182–3: General Dynamics; 183: Airfix (02057–2); 184–5: Airfix (02067–5); 185: Lockheed; 186: Airfix (00000–0); 186–7: MoD; 187: MoD; 188: Airfix (01036–2)/Airfix (03009–6); 188–9: Starless Collection; 190–1: Starless Collection/MoD; 192: MoD; 193: Starless Collection; 194: Imperial War Museum (3); 195: Airfix (05008–9); 196–7: Starless Collection; 197: Imperial War Museum; 198: USAF via MoD/Wardair; 199: MoD (2); 200: Boeing/Pilot Press; 200–01: Starless Collection; 201: Lufthansa; 202: Sikorsky; 202–3: IPEC/Starless Collection; 203: Tradewinds Airways; 204: Lufthansa; 205: CP-Air/Lufthansa; 206: MoD; 206–7: Airfix (09001–0); 207: MoD (3); 208: Lockheed; 209–19: Boeing; 220: Boeing/Avanca; rear endpaper: Sabena.